The Informer

The Informer
Confessions of an Ex-Terrorist

Carole de Vault with William Johnson

 Fleet Books, Toronto

A Fleet Book
Published by Fleet Publishers
A Division of International Thomson Limited
1410 Birchmount Road
Scarborough, Ontario, Canada M1P 2E7

Canadian Cataloguing in Publication Data

De Vault, Carole, 1945–
    The informer

Translation of: Toute ma vérité.
ISBN 0-7706-0001-8   (bound)
ISBN 0-7706-0056-5   (pbk.)

1. De Vault, Carole, 1945– 2. Front de libération
du Québec.* 3. Terrorism - Quebec (Province).
4. Informers - Quebec (Province) - Biography. 5. Quebec
(Province) - Politics and government - 1960–1976.*
I. Johnson, William. II. Title.

HV7911.D47A313   363.2'52'0924   C82-094707-5

EDITORIAL CONSULTANT: Barbara Hehner
DESIGN: Fortunato Aglialoro
JACKET PHOTOGRAPHS: Melinda Oksenhendler
JACKET ILLUSTRATION: Lorraine Aglialoro
TYPESETTING: Compeer Typographic Services Limited
COLOUR SEPARATION: Empress Litho
PRINTING AND BINDING: T.H. Best

Printed and bound in Canada

82 83 84 85 86 87 88   7 6 5 4 3 2 1

CONTENTS

PART ONE

CHAPTER 1
November 21, 1979

——————————— ❧ ———————————

To reveal that I had been a police informer was almost more than I could do. That morning, before appearing at the Montreal courthouse, I had taken several Valiums, but they seemed to have no effect.

I walked into the hall with my head high, looking straight ahead, a huge bodyguard on either side of me. In that crowded room, I saw no one except the Commissioner of Inquiry, Jean-François Keable, who sat on a raised bench at the far end, waiting for his star witness. I went to the witness stand in front of the onlookers, and my bodyguards sat behind me.

"Do you swear to tell the truth, the whole truth, and nothing but the truth?"

"Yes, I do." The truth at last, the whole truth, if it kills me. My hand shook on the Bible. My knees, beneath my black dress, knocked against each other.

Did my former companions in the Front de Libération du Québec begin to feel apprehensive when they saw me? Some were in the hall, I'd been told, including the man who had told me years before what would happen to those who betrayed the FLQ: "One day we will pay them a visit. We will put a bullet through their heart and pin a note to their body saying: "This is what happens to those who betray the FLQ!"

The counsel for the Commission, Mario Bilodeau, stood up. He was short, balding in front, with fair hair falling almost to his shoulders.

"Under the circumstances," he said, "I would prefer that we record only the name of Miss de Vault."*

No address, no date of birth, no employment. Now were my former companions beginning to catch on?

He could have said: "Carole de Vault, thirty-four years old, no fixed address, unemployed." In 1970, when British diplomat James

———————

* The quotations are translated from the official transcript of the Commission of Inquiry into Police Operations in the Territory of Quebec — the Keable Commission.

9

Cross was kidnapped, I was a student. For a few years, I was a lecturer in international relations at the University of Quebec and at several colleges. Then, I spent a few years in a bad marriage. Now nothing. I had lost my job, my home, my friends, and even my city. To protect me until I testified, they had moved me from Montreal to Quebec City, where I lived in a hotel under an assumed name. My bodyguards accompanied me everywhere.

Yesterday, they had driven me to Montreal to testify, and one had registered me as his wife. We had slept behind double-locked doors.

Mr. Bilodeau was speaking again. "Miss de Vault, before we begin questioning you, I think that you have a request to put to the Commissioner."

Seated at the witness stand, I clutched the microphone. "Yes, I want to ask the Commissioner to grant me the protection of the law."

"Very well. According to the Canada Evidence Act, your testimony cannot be used against you and is not admissible as evidence against you in a criminal trial, except a trial for perjury arising from your testimony."

A criminal trial! Yes, possibly I could be charged for some of my past acts. But that was not what had terrified me. I had asked to testify under the protection of the court. But would the FLQ respect the Canada Evidence Act?

Now the counsel asked the question I had been dreading: "Well, then, Miss de Vault, did you work in collaboration with the Montreal police during the year 1970?"

The silence in the courtroom was broken by a single whisper: "*Ah ben, maudit!*" I'll be damned! It was a few moments before I was able to answer; the words choked in my throat. Was it fear? No, though I was to know fear in the coming months. It was deeper than fear. For so many years, I had kept a secret buried deep inside me, I had led a double life. In a way, I had been a double person. Within the FLQ, I had been a respected member, a friend, and even a lover. With some, I had shared my days, my nights, my food, my apartment, and we had shared our secrets. All but one.

That secret was never to be let out. My mother and my sister never knew, even though they hid a bag of dynamite for me in an attic. They thought I was simply in the FLQ. My lovers never knew, except one; the man I loved when it all began. I told him, but he didn't believe me. Even when I married and left the police, I never told my husband my secret.

And now, in this courtroom, before strangers, before some of my former companions, I was being asked to admit that I had worked for the police, that I had betrayed the FLQ, that people had put their trust in me when I was working with their adversaries.

Behind me, listening for my answer, was Robert Comeau, the man who had recruited me into the FLQ, and Nigel Hamer, one of the kidnappers of James Cross. Long before they discovered where the hostage was hidden, I had told the police of an English-speaking person among the kidnappers. Later, I had found out his name. When the others traded their hostage for safe passage to Cuba, Nigel Hamer stayed behind in hiding; I had told the police where he could be found.

Would people understand? The reporters in the press gallery behind the Commissioner stared at me. They had never heard my name before. What kind of a person could be in the FLQ and yet tell all to the police? Artists were busy sketching me because the Commissioner had forbidden cameras.

And my best friend, Rose-Marie Parent. Would she now think that our friendship had been a sham? Would she understand that I liked her, that I had protected her as much as I could in my reports to the police, that I tried to steer her away from criminal acts? We had met in the FLQ, but when we were together we talked of everything except politics. What would she be thinking when she heard about me on the national news?

The counsel was speaking to me again. Had he noticed my long paralysis, or did it just seem to me such a long time before I could speak?

"Could you tell us the circumstances under which you came to work with the police?"

I took a deep breath. "At the beginning of November, 1970, I was visited at my apartment by Mr. Robert Comeau, who asked me if I could hide someone at my place . . ."

As I spoke, my trembling diminished. Dates, facts, names and places— this was material I was familiar with. Mr. Bilodeau asked about the first communiqué I worked on, which told how the assassins of Pierre Laporte had slipped through the hands of the police.

"So Mr. Comeau arrived at your place with a rough draft written in pencil, and asked you to make a neater copy of the communiqué?"

"That's right."

"Do you remember roughly the content of that communiqué?"

"It was the communiqué about the people of the Chénier Cell, the Rose brothers who were hidden in the clothes closet. Some policemen had forgotten their guns in the apartment."

"In the apartment where the Rose brothers were hidden?"

"Yes."

"It mentioned a closet, it mentioned guns?"

"Yes."

Mr. Bilodeau asked me how I had received the official paper of the FLQ, with its distinctive outline of a rifle-toting rebel, the toqued, pipe-smoking *Patriote* of the 1837 Rebellion.

"When you got that paper from Mr. Comeau, was anything else turned over to you?"

"Yes, I received dynamite, electric detonators, fuses and fuse detonators, and plans for making bombs or Molotov cocktails."

"And it was in February you received all that material?"

"Yes."

Dates, names, and places. There was a flat unreality to it all as the counsel questioned and I answered. October, November, December, 1970. January, 1971. The months when my life spun around, when everything changed for me, were now reduced in this courtroom to a kind of triviality.

"Between the first of December, 1970, and the beginning of February, 1971, did you, with the knowledge of the Montreal police, carry out activities in the name of the FLQ?"

"Yes."

The counsel questioned me throughout the morning. He thought that the police had done more than infiltrate the FLQ; they might even have become its accomplice through me. Or, worse still, the police might have been behind the events. Mr. Bilodeau was particularly suspicious of the man who had been my controller in 1970, Detective-Lieutenant Julien Giguère. Now promoted to captain, he was also in the courtroom.

"Miss de Vault, let me show you another communiqué, put out by the André Ouimet Cell [of the FLQ]. It is Communiqué Number 2, dated January 6, 1971, and it refers to an attack made the night before against the Brink's Canada premises. Could you look over the communiqué?"

I studied the document.

"Do you know who wrote this communiqué?"

"Yes."

"Who did?"

"I did."

"You did?"

"Yes."

"Are you also the one who delivered it?"

"Yes."

"Yes? This communiqué refers to a Molotov cocktail attack against Brink's."

"Yes."

"Were the facts as set forth in the communiqué made known to the police even before they happened?"

"Yes."

"You are convinced of that?"

"I'm certain."

At last, the counsel got to the point: he wanted me to implicate my friend and former controller, Julien Giguère.

"During that period, did you have from the very first — that is, from November 1970 until January 6, 1971 — did you have the same controller."

"Yes."

"Good. The controller is the person to whom you would have given this advance information?"

"That's correct."

"Is it correct to say that your controller was Mr. Julien Giguère?"

"Yes."

"And you would warn Mr. Giguère in advance about what was going to happen?"

"Yes."

What did Julien Giguère think of me now? We had shared the high drama of those days in 1970 when we were both obsessed with finding James Cross alive. He was always more concerned for my safety than I was. He thought that I took too many chances. He warned me to go slowly, not to ask too many dangerous questions. We would meet, often in the middle of the night, and I would make my report. Together we would try to piece together the meaning of what I had seen or heard since we had last met, and plan my strategy for the coming days.

The relationship between a controller and an informer is intense. There has to be trust, at least on the part of the informer who runs great risks. You need to rely on the judgment of an experienced person. And you carry an enormous secret that can be shared with no one but the controller. In a restaurant, I would often laugh with Julien about the serious business of the day. I could let go, talk freely. He was the one person in the world who knew what I was doing, and why.

With my lovers, even with my husband, I never again knew the intimacy of those meals at all-night restaurants when I reported to Julien. The 1970 crisis that so shook Quebec and Canada was for us a personal, shared experience, the most significant time in our lives.

Julien was married. But I was confident that even his wife did not understand as I did what the fall of 1970 meant to him. He had worked day and night to find the kidnappers of Cross, snatching a few hours sleep when he could in a sleeping bag in his office. I knew just how badly he wanted to find the British diplomat alive and return him safely to his wife and country.

Julien Giguère knew what I could tell no one else: that I had become an informer because I believed in an independent Quebec but could not condone violence to achieve that end. I believed in René Lévesque and Jacques Parizeau and in the Parti Quebecois, the party that would lead us to nationhood by democratic means. I thought that the FLQ with its violent methods would discredit the independence movement and destroy everything for which we had worked so hard in the elections of April, 1970.

But now, in a sense, I was betraying Julien. He had been adamant that I should not testify publicly before the Commission about my work as a police informer. In all the history of Canada, no one had ever before confessed publicly to being a police informer.

"The risks are too great," Julien had said. "It will end in a murder or a suicide."

I had decided to testify anyway. And now, to all appearances, I was incriminating him. The counsel for the Commission clearly thought that Julien Giguère had played a sinister role in 1970 and 1971, and this was revealed by his line of questioning.

"After you told Mr. Giguère when you were to receive the FLQ paper and dynamite from Mr. Comeau, did Mr. Giguère tell you what measures were taken by the Montreal police to find the dynamite or find the paper?"

"Would you repeat the question, please? I'm sorry, I did not understand."

The counsel came at it another way.

"Was there any question of your being put under surveillance at that time?"

"Mr. Giguère had told me that I would be under surveillance the morning I was to meet whoever was to turn over the communiqué paper and the other things."

"And do you know what came of your being under surveillance?"

"They— let's say that the surveillance team lost sight of the person who came to bring me the paper."

In the courtroom, it sounded suspicious that the surveillance team had missed the person who had contacted me and delivered the dynamite and the FLQ paper. That sort of thing happens sometimes. But could the counsel understand that? The questions continued.

"But is it clear in your mind that Mr. Giguère knew in advance that you would be receiving that kind of thing, namely dynamite and blank communiqués? Is that correct?"

"Yes, yes."

"And he knew the place?"

The counsel kept returning to the same theme. The police had been notified in advance that the FLQ was going to carry out certain operations, yet they did not intervene. Julien Giguère knew.

"Did Mr. Giguère try to prevent the people who wanted to commit that crime from acting?"

"Not at all."

"I will ask you to repeat your answer, because I want to be quite sure. You are convinced that none of the people who took part in that operation were bothered?"

"I believe so, yes."

"Believe?"

"Yes, I'm certain."

My testimony ended for the day. I would have to come back to go through the details and be cross-examined. But now I could go. The Commissioner reminded everyone that taking pictures was forbidden.

I got up and faced the crowd. My two bodyguards took up their positions beside me. I looked at no one, saw no one. Head high, I walked to the door. They whisked me through an office reserved for judges and into the elevator. I stood in the corner and my bodyguards made a wall in front of me. We got off at the underground garage level; I climbed into the back of a car and we drove off, preceded by a van. I was driven to a restaurant in the east end of Montreal to have my lunch, far from the courthouse. No reporter or photographer was able to get near me.

After eating, we got back into the car and took the highway for Quebec City. Back to anonymity, back to seclusion. On the radio, the news broadcasts kept repeating my name: "Revelations today at the Keable Commission . . . Ex-police informer Carole de Vault . . ."

My head began to get heavy as we rolled through the Saint Lawrence River valley toward Quebec City. Now the Valiums were having their effect. Like someone in the recovery room after an operation, I couldn't keep my eyes open. My secret was out. It had been removed like a cancer. Or was it a vital organ?

I had a strange sense of unreality. The private person I had been no longer existed. It had been replaced by that Carole de Vault splashed over the front pages of the newspapers, or shown in artist's sketches on the television news. I had become notorious and, at the same time, ceased to exist.

Who could I speak to now except my bodyguards? The people I had known in the FLQ must now see me as a traitor. Most of them were decent enough people, but I would never feel safe again.

My friends in the Montreal police would also feel that I had betrayed them. They distrusted this Commission, which they saw as a political gimmick. Some of them could not accept laymen poking into the techniques of fighting terrorism. Others saw the Commission as a ploy by the provincial government to embarrass the federal government that, by revealing the identity of police informers, would cripple the police in their fight against subversion. I was cooperating fully with the Commission, and my testimony today had cast suspicion on the actions of the police.

And the people I had worked with in the Parti Quebecois. They would think that I had been a spy infiltrating the PQ as I had later infiltrated the FLQ.

Would anyone understand? I had been the last person in the world likely to become a police informer. Even to me it still seemed incredible — as incredible as the year 1970, which had caught me up despite myself in its whirlwind and turned my life upside down. And now there was no going back.

CHAPTER 2
A Village Childhood
❧

I almost missed my rendezvous with the year 1970. Shortly after my birth in November, 1945, my mother went into a depression as many women do. She wanted to throw me off the bridge into the Sainte Anne River. My grandfather intervened, and so it happened that I spent the first five years of my life with my grandparents in Sainte Anne de la Pérade. When the time came to start school, I joined my parents and my little sister in Quebec City, but I always returned to La Pérade for the summer holidays, for Christmas, and whenever I needed to recuperate from the strains of family, school, work, or love. It was my real home.

Sainte Anne de la Pérade is a Quebec village settled more than three centuries ago, where the Sainte Anne river flows into the Saint Lawrence. I knew it before the Quiet Revolution came to Quebec to shake a whole society out of its torpor, its traditions, its certainties, its pious unanimities. The serpent hadn't yet slithered into La Pérade.

We lived in the house built by my great-grandfather and it seemed huge to me, full of interesting hiding places and storage rooms. The attic was a treasury of junk packed away in trunks and chests of drawers or stacked in the corners under the cobwebs. There were old dresses, old shoes, cradles, cow bells, bells for horse carriages and sleighs, catalogues, books, holy pictures, hats, a sewing machine, rugs, cloth, rosaries, statues, handbags, and shoe lasts that had belonged to my great-grandfather, who had been a cobbler. You reached the attic by a trap door in the ceiling of my grandfather's room. What excitement I felt when I was allowed in to explore!

We had running water and an indoor toilet, but no bathtub or hot water. We only took a bath three or four times a year. In the summer we waded into the Sainte Anne River. Fall, winter, and spring, we had our baths in a great wooden washtub usually used for soaking the dirty clothes. My grandmother filled every available kettle and pan with water and put them on the wood stove to heat.

The toilet had an overhead box full of water that was released by pulling on the wooden handle at the end of a chain. There was no roll of toilet paper: a spike held pieces of newspaper cut in four-inch squares. On holidays, when visitors were expected, we replaced the newsprint with pieces of silk paper.

The toilet was in such a little cubbyhole that when an adult sat there, his knees got in the way of the door and everyone had to leave the kitchen to give him privacy.

"Carole, go down to the cellar and get me a hunk of salt pork."

"Yes, *Grand-maman.*"

My grandmother was a tiny woman, always wearing silk dresses, woolen socks and slippers. She was a former teacher, and she never raised her voice. I loved her as my mother. She would lift the trap door in the floor of the kitchen and I would climb down the seven wooden steps to the bare earth. Traps were always set there for rats and mice. I would walk over to the row of earthenware jars and jugs filled with molasses, salt pork and my grandfather's wine made from dandelions, cherries, or rhubarb. I would lift the heavy lid, remove a piece of salt pork from the brine, and bring it to my grandmother. She cut it into little squares, boiled them and fried them, then served them with an omelet: she called them *oreilles de Christ*, Christ's ears, a popular dish in the village.

The village had been named in honour of Saint Anne, the mother of Mary and grandmother of Jesus. Its pride was the big, grey stone church, with its two great bell towers dominating the countryside. Everyone was Catholic, everyone went to church on Sunday when the great bells tolled. Crucifixes and holy pictures adorned the walls of all the homes. In my room, which had been my mother's girlhood room, there was a plaster medallion of the Virgin Mary. My Uncle Jules had a plaster bust of Saint Anne on his bureau. Each night before he went to bed, my grandfather would kneel for three minutes before a porcelain bust of the Virgin Mary.

In the stairway in a corner of the kitchen was a picture of the Sacred Heart: Jesus with a glowing red heart coming out of his chest. The picture frame held two palm branches, blessed and distributed at the church on Palm Sunday. We believed that blessed palms protected the house from all sorts of ills.

On Holy Saturday, my grandmother brought a jug to church and filled it, as all the villagers did, with the newly blessed holy water. She kept the jug in the kitchen, and whenever there was a thunderstorm, she took a palm branch from the picture of the Sacred Heart, wet it in the holy water and went about the house sprinkling the doors and windows. Holy water, as everyone knew, was a powerful protector against lightning. Our house had no lightning rod.

Holy water had other uses too. My Uncle Jos lived next door

when he came from Ontario for the holidays. When he was far gone in drink and English songs, my grandmother would fetch her palm and holy water and sprinkle Uncle Jos to rid him of the Devil.

When I was older and again living with my parents, I sometimes had terrible quarrels with my mother who became convinced that the devil had possessed me. She sprinkled me copiously with holy water. Despite her best efforts, the Devil proved tenacious.

As happens in every Catholic country — and Quebec was surely the most Catholic of all — the figures and the objects of religion permeated daily life. Many people in La Pérade punctuated each sentence with invocations to Jesus, the Virgin, the Host, the Tabernacle, the Ciborium, and the Chalice. The priest from his pulpit denounced his flock's profanity. Our family considered these words vulgar as well as blasphemous, and we avoided them.

But we did use other words which were acceptable, such as *târrieu*, perhaps because we did not recognize the medieval curse *tord-dieu* (twist God), and we were on familiar terms with the Devil. We pronounced his name *yâble* rather than *diable*. He came up all the time, usually as a metaphor rather than as an actual evil being. We had mixed feelings about the *yâble*. Sometimes we used his name humorously, sometimes all too seriously. A good fellow was called "a good *yâble*," someone else was "as ugly as the *yâble*." When it thundered, my grandfather would say "the *yâble* is making himself some pancakes," and, when the rain poured down, "the *yâble* is beating his woman and making her cry." To be terribly poor was "to pull the *yâble* by the tail." Someone who indulged in fast living — especially with alcohol and women — was "going straight to the *yâble*." When someone was overambitious, he was said to have "plans to frighten the *yâble*." If a woman suddenly came into money in a way that no one understood, it was said that she "sleeps with the *yâble*." To be really angry was to be "*en yâble*." If you were talking about someone and the person showed, you would say, "speak of the *yâble* and you will see his horns."

There were hundreds of expressions, acceptable to God and the parish priest, which daily invoked the Devil. Then, there were the stories my grandfather told about the Devil. A man ploughed his field on a Sunday and the potatoes turned to stone. A girl went to a dance and a handsome stranger all in black rode up in a sleigh pulled by coal-black horses. She danced with the stranger in a growing frenzy until they disappeared through the wall in a burning flash. My grandfather described in detail the charred hole in the wall.

Although these tales filled me with dread, at least I knew how to take precautions against the Devil. At home, holy water was known to be very effective. And I knew that if you were walking alone far from home on a dark night, you could make the Devil keep his distance by tracing a sign of the cross in the air.

Besides holy water, every well-stocked household had its jug of Easter water. In the Christian calendar, Holy Saturday evening, when Jesus rose from the dead, is the holiest night of the year. Before sunrise on Easter, each family went down to the river to get its year's supply of Easter water. On Holy Saturday, my grandfather would consult his almanac to see what time the sun would rise the next morning, because water collected after sunrise was worthless. He would come to waken me on tiptoe while the whole house was asleep. I dressed quickly and we crept out, hurrying down the path some three hundred yards to the Sainte Anne River. In the darkness, he scooped up the water and we returned to the house. It was stored in the kitchen beside the holy water, each jug labelled carefully because they had different uses.

When I had a sore throat, my grandmother poured out a quarter of a glass of Easter water and I drank it. When I had a fever, she would dip her fingers in the Easter water and apply it to my forehead. When my chest was congested, she spread the water on it. My grandfather sometimes suffered from headaches: my grandmother applied Easter water. Once when her sister Cécile had fallen going down to her cellar, my grandmother treated her injured knee with Easter water. In our village, it was the accepted medicine for all the common ailments. Doctors were called in only rarely, for great emergencies. Easter water worked as well against the infirmities of the body as holy water did against dangers from lightning and the Devil.

We had other protectors against the vicissitudes of life. Each house had its statue of Saint Anthony of Padua, recognized for his powers in locating lost objects. If I lost a key or a two dollar bill, I invoked the Saint: "Dear Saint Anthony, help me to find my key." I would then take my rosary by the crucifix, twirl it in the air and let it fly. I checked to see in what direction the crucifix pointed: that was the direction in which Saint Anthony wanted me to search. Countless lost objects have been found in Sainte Anne de la Pérade thanks to the intervention of Saint Anthony!

Each house had its statue of Saint Jude, patron saint of desperate causes beyond the competence of most other saints. I remember once in particular, one of my grandfather's cows was very sick. We made a novena to Saint Jude: for nine days we burned a candle before his statue. Each evening my grandmother said the same prayer: "Dear Saint Jude, please cure our cow." Alas, Saint Jude did not answer our prayers and the cow had to be slaughtered.

"Saint Jude is busy elsewhere," we rationalized.
My grandmother turned Saint Jude's face to the wall.
"He is being punished," we said.
We had seven statues side by side on a shelf above the doorway
to the toilet in a corner of the kitchen. Saint Francis of Assisi, standing between Saint Anthony of Padua and Saint Jude, was often
invoked: we would write our request on a piece of paper and slip it
under the base of his statue.

Once, when I was about ten years old, I went to the toilet at an
aunt's house and when I closed the door a piece of paper flew down
from the shelf. As I returned home, I read what was written on it:
"Dear Saint Francis, grant that my brother die soon, for he does
not deserve to live with me." That particular brother did not die
until many years later, and Saint Francis of Assisi spent several
years in penance with his face turned toward the wall.

How I remember the Feast of Saint Anne, patron saint of the parish and the village! The feast day was preceded by a novena: for nine
days we went to church to say the rosary, adore the Blessed Sac-
rament, recite the litany of Mary's praises, and hear the pious and
terrible words of high-powered preachers who were brought in for
the occasion. How they would evoke the eternal sufferings of hell!
They assured us that the flames would burn sinners without res-
pite day and night for a year, a century, a millenium, for eternity.
What remorse all this suffering will bring! The preachers warned
us against dancing. Many a lost soul first took the road to hell at
a dance amid laughter and flirtation. When people of the opposite
sex clung to each other in public, who knew to what it would lead?

On July 26, the feast day, the bells rang merrily, hell was forgotten and all was joy. The church was festooned with great banners
that came together in a crown at the highest point of the nave.
Each pillar had its brilliantly coloured pennant. After evening mass,
the whole village walked in a candlelight procession with everyone
carrying a candle set in a paper shield to protect the flame from
the wind.

At the front of the procession, a priest and altar boys in splendid
vestments carried cross, censer, pennants, and tapestries. The tapestries were adorned with scenes from the life of Saint Anne, her
husband Joachim, her sister Elizabeth, her brother-in-law Zacharias,
her daughter Mary, and the Sacred Heart. The citizens of Sainte
Anne de la Pérade walked behind their respective banners: the children of Mary, the Crusaders, the Women of Saint Anne, the Third
Order of Saint Francis, the Knights of Columbus, the Lacordaire
Temperance Circle, the Daughters of Isabella. Above them all billowed
the colours of Mary, heavenly-blue and white. Six sturdy men in

their Sunday clothes carried at shoulder height a dais on which the statue of Saint Anne was enthroned, surmounted by a canopy of gold-coloured satin. From each corner of the dais hung a ribbon held by a woman of Saint Anne. There were two or three Zouaves in grey, red, and gold baggy trousers. They has sworn to defend the Pope to the death; since His Holiness was faring well, our Zouaves guarded the church on solemn occasions against all attacks by Protestant or pagan. We had neither in Sainte Anne de la Pérade but we were prepared.

As we walked through the familiar streets of the village by night, everything and everyone was transformed. The lights from the candles flickered on the houses decked out with the flags of the Pope, of the Sacred Heart and of Quebec. Holy terrors were changed into altar boys, walking with joined hands, slicked down hair, scarlet gowns, and white surplices. They sang the praises of good Saint Anne. Our matrons were radiant with piety and finery in the wavering light. Our parish priest no longer wore his ordinary black soutane: he was resplendent in his white alb, gold chasuble, and gold cape. His eyes were raised to heaven. The parishioners, our neighbours and our relatives, had temporarily left their daily drudgery, their gossiping, their quarrels, and their jealousies. Now forming a guard of honour to accompany the celestial visitor through the streets of the village, they rose to the occasion and shone with the light of heaven reflected by the candles.

The next day, of course, everything returned to normal, like Cinderella's coach after midnight. The flags came down from the houses, the farmers returned to their cows, their chickens, and their pigs. Everyone returned to gossiping and spying on the neighbours, the village's favourite activities.

Proud as we were of our church, which had cost so much and which drew people even from Saint Casimir, twelve miles away, I must confess that our patron Saint was revered more splendidly elsewhere, especially at Sainte Anne de Beaupré, a hundred miles or so down the Saint Lawrence River. There, miracles abounded, and July 26 brought sick or crippled pilgrims from all over Quebec, Ontario, New Brunswick, and even the United States.

Our village church met the ordinary needs of the liturgical year. When the need was very great, however, we went elsewhere. Our favourite place of pilgrimage was Notre-Dame du Cap Basilica, in the city of Cap de la Madeleine, twenty-two miles from Sainte Anne de la Pérade. Miracles happened routinely in that enormous church, several times the size of ours. Hanging from the stone wall were crutches, wooden legs, glasses, orthopedic devices, and plaster casts left behind by the grateful cured. I have a cousin who was miraculously cured there. She had fallen while climbing and the wound on her hip would not heal. For ten years she was unable to walk and remained in bed. Finally, one year, she insisted on being taken to Notre-Dame du Cap for the Feast of Saint Anne. There, during the blessing of the sick, she stood up and took a few steps. Within days she could walk. After this miracle, she entered a convent and became a Carmelite nun, in accordance with the vow she had made when she had prayed to be cured.

In a village like Sainte Anne de la Pérade, human nature reveals itself as it rarely does in a big city. Generations live side by side. One is initiated into the Family Secrets, terrible stories about a cousin, an uncle, a great-aunt, a neighbour, and the neighbour's ancestors. The transmission of the Family Secrets is a solemn occasion: sometimes it takes years of hints, of veiled references, of refusal to share the secret because it is too horrible, before the skeleton finally comes out of the closet, amid pledges of eternal silence. It is a mark of the greatest friendship when two people of the same age trade their Family Secrets.

So I learned of the woman in the village who became pregnant by her brother and lover. A boy I knew had a priest as his natural father. An old maid had an abortion at home and kept the fetus in a jar on a shelf in her kitchen. There was the man who shut himself up alone in his house to dress in corset and panties. A man, years before, had murdered his friend: everyone knew about it, but he was never prosecuted. There were the two simple-minded sisters: although they were adults, they wandered around with dolls and a stuffed bear. Local men picked them up and they were always getting pregnant. They liked to raise their skirts and show their panties.

"Look at the pretty panties my boyfriend gave me," they would say in childish voices.

After each had produced half-a-dozen babies for adoption, arrangements were made to have them sterilized.

There were the dirty old men who chased young girls and tried to get them to undress. Our parents warned us not to get into their cars. When I was about nine, the parish priest tried to touch me on my private parts. I poured a bottle of mineral water over his head. How he roared! One little girl of eight was encouraged by her mother to be especially friendly to this same priest.

"Give a big kiss to *Monsieur le curé*," she would say when he came visiting. As he left, she would send the girl alone into the dark front hallway to help him on with his coat.

"I hoped he would remember you in his will; he was quite rich," she explained years later.

The same people lived side by side for generations. They kept the same names — not just the family names, but even the nicknames. A man some generations back who kept sheep had both their smell and their curly hair. He was called *Mouton*, and all his descendants were called *Mouton*. The Mouton-Charest family is well known in Sainte Anne de la Pérade.

The local fire brigade was made up of volunteers. Its equipment consisted of a red wagon with a barrel on it and a pump. When there was a fire, the chief hitched himself between the two traces and ran at top speed towards the fire.

During my early years, the political machine of Premier Maurice Duplessis ran Quebec. Our neighbours were ardent supporters of his Union Nationale party. When one of the young women got married, a gift of a stove or a refrigerator came from Duplessis. Families that "voted the right way" received truckloads of gravel for their yards. We Liberals were neglected. On the back roads outside the village, you found alternating stretches of asphalt and unpaved gravel. The asphalt ran along the farms of Duplessis supporters, the unpaved roads indicated a Liberal's farm. You knew at a glance people's political affiliation. Jobs on the provincial roads went to supporters of Duplessis. My family had no claim to the regime's largesse: my Uncle Jules was active in the Liberal party, and the morning after one election my grandfather awoke to find a funeral wreath hanging on our front door.

Another uncle, my father's youngest brother, hid out to avoid conscription during the Second World War. It was a kind of tradition in Sainte Anne de la Pérade. There were men in the village who had hidden in the woods during the First World War. The people of La Pérade understood: they had little use for wars in distant countries that no one had ever seen. They preferred to die at home. So Uncle Jean-Robert kept moving from the house of one sister to another sister's, or to his mother's house. When the military police came to La Pérade, the word was passed around and my uncle disappeared. He was never caught.

In winter, we would go ice-fishing. Around Christmas time, swarms of little fish swam up the Saint Lawrence and into the Sainte Anne River to spawn. The whole village moved onto the ice to catch the tomcod, also known as frostfish. People hauled special fish huts onto the frozen river, and in January you could see hundreds of them on the ice, a whole portable village.

Each fish hut had its own wood-burning stove and the plumes of smoke rose in the cold air. There was a gap in the floor on either side of the stove, eighteen inches by three feet. My grandfather would saw two holes through the ice and we would dangle our lines from pegs on the wall. The hooks were baited with pig liver, and a matchstick was knotted into each line at eye level. When a fish would bite, the match jerked about. We lifted the fish out of the water, unhooked it and tossed it through the window to freeze on the ice outside. We would catch as many as a thousand little fish in a day. My grandfather would gather them into a jute sack and store them in a shed behind our house.

Sometimes we would invite all our relatives from neighbouring villages for a feast. Grandfather would bring in about a hundred fish from the shed to be thawed and cleaned. Grandmother and her two sisters prepared them. Cooked with little, yellowish eggs they made a delicious omelet. The fish, head and tail and all, were dipped in milk and flour and fried. When the meal was over, we could scarcely walk away from the table.

The fish huts were not only used for fishing, as everyone knew. In February, they were pulled back to their usual place in the back yards. Curtains covered the windows. The cabins were favourite meeting places for lovers, and many a citizen of Sainte Anne de la Pérade owes life today to a rendezvous there.

My own first, furtive explorations took place in our fish hut. My cousin, a girl my age, and I used to pick the seed pods of a vine called climbing cucumber that grows along river banks. Ripening in August, these fruits look like tiny cucumbers covered with down. They exploded with a vulgar sound when struck against the palm: to our childish ears it was the height of daring, and we would burst out laughing. Inside each pod is a little seed. After bolting the door of the cabin and drawing the curtains we would play doctor and patient, using the seed as a treatment. Even today, after thirty years, I blush when I recall those forbidden games.

I learned about life in a very small world between 1945 and 1950 in Sainte Anne de la Pérade. Some will find it backward, even comic, but it had a long tradition. My ancestors lived there long before Confederation gave birth to Canada in 1867, long before the Treaty of Paris in 1763 confirmed the conquest of New France.

My father's family had lived in Sainte Anne de la Pérade for about three-and-a-half centuries. On my mother's side, Pierre Duval had accompanied Champlain in 1608 and, shortly after arriving on Canadian soil, was hanged by the famous explorer for mutiny. In La Pérade, about half the inhabitants were my relatives. Here you could see the ruins of the manor where Madeleine de Verchères, wife of the Seigneur de la Pérade, who gave his name to the village, had lived. At the age of twelve she became a heroine of New France by defending alone a fort attacked by Indians. Even more of a heroine to me than Madeleine de Verchères was

Jeanne d'Arc. One of my earliest memories is of a picture of Jeanne that hung at the top of the stairs. She seemed beautiful to me with her short, straight hair, and the armour that covered her from her shoulders to her feet. I was fascinated by the story of this shepherd girl sent by heaven to fight *les Anglais* and drive them out of France. Long before I could read, I listened to my visiting mother tell me the tale. Mother's name was also Jeanne, and she had taken Jeanne d'Arc as her patron saint. Five or six books around my grandmother's house had pictures of the main episodes of Jeanne's life. I would thumb through them by the hour.

One picture showed a shepherdess sitting under a tree whose branches were bathed in a radiant light. My mother explained: "That's Saint Margaret and the Archangel Michael telling Jeanne, 'You must drive the English out of France.'"

Another picture showed Jeanne on horseback, brandishing a sword in battle. "Jeanne is at Orleans, fighting the English."

A few pages later, a proud Jeanne, in armour, was presenting a man on his knees to the bishop. "Here, Jeanne has Charles VII crowned King of France after defeating the English."

Then the most dramatic picture of all: a woman in a long dress, tied to a post. The flames at her feet rose from burning branches. Around her were smirking, evil-looking men. A priest was holding up, on the end of a long stick, a crucifix for Jeanne to kiss. "This shows the English burning Jeanne d'Arc. They say she is a witch, but really they want to put her to death because she defeated them."

How I admired Jeanne, how I hated *les Anglais*. For me, *les Anglais* who burned Jeanne were the same *Anglais* who had taken over Canada.

"*Grand-papa*, who are *les Anglais*?"

He would answer: "*Les Anglais* are those who stole our country at the Battle of the Plains of Abraham."

They were somewhere around us, *les Anglais*, but where? I never saw a single English person in my ancestral village, where everyone spoke French. The closest I came to the English was Uncle Jos, my grandmother's brother who worked for a railroad somewhere in Ontario. There, we knew, everyone spoke English. He would come visiting and, when he had had a few drinks, he would take his bath in the washtub and sing in English, "You are my sunshine, my only sunshine . . ." Or, sometimes, "It's a long way to Tipperary . . ."

At first, those strange words astonished me.

"It's because he works in Ontario with *les Anglais*," people explained.

He liked to dress up and wear ties on which appeared bikini-clad girls standing in a martini glass. General disapproval! I used to imagine Ontario as a place filled with *les Anglais* working along a railway track and half drunk on the top of the telegraph poles singing, "You are my sunshine . . ."

I didn't want to go to Ontario.

Though there were no *Anglais* at Sainte Anne de la Pérade, they had left their traces everywhere. My grandmother would ask me to bring her the *thé-pott* to make tea; she gave me a nickel to buy an ice cream *cone*, my grandfather ate his *papparmannes*, we washed the dishes in the *sink*, we were never to play on the *track*, my grandmother made her cakes, not with *farine* but with *fleur*, the French word for flower. We didn't go to the *toilette* but to the *closettes*. I thought all those words were French. Later, when I studied in Montreal and discovered that they were English, I was indignant. I would try to correct my grandmother and tell her to say *théière*, rather than *thé-pott*, but without success. I still wonder how so many English words invaded the French spoken at La Pérade. No one understood a word of that language, and no *Anglais* had ever settled in the area. Not an *Anglais* at Grondines, not an *Anglais* at Batiscan, not an *Anglais* at Saint Casimir, not an *Anglais* at Saint Alban, not an *Anglais* at Saint Narcisse; no *Anglais* until you got to Trois Rivières or Shawinigan!

For us, *les Anglais* remained foreigners and alien residents, even though they had started to call themselves Canadians after a century or two in residence. We didn't like their language and, as far as possible, refused to speak it.

My grandfather would bounce me on his knee and sing songs that our ancestors had brought from France.

"*C'était Anne de Bretagne, duchesse en sabots . . .*"

"*Grand-papa*, who is Anne of Brittany?"

Or he would sing: "*Sont les filles de la Rochelle . . .*"

"*Grand-papa*, what is la Rochelle?"

"It's a city at home in France," he would reply.

My grandmother brought me to the Place Royale in Quebec City, which dates back to the early years of New France. In the middle of the square there is a bust of Louis XIV.

"*Grand-maman*, who is that?"

"It is Louis XIV, the greatest of our kings."

"Our kings" were the kings of France. When George VI died and Elizabeth succeeded him, I asked my mother who they were.

"George VI was the king of England. Elizabeth is his daughter, and she is now queen of England." He was not our king, she was not our queen, whatever the rest of Canada might say.

One day I was taken to the Plains of Abraham, beside the walls of Quebec City, where the English under James Wolfe defeated the

French under the Marquis de Montcalm. It saddened me to see the place where New France had been so terribly wounded. But I admired the massive statue of Jeanne d'Arc on horseback, her sword high, that overlooks the Plains. Is it a warning to *les Anglais*? Have the Quebecois been waiting all those years for a Jeanne d'Arc to return and drive the *Anglais* out of Canada?

CHAPTER 3
Education of Various Kinds

——————————— ❦ ———————————

At the age of five, I left Sainte Anne de la Pérade and my grandparents to move to Quebec City with my parents and younger sister. We stayed there for three years and then settled permanently in Montreal.

I missed my grandparents and returned to stay with them at every opportunity. They were like my real parents. My relationship was distant with my father, who worked for Canadian Pacific Railways as a station agent and later a superintendent. He seemed uncomfortable with the women in his family. As for my mother, the rift between us at my birth was never entirely mended. Our relations were troubled and often stormy.

I was a lonely, uncommunicative child, painfully sensitive. I could not bear to be laughed at or to be seen making a mistake. So I shunned games of skill such as skipping or hop-scotch. I was simply too vulnerable to risk making friends. If someone scolded me, I would burst into a flood of tears. Once, when my mother was angry at me, I decided to put an end to my life and drank chlorine bleach, but fortunately the first mouthful so burned my throat that I retched and reconsidered.

Like many other little girls of bourgeois families, I attended a convent school, first in Quebec City, then Regina Assumpta convent school in Montreal, and was taught from Grade One to the age of eighteen by the nuns of the Congrégation de Notre-Dame. I had learned my letters before starting school and excelled in every subject except mathematics. Reading was my favourite pastime and I whiled away the hours daydreaming about what I had read. I had devoured many books on ancient mythology by the time I was twelve. At thirteen, I discovered a forbidden treasure in the basement in a padlocked trunk. Curious, I unscrewed the trunk's hinges and found it full of books: many racy love stories that my mother did not want her children to see, as well as biographies of Mazarin, Richelieu, François I, Louis XIV, and Jeanne d'Arc. What a delight!

I shoved aside the love stories, which were soon to absorb my younger sister Agathe, and plunged into the furtive reading of history. A marvellous world opened before me, so much more entrancing than my daily round of convent and home.

My mastery of the dynastic intricacies of the kings of France became legendary at school. No wonder. In my dream world, I invented elaborate courtships between Louis XIV and me — transformed into the French noblewoman, Marie-Caroline de Valbrune. This lady of my creation was more real than my teachers or my schoolmates. I haunted the library so that every detail of my elaborate imaginings would be authentic. I began reading about A.C. Boulle, who made Louis XIV's furniture. I learned all I could about the family of Louis and their quirks. Versailles held no mysteries when finally I was presented at court on the king's own insistence, and the ladies wondered enviously who this stranger might be.

"Miss de Vault, could you tell us the last words of Montcalm?"

I was always too bashful to ask a question, or to raise my hand to volunteer an answer, and to be questioned in class struck me with terror. I would blush scarlet.

"Miss de Vault, what were the last words of Montcalm?"

At the front of most classrooms, both in Quebec City and Montreal, there hung a picture of a wounded general of the French regime, a bandage wrapped around his head, attended by a Jesuit, a nun, and a peasant. It was the Marquis de Montcalm, fatally wounded during the battle of the Plains of Abraham. At the bottom of the picture were printed his last words.

I blurted out the sentence: "I die happy, for I shall not see Quebec in the hands of the English."

The world of the convent was as unreal, in its own way, as the imaginary world of my daydreams. Every day, the nuns taught us to live in a time and place that bore little resemblance to Quebec in the twentieth century. They did their best to turn our thoughts and aspirations to heaven. In secondary school, we concentrated on the study of ancient Latin and ancient Greek. Contemporary Greece and Rome didn't exist. We studied the history of France before the Revolution as though it were our own. For us, the Golden Age was the era of New France, when Catholic Church and State were one. Everything since was decadence, Eden after the Fall.

I have before me my class picture from May, 1961, when I was fifteen. It speaks volumes to me today! Twenty-three girls, all dressed in the identical convent uniform: heavy navy-blue dress, white plastic cuffs, white plastic collars, heavy cotton stockings and heavy brown shoes. They all sit with the same straight back, right hand resting palm upwards in the left hand, the right heel lodged at a forty-five degree angle against the left instep. The desks are all cleared. The nuns had a passion for order and uniformity. In her desk, each girl had the identical black veil for going to chapel on ordinary occasions and a white veil with white gloves for solemn occasions, as well as school books, a prayer book, and a rosary.

In the picture, I'm the second girl in the second row, looking out sadly at the world with a frozen face, no trace of a smile.

At the back of the room on the blackboard, you can see a drawing of the Virgin Mary with a faun, and the words of a prayer to Our Lady of Adolescents. On one side of the room there is a map of Gaul at the time of Clovis, on the other side a poster of a medieval cathedral with the single word: FRANCE.

You can't see the front of the class in the photo, but I remember a crucifix and a picture of the founder of the Congrégation, Marguerite Bourgeoys, her hands joined in prayer. She was constantly put forward as our model.

One day she was at her father's home in France when the Virgin Mary appeared to her and said: "Marguerite, go to Canada." She came, helped found Montreal, and became the colony's first teacher, with French and Indian girls as her students. The nuns of the Congrégation led us in prayers for the canonization of their founder.

Each day, we filled in beside our names on the blackboard three columns: the number of masses we had attended, the rosaries we had recited, the sacrifices we had made. At the end of the week, the nun would reward the most deserving students by putting on the tongue of each a little silk-paper image of Marguerite Bourgeoys. It was hard to swallow without water, but it was hoped that the holy lady might reward some of us with a call to the Congrégation de Notre-Dame.

Like so many girls, I felt a call for a while, but to the contemplative and austere order of the Carmelites. Louis XIV and Peter the Great disappeared from my life. I renounced Prince Orlov, thinking only of taking the veil and devoting myself to God. To begin my ascent of Mount Carmel, I got up at five-thirty to attend six o'clock mass at the parish church. I arrived early at the convent, went to the chapel for prayer before and after school, morning and afternoon. My daydreams were taken over by Saint Teresa of Avila, the great mystic and reformer of the Carmelites, whose biography I had read. Daughter of a noble family, she lived in a castle, was in love, and wore splendid clothes. Then came her conversion. Each nun in her order received just one robe which she was to wear till death, and slept nightly in the coffin which was to be in her grave. A skull glowed in every cell. With what passion I set about emulating the Carmelites.

At home, I was considerate with my sister and ate everything my mother served me, even the fish that I hated. To practise sacrifice, I burned my toast and ate one egg instead of two. Before falling asleep I recited the rosary, to my mother's surprise. My favourite book was *The Confessions* of Saint Augustine. I prayed and prayed, and awaited a vision, sometimes studying the moonbeams on a cloud for signs of an approaching celestial visitor, but none came.

I soon wearied of sanctity. I lost heart at the prospect of a long diet of fish. My visits to the chapel fell off. Richelieu returned to see me. Soon I was Charlotte Corday, that young noblewoman who assassinated Marat in his bath, then Josephine de Beauharnais and Maria-Theresa of Austria. I married Bismarck. I was the wife of Montezuma and punished Cortez for the death of my husband: it was I who led the revolt against the Spaniards.

It seemed I lacked a true vocation. The prudery of the nuns put me off. They warned us not to sit on warm radiators for fear of carnal pleasure. We were to sleep at night on our backs, with hands outside the blankets. Recklessly, I slept on my stomach, my arms wrapped around my pillow. The boarders at the convent took neither bath nor shower. They washed with a face cloth under an ankle-length nightie, and dressed and undressed under the same nightie to avoid catching a glimpse of their own bodies. I particularly disliked a piece of clothing we wore for gym called *bouffants*, bloomers with an elastic belt and loose legs that ended at the knee. They were worn over top of our long cotton stockings to make sure that no one could see our panties when we stretched our legs. After gym, we had to remain in our bouffants for the rest of the day with no shower or change of clothing.

The constant admonitions against consorting with boys were lost on me: I was far too shy even to speak to a boy, much less respond to amorous advances.

One day, I read an article about Mata Hari, the famous spy of the First World War. That night I became Mata Hari, though it wasn't easy: I was required to betray the French for the benefit of the Germans. But war is war, and I rather enjoyed the life of a spy. I became a singer in a cabaret frequented by French officers. Soon a lieutenant courted me and I accepted his favours: he had a strategic posting, and of course confided to me the plans for military operations. I left the coded information in milk bottles to be picked up by an accomplice disguised as a milkman.

Sometimes I almost fell in love. What anguish! But of course I couldn't afford to love someone I was betraying.

The French officers came to arrest me at last. Some had been my lovers. What a painful, passionate scene! They offered to spare my life if I agreed to work for them. But I could never betray my country, Germany! They sentenced me to death, but out of respect for my intelligence and daring they let me choose the time and place of my execution. It took place at dawn under an oak tree. I died with my head high, while my former lovers wept.

"*Mesdemoiselles, faites la révérence!*" The voice of Mother Saint Cecile, ordering us to curtsy. From the courts and intrigues of Europe to Regina Assumpta Convent was a painful transition, though the nuns practised a protocol as punctilious as that of the Bourbons or the Romanovs. Its triumph was the annual visit of the Mother Superior-General of the Congrégation.

For two weeks, the convent's 400 girls were drilled as we prepared to honour the distinguished visitor in the assembly hall. To please her eye, we had to be seated in three sizes, small, medium, and tall. Age or grade made no difference. The nuns corrected the inconsistencies of nature by making us sit on books of varying thickness. We were a geometric wonder to behold.

Four hundred girls waited, all identically dressed, all level, all sitting straight-backed on the edge of the chair, chin high, every right hand in white lace glove resting palm upward in the left hand, every right foot flat on the floor at the same angle to every left foot. Mother Superior-General swept in with her attendants and took her place on the stage.

Mother Saint Cecile appeared behind her. With imperious hand, she directed the magic of our movements, though she no longer counted out the beats as she had during rehearsals. We had been trained like a corps de ballet.

At a signal we rose from our seats. One! Two! Three! The same smile appeared on 400 faces. Then began the curtsy. Each hand raised a corner of the navy-blue dress. One! Eight hundred knees bent. Two! The knees parted. Three! Each girl, back straight, chin up, had dipped to the same depth and 400 voices chanted, "*Bonjour, Mére générale!*"

Another signal from Mother Saint Cecile's hand. One! Two! Three! Up again, then seated. The look on her face told us when we had succeeded, but what a frown appeared there when a small girl knocked over her dictionary!

Mother Superior-General, too, was well rehearsed. She smiled. She gave us a little speech on a pious subject. We listened, 400 pairs of eyes on her. If she had delivered a pleasantry we would have known how to laugh: the nuns had taught us to laugh, neither too loud nor too low, making the sound "hee-hee-hee," but never "ha-ha-ha" nor "ho-ho-ho," which were considered vulgar.

In fact, Mother Superior-General's homily never gave rise to levity. Nor did we applaud when she finished, though the nuns had also taught us how to applaud, the left hand held motionless, the lower fingers of the right hand tapping gently against the palm of the left. Mother Superior-General always asked us to sing. One! Two! Three! On our feet, we sang in honour of the founder of the Congrégation. "O Mother Marguerite, you who came from France . . ."

When I was sixteen, I wrote a paper on the poet Charles Baudelaire that was a labour of love. No poet had ever inspired me with such a passion. Somehow, I had come across a copy of *Les Fleurs du Mal*. My mother disapproved of my reading a book on the Index, the list of books forbidden by the Catholic Church, and she hid my copy under a leaf of the kitchen table. After discovering the hiding place, I would read my book crouched under the table, then put it back so she would not be inclined to change the hiding place. Soon I knew some thirty poems by heart. Baudelaire's aestheticism and his sensuality seduced me. Perhaps, too, feeling myself different from my schoolmates, unable to communicate my thoughts and feelings to anyone, I recognized in him a kindred spirit, a lost soul.

Eventually we studied Baudelaire at the convent. Of course we could not read *Les Fleurs du Mal* itself; we sampled the author by only the chaste poem "L'Albatross." No mention was made of the poems that had awakened such a rapturous response in me. The nun spoke of Baudelaire's platonic love for the society woman, Madame Sabatier, but not a word about his passion for Jeanne Duval, the mulatto woman who became his mistress.

When the nun asked us to write a ten-page essay on a nineteenth-century poet, I chose Baudelaire and wrote twenty pages, after devouring every book on him in the Montreal library. I was proud of my work which had caught, I was sure, the very essence of Baudelaire's poetry, his sensuality, and his mysticism.

My paper came back with a grade of 67 percent. I was used to 90 percent for less ambitious work. Despite my shyness, for once I went and spoke to the nun to ask why she has assigned such a low grade. Her lips were tight as she replied, "Why, Carole, I admit that you did very good work, but you seem to have forgotten that, at the end of his life, Baudelaire felt the call of Catholicism. He wanted to return to his religion, but died before he was able to see a priest. It is from his death that Baudelaire's work takes all its meaning."

A moment of repentance that existed only in her pious imagination was much more significant for her than everything the poet had written; his return to Catholicism meant more than his long revolt against the pieties of his times. I was disgusted.

That was how we studied literature. And there was only one great literature — French literature.

"*Mesdemoiselles,* of course other nations have their great writers. England has Byron, Milton, the Brontë sisters, and Shakespeare. It is not certain, though, that Shakespeare existed; his name is said to have been a pseudonym for several playwrights. Germany had Goethe and Schiller. Italy, Dante, Boccaccio and Petrarch. Spain gave birth only to Cervantes. Russia, more fortunate, had Dostoevski, Tolstoi, Gogol, Pushkin, Turgenev, Chekhov. But none has a literature to compare with ours. What land can boast of a Villon in the Middle Ages, an Anatole France or a Paul Claudel in the twentieth century, and in between, a Ronsard or a du Bellay during the Renaissance, a classical period with Racine, Corneille, and Molière, a romantic period with Balzac, Lamartine, Vigny, de Staël, and Chateaubriand?"

In Quebec, our literature was French literature, just as our history was French history. The literature of England or of English Canada was as alien as their kings and queens.

Of course we could not read books on the Index. We read authors only in expurgated editions. We could not read *The Hunchback of Notre-Dame* because Victor Hugo was on the Index, as were also Balzac and Stendhal. There was no question of reading Molière's *Tartuffe,* in which he mocked pious hypocrites; we made do with *Le Misanthrope*. Voltaire was the Devil personified; Rousseau, Montesquieu, Diderot, and Zola were all on the Index. Even reading the Bible was forbidden: the Holy Spirit did not write for convent girls. We studied the world's greatest literature only through the fragments that escaped the Index.

When I was sixteen, a girl in my class invited me to go with her to La Paloma, a downtown café. It opened up for me a world completely different from the stifling atmosphere of the convent: a world of semi-darkness, of irregularity, of the present, of spontaneity. A world that Marguerite Bourgeoys would not have recognized.

From the street, we went down three steps into a room where two people sat at a games board. Down several more steps was a dimly lit room with five tables. Ahead, an archway led into a bigger room with refectory tables. No windows. There was a mural of a bullfight on one wall. On another wall, a painting of the Costa del Sol. Here and there, theatre posters. La Paloma was run, we were later to learn, by a Spaniard called Diego, who was said to be a refugee from the Spanish Civil War. Here, in 1962 and 1963, I spent many hours supplementing my convent education.

The people there struck me at once. Girls with long, free-flowing hair, their faces pale with make-up, listened to bearded young men with wooden crosses around their necks. It was still startling, in 1962, to see a man under sixty-five wearing a beard.

They spoke of Camus, of Simone de Beauvoir, or of Jean-Paul Sartre. "You must read *Nausea*. It's all there. Sartre said it. There is nothing to justify existence."

What sadness, what world-weariness at those tables! They sipped espresso coffee or Brio, an Italian soft drink. No one would have thought of asking for a Coke, a Pepsi, or a Seven-Up. Above the counter was a poster of Sophia Loren holding up a bottle of Brio like a torch.

I happened on an evening of poetry recitals on my second visit. A short, scrawny young man declaimed his verse from his seat at a table. Suddenly he leaped up, seized a bottle of Brio, and threw it to the floor, then overturned the table with a flourish. The Brio splashed a few patrons and formed a puddle at their feet.

"Ah, life! There is life . . . spilled on the floor," he exclaimed. "Nothing binds us to life: it must be spilled."

The imperturbable Diego mopped up the Brio while the poet, still glowing with the aftereffects of inspiration, called for an espresso and lit a cigarette. He was with a girl as skinny as himself. Her blonde hair fell almost to her waist and her pale skin contrasted with her black clothes. She worked, it seemed, as a telephone operator and her companion's poetic outburst left her unfazed. But she had a world-weariness of her own.

"I'm so damned tired of plugging at the Bell!"

I learned later that the poet, Christian, belonged to a very aristocratic family. He had rejected everything: his family, his house, his bourgeois upbringing, and his college friends, all in the name of poetry and of existentialism. He lived in a cheap room, foreswore gainful employment, and was always broke. Others paid for his coffee and he rewarded them with poetry. He enjoyed second-rate American movies and went regularly with a woman who paid for them both. He fathered two or three children by different women. One day, he disappeared. When he showed up again, he told us he had gone to the far north and married an Eskimo woman, according to the rites of her tribe. For weeks he discoursed on the life, manners, and customs of the Eskimo. He explained that his wife, refusing to live in Montreal, remained in the north. Some cynics suggested his only trip north had been made on drugs.

A jukebox played the songs of Jacques Brel: "The bourgeois are like pigs, the older they get, the more beastly they are." Over and over, we listened to the songs of Juliette Greco, protegée of Jean-

Paul Sartre. Her voice was deep, tragic, languorous, her eyes black pools of mascara, her black hair framed a pale face. She sang a warning: "If you imagine, young girl, young girl, if you imagine that it will, it will last . . ."

We disdained American pop songs, preferring Léo Ferré singing the poems of Louis Aragon, Verlaine and Baudelaire. We tried to live Saint Germain des près in Montreal.

The style ran to leather. Girls wore skirts of black or brown leather, boys wore leather trousers. The goddess of leather at La Paloma was the singer Ginette Ravel: she wore black leather trousers, a black leather vest, and leather belt. It was even whispered that she had a black leather bikini. She was often with the sculptor Armand Vaillancourt, who had not yet caused a sensation in Toronto by leaving his pile of pieces of metal unassembled, or in San Francisco by inscribing on his commissioned fountain: *"Vive le Québec libre!"* In 1962 he, too, wore black leather pants, vest, and tie. He tried to explain to us the beauties of modern sculpture, without success.

What a contrast with the frozen world of the convent! Here, everyone devoured Albert Camus. One Friday, I had left in my school desk my copy of *The Outsider*. I should have remembered that the nuns routinely rifled our desks. By Monday the book had disappeared. I did not ask for an explanation, knowing that the teacher had taken it. Some time afterwards, she passed me in the corridor as I was lost in a book. Her tone ominous, she asked: "Carole, what are you reading this time?" She looked at the title; Dante's *Divine Comedy*. Embarrassed at her mistake, she said hastily, "Ah, that's good, very good."

The nuns tried to keep us in a walled garden, protected from all the winds sweeping the world. The Quiet Revolution was underway all around us. The old certainties had begun to crumble. Within a year, control of education was to be taken away from the Church and given to the State by the establishment of a ministry of education. Soon, in the spring of 1963, the first bombs of the FLQ would explode in the mailboxes of Westmount. But the nuns continued to cultivate their charges like delicate flowers in a fragile greenhouse.

At La Paloma I was running away from the convent, and away from Sainte Anne de la Pérade. Much of Quebec was running away from its past at that time, four years after the death of Maurice Duplessis.

Spain and Spaniards were in. We read *Blood Wedding* and *The House of Bernarda Alba*, by Federico Garcia Lorca, and *The Master of Santiago* by Henri de Montherlant: the action took place in Spain. Diego would approach the refectory tables where we sat and recite in animated Spanish the poem by Garcia Lorca, *"Cinque horas de la tarde"*; the blood of the civil war victims ran in the streets. Some of us understood, others pretended to follow. Knowing Spanish was very chic.

We thought of ourselves as "beatniks." None, as far as I know, had ever been to San Francisco, but some had seen Greenwich Village.

The most "beat" of all was a fellow usually to be found alone at a table for two in the darkest corner of La Paloma. He rarely spoke. His eyes, deep-set, conveyed a constant sadness. His hair fell down his shoulders at a time when the most daring wore their hair ear-length, and his beard reached his chest. He wore sandals without socks, even when snow covered the ground. He spent his time reading or carving out wooden crosses that he sold on the street: they were worn around the neck on a shoelace. If you spoke to him, his only answer was an enigmatic smile. He lived as an ascetic. He ate little, was terribly thin, constantly frozen except in summer, often afflicted with a cold. How old was he? I couldn't tell. Perhaps twenty or thirty, but he looked older.

His name was Jean Roy. He was later to be a Director of the Company of Young Canadians during the period when its Quebec branch advocated revolution. He became a printer. During the FLQ crisis, he was arrested and jailed under the War Measures Act. Now he sits on the Montreal city council. I got to know him quite well.

Another regular was Louis Lépine. Red-haired, bearded, barefoot, he also sold wooden crosses. During a summer visit to the Gaspé, he discovered agates on the seashore. He turned them into earrings, pendants, or pins and sold them instead of wooden crosses. Soon Jean Roy's trade suffered from the competition of Louis's agates.

The poet Gaston Miron would come by too, and I remember the nationalist poet Paul Marie Lapointe, who carried with him designs for a proper Canadian flag. His favourite among his sketches was green, with a field of flowers. He took it all very seriously; this was before separatism had become the artists' creed.

These people cared about books and ideas, as I did. I soon felt more at home at La Paloma than in the stifling moralism of Regina Assumpta Convent. The refectory tables, seating twenty, encouraged mixing. I lost some of my shyness. I bought a black turtleneck sweater and black slacks. Slacks! If the nuns could see me! On weekdays, I wore the convent uniform. On weekends, I undid my braids and let my hair fall down my back.

I fell in love. At least, I thought it was love. His name was Gaston, and he was a student a few months older than I, who lived a block away from my home and also went to La Paloma. It was more than an hour by bus from my home in Ahuntsic. Soon, we made the trip together. He would speak of Verlaine, of Aragon, of de Montherland, Malraux, and Camus. I thought he was very handsome, with his blue eyes and brown hair.

We walked along the street hand-in-hand, reciting verse by Prévert. His hair was long for the time and he had a trim beard. People would stare at us and whisper, "They are beatniks." We would kiss openly in the streets.

Sometimes, we left La Paloma in a group and hitch-hiked into the Laurentians, to Val David. There, at the *boite* (café) called La Butte à Mathieu, we listened to Pauline Julien, just back from Paris, singing French songs. She discovered Quebec some time later. We also heard Ginette Ravel, Pierre Létourneau, Claude Gauthier, Félix Leclerc, and Tex Lecor, seated on cushions on the floor in reverent silence. When the performance was over we hitch-hiked back, sometimes in the rain. I always travelled with Gaston.

One day, I ran away from home after a fierce quarrel with my mother. I took a taxi to La Paloma and met Gaston. I told him I was never going home again, so he decided to stay with me. Though he lived at home, he took me that night to the apartment of some friends, where we spent the night in separate beds. The next day we wandered together through the streets of Montreal, stopping now and then to visit friends. We planned to spend our lives together. He would teach and I would become a nurse.

It was November 7, 1962: the next day would be my birthday. Snow fell on Sherbrooke Street, I was cold and hungry and began to feel sorry for myself. We again spent the night with friends. The day I turned seventeen, we both felt sad. As we sat over coffee in a restaurant, Gaston suggested I call my mother. Soon he and I were back in our respective homes.

Despite emancipated talk, I was still a virgin. If Gaston had insisted on our making love, I would have been willing, but he wanted to imitate Jean Roy and his asceticism. He rejected the pleasures of the flesh in favour of poetry, which he hoped some day to write.

I continued to see him and to suppose we were in love. True, he was now frequently in the company of a plump girl who worked as a nurse and modelled nude at the art school. Her name was Monique. Gaston assured me that she was just a friend. One day at La Paloma, I learned that she was pregnant by Gaston. The ascetic had relaxed his stern principles. I was crushed. For three weeks, I cried myself to sleep. When I saw him at La Paloma I looked away, my head high, and refused to speak to him. It took four months before the hurt ended.

Five years later, on my way to the Saint Jean Baptiste parade which was to end in a riot, I stopped off at La Paloma after a long absence. Gaston was there and we chatted. I found him a dullard and wondered what I had ever seen in him. He scarcely remembered me from the past.

It was unfashionable to be a virgin. All the girls wanted to lose their virginity. When we saw a girl often with the same man, it was quite proper to ask, "Have you slept with him?" If she answered no, she was considered a hopeless case, she was *niaiseuse*, someone who didn't know the score. If a boy was still a virgin, he was called by the medieval word for virgin, *puceau*; no one wanted to carry the name. Boys sometimes told the story of how they had been sexually initiated, but the story often changed from one telling to the next.

If a girl wanted to become an actress, she was told, "You will have to lose your virginity if you want a role. How do you think Marina Vlady became what she is?" Vlady, of Russian origin, was the French actress of the hour, the idol of La Paloma.

As for me, I did not know exactly how you lost your virginity. I knew you had to do something with a boy, but what, I couldn't have said. At Regina Assumpta, most of the girls were as ignorant as I was.

Sometimes at La Paloma a girl would announce: "Tonight I'm going to lose my virginity." She left, and the next time we saw her she would say simply, "It's done."

"Who with?"

"I don't even know his name. Now that he's done what I wanted of him, I don't intend to see him again."

"What was it like?" we would ask.

"There's nothing to it. I expected it to hurt, but I hardly felt a thing."

Most of these people were in revolt against their strict religious upbringing, against convent and home. I remember one girl who arrived at La Paloma in a Jaguar, and there she railed against the bourgeoisie, of which, of course, she was a member.

It was fashionable to live in "pads," or *piaules*, run-down rooms on Sainte Famille, Coloniale and Saint Urbain Street near Sherbrooke. Some told their parents that they needed a room to be close to their college. But the real reason for having a *piaule* was to reject the comfort of the family house and its bourgeois morality. For fifteen dollars a week you could rent a room with a single bed, a chair, and a dresser, a sink and a towel rack. The toilet and bath were off the corridor, shared by everyone on the floor. It was "in" to be poor, badly dressed, and to eat meagrely, especially since there was no cooking in the rooms. People survived on hamburg-ers, hotdogs, eggrolls, and peanut butter sandwiches, and the French-style sandwiches of La Paloma with ham, pâté de foie gras, and lettuce on French bread.

The police came by looking for drugs or for runaway girls of sixteen. By mid-1963 they would come for FLQ revolutionaries who hung out there.

Diego, broom in hand, a white apron tied around his waist, would lament, "Don't just sit here doing nothing. This is a café, not a place to loaf. If you want to stay here have a coffee, eat something. Think of me. I tell you, the police will come and they will close down La Paloma. And when you run away from your parents, don't come to see me. You are going to get me in trouble with the police. I don't want to see you here when you run away from home, do you understand?"

He had his living quarters behind a door at the back of the café. When the police came looking for a girl, he would send her quickly through that door and through another door to the street.

One waif who haunted La Paloma would later become an actress and play in soft-core pornographic films. She was about sixteen, blonde, blue-eyed, freckled, with the naïve face and coy ways of a kitten. She recited the lines of Louis Aragon or Jacques Prévert, exclaiming about their beauty. She admired men, complimented them on their looks, and of course they found her special.

One day she arrived with torn clothing, her arms scratched and bleeding. She told us she had just escaped from a house of correc-tion by climbing over the barbed wire fence. Shortly afterwards, the police appeared. Diego, who had been warned, drew her by the hand to the back, where she made her escape.

In the spring of 1963, the Mother Superior of Regina Assumpta summoned five girls to the parlour and delivered a lecture that left us astounded.

"*Mesdemoiselles*, I know that you frequent a place where a membership card is required to enter. I know, too, that it is reserved for young women from the classical colleges."

It was clear that she thought we were part of an upper-class pros-titution ring. She delivered her admonitions for about fifteen min-utes. If we returned to "that place" she would hear about it, for she had her ways of finding out and she would be forced to take action.

As soon as we were excused from her presence, we burst out laughing. How could she believe such nonsense? What tales had reached her?

Some time before, the French-language service of the CBC had run a series of television programs on youth, and had come with its cameras to La Paloma. I appeared two or three times in close-up. Jean Roy was also shown, silently reading a book of poetry. The subject of the program, as I recall, was young people's interest in poetry. My mother saw the program and was aghast that I was filmed in such company. For months and even years, she railed at me, "What will everyone think? You should be ashamed to be seen on television in such a dump, with your hair hanging down your back."

Some girls at Regina Assumpta had also seen the broadcast. Was that the origin of the gossip? One day, the nuns invited my mother to the convent to tell her that her daughter would not be welcome back in the fall. I had three years to go before getting my B.A. My mother happened to have read an article in a newspaper about a private college, Saint Denis, that was co-educational, run by lay people, and non-sectarian. Religious classes were replaced by a course in the history of religions. How daring for Quebec in 1963!

I arrived at the college in September wearing my hair in braids, as was usual at the convent. How my fellow students laughed at me! They pulled my hair so much that at last, in self defence, I had it cut. The atmosphere at Saint Denis was entirely different from that of the convent. We were a class of twenty-four, and only two girls. Teasing and joking were the order of the day. My handbag would be seized and its contents spread to the four corners of the room. A boy grabbed my shoe and hung it from a pipe that ran just below the ceiling. Everyone laughed: how could I stand on a desk and retrieve my shoe without having everyone see my panties? To survive at Saint Denis, I had to lose my shyness. Eventually I asked a question in class, my first ever.

At Saint Denis, they did not worry about whether books were on the Index. Professors seemed to care about their subjects, without the fear of heresy or sin that prevailed in the convent. The students were largely those who had been expelled from the classical colleges of Montreal or were the children of families in revolt against the clergy's domination of society.

One of these students was Jacques Lanctôt, later to lead the FLQ cell that kidnapped James Cross. He was my age — seventeen; we were born in the same month of 1945. He kept to the back of the classroom. André Brassard and Claude Turcotte usually sat beside him. Brassard was to make a career in the theatre and direct most of the plays of Michel Tremblay. At that time, he used to play with pieces of string a foot long, to which he gave names like Marguerite, Armande and Antoinette. In his room at home, about a dozen strings hung from the wall, and he had a story to tell about each. Claude Turcotte considered himself a poet; he sang the songs of Léo Ferré and swore that Ferré was the greatest poet of the century. Lanctôt wore his hair short, parted on the left side. He had French-style glasses, big melting brown eyes with long lashes, and a constant smile. I found him pleasant, gentle, a little shy. He had the look of a choir boy. Though bright enough when he gave answers in class, he wasn't much interested in his studies. His assignments came in late. Two blocks from the college was a tavern which we called *l'Eglise*, the church. Lanctôt and Turcotte would go there over the noon hour and return late for their Latin class, taught by Dr. Charles Borromée Tanguay. Dr. Tanguay would address them as they strolled nonchalantly to their chairs at the back of the room.

"I suppose you two are returning once again from l'Eglise?"

"Well, sir, we had ordered three Molsons. We couldn't just leave them there. But don't worry, we prepared for your class at l'Eglise. We have it all down. We'll just go and take our seats and we won't disturb you."

They were often slightly tipsy. On one occasion Dr. Tanguay waited till they were seated, then called on Turcotte to translate from a poem by Catullus, the line *Passer mortuus est meae puellae*, the swallow of my sweetheart is dead. Turcotte translated *puellae* (sweetheart) as *poil* (hair). The class burst out laughing. Then it was Lanctôt's turn to try his luck at the line, also without success. Dr. Tanguay was generally good humoured about the flippant behaviour of the two class buffoons. One day, though, Lanctôt walked in late carrying a barbecued chicken. Dr. Tanguay made him dump it in the waste basket.

A morning came when Lanctôt did not show up for class. A teacher told us that we would not be seeing him for a while, because he was in jail. He and two others had belonged to a cell of the FLQ that had planted a bomb under the Victoria Bridge and thrown Molotov cocktails at two military armouries in Montreal. We were astonished. Lanctôt, when I knew him, never talked politics. He had been arrested on August 27, 1963, just before the school year started at Saint Denis, and had been out on bail. Because he was a juvenile, his name had not been made public, and it was only when he began serving his sentence that we learned he belonged to the FLQ.

He never returned to Saint Denis. He had two sisters studying there: Marie-Claire, a year older and considered quite a philosopher, and Louise, who was a year behind me. Louise later married Jacques Cossette-Trudel and both took part in the kidnapping of James Cross.

A few months before his arrest, Jacques Lanctot had written a poem, "The Deserter," which I only read many years later.

> On my forehead, a sunset,
> In my eyes, a hope flown away,
> On my lips, a smile faded
> And in my pockets . . .
> A machine to extinguish a life . . .
> And that is how the sun sets
> And how hope flies away
> And the smile fades . . .
> I ran
> Through all the streets of the city
> I had been told
> That I would find there happiness
> Love and peace
> I saw only hatred
>   and contempt
> Then I lost myself among the crowds
> I made myself into a child
>   for a few moments
> And I found again the road of my dream.

That was the year the FLQ began. The first Molotov cocktails were tossed at three armouries on March 8, 1963 and the letters FLQ were smeared on the walls. Soon, bombs began exploding. On April 1, one blew up a section of railway track a few hours before Prime Minister John Diefenbaker was to pass by; the letters FLQ were painted on a nearby barn. Then, three weeks later, someone was killed when a bomb set off at an army recruiting centre blew up the night watchman. On May 17, an army demolition expert lost an arm when an FLQ bomb he was defusing exploded in his hands. The first wave of bombings ended on June 2, when police swooped down and arrested fifteen people, with more arrests to come later.

I did not then take the FLQ seriously, nor did most people in Quebec. Most of the bombs exploded during the night in mailboxes, in the very English and very rich suburb of Westmount. Like many French-speaking residents, I felt some pleasure at the thought of an English gentleman in his satin dressing gown suddenly hearing an explosion outside his window, and his mail going up in smoke.

Quebec was awakening, demanding new terms of coexistence with English-speaking Canada. Where it would lead, no one knew. So many grievances, so many humiliations had accumulated over the centuries. It was time to make English Canada sit up and take notice.

The bombs were only some of the messages of discontent which, later that year, convinced the new Prime Minister Lester Pearson that he should appoint a Royal Commission on Bilingualism and Biculturalism. I didn't think that a few bombs planted in mailboxes or near federal buildings would take us very far. I thought the *Felquistes*, as we called them, were idealists and romantics. Quebec was not Algeria.

Among those arrested in that first FLQ wave were a few people I had known at La Paloma. One was François Bachand, whom we had called Mario. He was sentenced to four years in the penitentiary. In trouble again with the police in 1969, he fled to Cuba, then moved on to Paris where he was assassinated in 1971 by a bullet in the head. No one ever determined beyond a doubt who murdered him. The police cannot prove it, but they think he was executed by two other members of the FLQ for reasons unknown.

I had often met him on the street when I was coming home from the convent. He lived on the next street over from us. He was a few years older than I, a skinny fellow with dark brown hair and a moustache. I saw him a few times at La Paloma, in the company of Jacques Lanctôt. There we spoke, though not always pleasantly. I remember once he said to me: "What you need, Carole, is something between your legs." How humiliated I felt! Jacques Lanctôt and the others at the table laughed. He never changed all the time I knew him: he smoked a lot and talked constantly. He was loud, opinionated, sometimes very arrogant. If he didn't like someone, he would not hesitate to humiliate the person publicly. We spoke occasionally, but I avoided him when I could.

Richard Bizier was another arrested in that first wave. He was a little older than I, perhaps nineteen or twenty. He had emigrated from France three or four years before. Rather stout, clean-shaven with short hair, quiet, and introspective, he lived in a *piaule* on Clark Street where I sometimes visited him. His room, like most *piaules*, was sparsely furnished, with a beige hide-a-bed, an armchair covered with brown corduroy, and a record player. Seated on the floor we listened to his records, including his favourite song, banned in France under de Gaulle: "*Monsieur le président*, I don't want war . . ."

He was friendly toward everyone, but showed no interest in women. He held a job as a technician in a hospital, if I remember correctly. Because he didn't have a single book in his apartment and never talked politics, I was astonished when he was arrested for setting off bombs for the FLQ.

One evening, a woman I knew invited me to La Crêpe Bretonne on Mountain Street, where she was to meet a friend. Nicole and I sat sipping Manhattans, which was the style at the time. Her friend arrived: rather short, about eighteen or twenty, a Frenchman with the supercilious manner that French ex-patriates often affect. "In Paris, that's not how it's done. Such a thing would be unheard of in France. Back home, I wouldn't want you for a friend."

His name was Richard Bros. He was to be arrested with Jacques Lanctôt for planting a bomb under the Victoria Bridge.

I saw him often at La Paloma during 1963. He spent most of his time trying to pick up every woman he encountered. Each time I saw him, he was with a different one.

I remember one day discussing the French Revolution with him. When I suggested that it had been a bourgeois revolution, he replied sharply: "You're wrong, it was the common people who revolted against the monarchy." I argued, but without success. Richard was always right, those who disagreed with him were always fools.

Another time, I was taking the train to Sainte Anne de la Pérade with my mother and my sister, and we met Richard Bros on the train. He was on his way to Quebec City to spend Christmas there, and we travelled together. "How slow and uncomfortable the trains are here. In France they really move, and the ride is so much better." Neither my sister nor I could stand him, and we couldn't wait to reach La Pérade.

I was at La Paloma one day when Nicole, who had introduced me to Richard Bros, arrived in tears. She sat down beside me.

"What's the matter?"

"Richard Bros attacked me."

She told me she had gone to his room where she found him with another man. They grabbed her, stripped her, tied her to the bed and gagged her. Then they spread peanut butter all over her and licked it off. She was choking with anger and humiliation as she told me about it. She drank an espresso, cursing Bros and his "bloody gang of Frenchmen." I suggested she go home and have a shower.

Soon after, I met Bros. "How could you do such a thing?"

"Oh, that girl is an idiot, she has no sense of humour."

When I defended Nicole, Bros told me that I was being stupid. I answered heatedly: "I don't know what Nicole ever saw in you. You're such a jerk!"

In 1971, he was arrested in England for drug trafficking and hanged himself in his cell. On his wrist, after he died, they found a bracelet with three engraved letters: FLQ.

CHAPTER 4
The Splendour of Expo

Montreal was the crossroads of the world in the spring and summer of 1967, when a fairy-tale kingdom rose like a mirage on the islands in the Saint Lawrence. The sun struck the glittering bubble of the American pavilion, designed by Buckminster Fuller. It also shone on the glass and aluminum boat of the French pavilion and the British pavilion rising from an island of lagoons. Gliding through it all like a sea serpent was the monorail.

Expo 67 was Quebec's debutante ball, where each nation came to be presented. We Montrealers opened our arms to the visitors of the world.

My friend Ginette lost her heart to a *gendarme* named Pierre, on duty at the French pavilion. After a few days he lost interest in Ginette and took up with her friend, Lucy. A couple of weeks later, he abandoned the ladies of Quebec for a pretty hostess from Paris. Lucy, meanwhile, had a fling with a Bavarian who was manager of the beer garden. She dreamed of moving to Germany and living there happily ever after. Alas, once she was pregnant, her Bavarian Prince Charming ran off to Mexico. Would she have been happy in Munich? I doubt it: I learned through a German who went out with my sister that Lucy's Bavarian worked as an undertaker in his native land.

Barbara, another friend, discovered Paulo, a chocolate-coloured mulatto from Trinidad or Tobago, always smiling with pearly teeth, always in a shirt printed with palm trees, always wearing a huge straw hat.

Nicole outdid us all. Her constant companion at Expo was Abdallah, from the Yemen pavilion. He was a Moslem, and wore flowing white robes and a white headcloth kept in place by a band across his forehead. She called him her "lord of the desert" and had decided to return with him to Yemen, but she was never to see more of Yemen than its pavilion.

We became citizens of those enchanted islands and spent every spare moment there, every evening, every weekend, with Expo passports that contained our pictures, names, and addresses. We crossed out the line marked "province" and wrote beside the entry for "country": Quebec.

I had a great need of magic that summer. I was twenty-one, a year out of Collège Saint Denis and employed. I was to begin the study of law at the University of Montreal in the fall, but I had taken a year away from studies to learn something about the work world. After the rarified atmosphere of the convent and the college, work was a disenchanting experience.

Imagine a room with a long table at which two rows of plump women between the ages of forty and sixty-three are seated side by side. My first impression was that they all looked alike: stout, with ample posteriors, short hair dyed blonde and set in the same permanent. They wore the same glasses of brown tortoiseshell, gave off the same odour of Yardley's Lavender.

This was the complaints department for the Steinberg supermarket chain. Each woman had a phone in front of her with twenty buttons. Whenever someone had a complaint about the service at any of the 143 stores on the island of Montreal, that person phoned a central number, and the complaint was handled by one of the women of the complaints department.

"Good morning, Steinberg, *bonjour.*"

"Miss, my order was delivered without the bag of potatoes."

Steinberg stores used to deliver in those days, and most complaints came from people waiting for an undelivered order, or who claimed that it had arrived with broken eggs or some articles missing. Sometimes the order had gone to the wrong address.

"At what store did you shop?"

"*Your* store. That's why I'm calling you."

"But sir, this is not a store, it's the head office. Where did you shop?"

Once the details had been taken down, a woman in the complaints department would call the manager of the appropriate store, make arrangements for the delivery of the bag of potatoes, and then get back to the aggrieved customer to tell him relief was on the way.

The woman who presided over the complaints department was named Anastasia Kowalchuck, though everyone called her "Mrs. K." She was of Ukrainian origin, and soon made it plain that she liked neither Russians nor French Canadians.

On my first day, a woman by the name of Rita Masson was explaining to me in French how I was to handle the complaints. Mrs. K approached and said to her, in English:

"You can speak English. She understands English."

Mrs. K 's pet complaint, as it turned out, was that some French Canadians refused to speak English.

"Why don't they learn English? Remember, Carole, you're a minority here in Canada."

"Yes, but remember that you are a minority here in Quebec," I retorted one day.

The women were not always busy on the phone handling complaints. They found a good deal of time to chat and complain to each other. They shared a compelling interest in the sordid crimes committed in Montreal or abroad, and read *Allô Police* and other tabloids specializing in crime and violence. Between the two calls to track down someone's missing cheese, they would savour the gory details: "My God, how could a person do that to someone else? Just look at this picture, Madame Meilleur. His face is completely crushed. Good God in holy heaven!"

"Isn't it sickening? But just wait, Detective Latournelle will find the killer. He's really something: he's already solved four murders in the past two months. I think he'll get a promotion any day now."

"Listen to this — they've found the body of a seventeen-year-old girl in the Lachine Canal! Another damned man! Aren't they disgusting? I suppose the rat did what he wanted with her, and then killed her! Now that they've taken away the death penalty, there's no stopping these perverts. They should bring it back, it's what we need."

Many conversations turned on the marital and extra-marital lives of the stars. They read *Echoes-Vedettes*. A discussion that began with Brigitte Bardot's latest man often led to confidences much closer to home. The conversations ended with the fat women on one side of the table shaking with laughter while those on the other side, separated by a glass partition, demanded to know what they were missing.

"Brigitte Bardot has gone and changed her man again. Those women change men like they change shirts."

"I think they've got the right idea, Madame Turcotte. You get tired of one tool and feel you'd like to try some others."

How they all shook with laughter! Almost all had a rather low opinion of men, especially their husbands. The only one who seemed satisfied was a thirty-seven-year-old widow who had lost her husband a month before. He left her with a house and swimming pool and a lot of insurance money. She was the envy of the complaints department.

The marital life of these women was, to all appearances, somewhat lacking. When one of the women had been approached by her husband in bed, the good news spread along both sides of the table.

"Well, ladies, it's been four months in coming, but last night my husband finally made the big move," she would titter and blush.

The reactions of the other women were not long in coming.

"Why don't you tell yours to have a talk with mine? He's been out of commission for months, and I'm going to go looking elsewhere if things don't improve soon."

Then the widow would pipe up from across the table. "I'm so happy. No husband to tie me down. Now I can take as many lovers as I please, and I've got a lot of catching up to do. Lovers, yes, but I'll never get caught like that again. I've been so happy since God took him away from me."

They considered me, at twenty-one, to be a poor innocent student who did not yet understand the ways of the world, and they often ended one of these conversations by turning to me:

"Do yourself a favour, dear, and don't ever get married!"

At Steinberg, the aesthetics of sex were not a major preoccupation. The women in the complaints department seemed to derive satisfaction from the grotesque, the cruel, the bizarre, the shocking. They claimed to be appalled by the horrors they read in *Allô Police*, but relished every gruesome detail of the murder of a prostitute, or the sufferings of a woman forced by her husband to submit to bestial acts at the hands of his friends. Sex itself seemed boring and only became interesting when spiced with danger, with scandal, with betrayal, or with the cruelty that is latent in every human being.

I didn't spend all my time in the complaints department. I also worked in public relations, where I scanned newspapers for any mention of the supermarket chain, its owners, or directors. Hardly an inspiring task.

Another duty put me in contact with the public. Steinberg had a vast bakery in the east end of Montreal which was its pride and joy. Groups of men and women would come for a tour of the bakery. When they arrived, I greeted them with a little spiel in English or French depending on the group, and then I took them on a tour.

"Good afternoon. My name is Carole de Vault. This bakery is the largest bakery in North America . . . Please follow me . . ."

It was a miracle of technology. No human hand touched the ingredients. In the lab, a man in white explained quality control.

"Now follow me into the bakery, where every hour, 700 loaves of bread are baked, sliced, wrapped, and stored."

"Ooooh! Aaaah!"

What awe I saw on those upturned faces as they walked through the modern-day equivalent of a cathedral. They saw the bins full of flour, stared at the pipes through which the flour flowed, then at the vats where the dough was mixed, plopped into a mould, conveyed through the oven, cooked for twenty minutes, and removed from the mould by suction. Bread, untouched by human hands. The multiplication of the loaves. An automated miracle.

They were amazed, but that was nothing. On to the area where, in one hour, 2,700 pies were mixed, cooked, and packaged. That was nothing. Onward! Here, 300 cakes were baked in an hour. There, 29,000 donuts! Pistons pounded, the flour puffed and sizzled in a river of grease.

"Did you see that, dear? Isn't it marvellous? Marvellous!"

I knew that the bread, if you squeezed it, collapsed to the size of a baseball. The donuts and the cakes tasted more of preservatives than of dough. The pies were two thick layers of paste with a thin filling.

"Fantastic!"

After an hour of contemplating the mysteries of the bakery, the faithful were served communion: donuts sprinkled with powdered sugar and coffee, or donuts sprinkled with cinnamon and coffee.

I must have introduced several thousand people to the marvels of the Steinberg bakery, and I had disciples. I trained other young men and women, all of them students, to prepare them for the stations of the guided tour. I can truthfully say that I have never since eaten one of Steinberg's cakes, pies, or donuts. Devotion can only go so far.

Mrs. K's women worked on the twelfth floor of the head office, past the cafeteria. The public relations department was on the eleventh floor, as were the offices of senior management. The men here were often rich, the women young and attractive. Here was another view of the relations between the sexes. The men were English-speaking and married. They found it a diverting change from their spouses to chase the French-Canadian women who worked on the same floor.

A pretty receptionist had a summer-long affair with one of the managers. She was about twenty-one years old and lived with her parents, so her middled-aged lover rented a downtown bachelorette for their trysts. Sometimes they made love in his office after five o'clock. Eventually he tired of her and took up with an airline hostess. To console the receptionist, he bought her a beauty shop.

Another woman, Suzanne, who was a secretary, had an affair with her former boss, no longer employed at Steinberg. He rented an apartment for her and furnished it. She left her parent's house. A year later she left the company, to be supported by her lover.

He was about twenty years older than she, pudgy, not very handsome, but Suzanne loved him because he was rich. He took her on trips to Florida, Puerto Rico, Las Vegas. She began to dream of becoming his wife.

I lost touch with her for a couple of years, till one day in 1970, at the height of the October Crisis, I received a call from her. Suzanne was tearful and depressed, felt no one loved her, and spoke of committing suicide. I invited her to my apartment for the weekend and saw her several times afterwards.

She had convinced herself that her lover would marry her if his wife were out of the way. She told me of consulting a "witch" who told fortunes and could cast spells. Little by little, the story came out. She was paying the witch several thousand dollars to cause the death of her lover's wife. Suzanne asked her lover to borrow a hat from his wife, because the witch needed something that had been part of the woman's body: the hat would carry loose hairs. She also turned over a ring that belonged to her lover. She paid for rare herbs that the witch needed for the spell. At one time, Suzanne gave her $600 so the woman could go to her native Italy to find herbs not available in Canada. Poor Suzanne! I tried to tell her that she was being swindled, but she believed in the powers of the witch and also feared her. One day, I went with Suzanne while she turned over $3,000 to the woman.

Needless to say, the wife, who had briefly been in hospital, recovered. Suzanne had wasted her money. Her liaison ended in 1975 when her lover found another woman. He threw Suzanne out, called her a whore, and threatened, if she made trouble for him, to show her family pornographic pictures that he had taken of her.

In the public relations department on the eleventh floor, the talk was about affairs, just as on the twelfth floor it was about violent sex and sluggish husbands. I found most of these flirtations sad because they were essentially vulgar. The clichéd scenario, repeated over and over, was the rich, older, English-speaking man hustling the pretty young French-speaking woman. Most of the men had very little culture or charm. A crass, repulsive materialism pervaded the eleventh floor.

Sometimes, on my way to the bakery in the east end of Montreal, I rode with one of the executives, who had a chauffeur-driven car. He was an ugly little man in his sixties, bald, paunchy, and ignorant, who spoke French with a terrible Eastern European accent. We sat in the back seat of the car, and he would move closer and closer until I was crushed against the door. I had to remove his hand from my thigh.

One day he summoned me to his enormous office on the eleventh floor. He locked the door behind me. "Have a candy," he said in his broken French. He sat me in an armchair at the far end of the room, and then came up behind me. He put his hands around my neck and began kissing me from behind. Half turning, I brought back my hand and swung it in an arc that ended at his face. I stood up, unlocked the door, and marched out. I fully expected to be fired, but he must have been afraid of drawing attention to our little scene.

Expo 67 offered a stunning contrast to the varied ugliness of Steinberg's bakery and eleventh and twelfth floors. Expo was a world of beauty and harmony. Serenity came over me when I walked in the Expo grounds, with the spray tossed in my face by the wind playing in the fountains. Every nation had pondered what contribution of beauty and cultural wealth it could make to this microcosm of the earth at peace, to this *Terre des Hommes*. The concern for style touched everything, from the architecture of the pavilions to the curving plexiglass of the telephone booths.

Expo was a revelation for me. All my life, I had tried to live in my imagination, amid the ancient splendours of Europe as conveyed through books. I felt like an exile on this continent that spoke of materialism in English. I could not accept a country, Canada, that had refused for 200 years to recognize its French heritage. As a French Canadian in Canada, I was made to feel like a perpetual immigrant, although my ancestors had lived nowhere else for three-and-a-half centuries. I was an exile without hope of finding my own country, because my country did not exist.

For French Canadians, Expo was a message. Throughout most of our history after the Conquest, we had looked to the past. New France was the Eden from which we had been expelled. France had abandoned us, more concerned about the sugar of the Caribbean than the "few acres of snow" in the northern hemisphere. Even the motto of Quebec looks back: *Je me souviens*, I remember. The novel that, for decades, typified us was *Maria Chapdelaine*, the story of a farm girl who rejects the city and who insists that nothing must change in Quebec, neither language, nor faith, nor songs, neither virtues nor vices. We must learn nothing, forget nothing. "That is why we must remain in the province where our fathers remained, and live as they lived, to obey the unexpressed command which formed in their hearts, which was passed into ours and which we must transmit in turn to our many children: in the land of Quebec, nothing must die and nothing must change . . ."

Expo was proof that Quebec could change, could turn toward the future. In the past, industrialization had come to us from outside as something alien and threatening. But now we would never again be excluded from modern technology. Expo proved that we could be at home in the modern world.

I met a French *gendarme* at Expo named Jean Causse. One sunny day, I was sitting at a table with my friend Ginette and her young *gendarme*, Pierre, on the terrace of the French pavilion, looking out over a lagoon to the British pavilion on the other side. As we sipped vermouths and chatted, an older man approached, dressed in the navy-blue uniform, with red, white, and gold braid, and white gloves, of the *gendarmerie*. This was Pierre's commanding officer. He was in his late forties, with distinguished grey hair, a dignified bearing and kindly blue-grey eyes. He introduced himself and sat down. I liked him at once.

We spent many hours walking and talking during that sun-drenched summer. Ours was a platonic relationship. We enjoyed being together to explore the byways of Expo. He had a calmness and a strength of character that made him pleasant to be with.

We discovered a coincidence. His mother's maiden name was Duval, as was mine. We joked about being cousins, though far removed. I told him about my mother's first ancestor in Canada who had been hanged by Champlain: an inauspicious beginning for the Duvals in the New World.

I suspect that part of his attraction for me was that he was older and French. In a sense, he represented a return to France for me, the healing of a rupture in the distant past. Father and daughter met again as adults and got to know each other in the enchanted setting of Expo.

There was a stepmother. Canada did its best to be obtrusively present that summer. It was the centennial year of Confederation. Everywhere you saw the reminders: 1867–1967. I suppose that on July 1, there was an outburst of festivity amid the noise and colour of the greatest display of fireworks in the history of the country.

But I did not go to Expo on that day. I didn't want to see those celebrations. For me, there was nothing to celebrate. The separatist slogan that summer, painted here and there in protest, was: *1867–1967: One Hundred Years of Injustice*. That was how I felt about Confederation.

The Queen of Canada visited Expo early in July, her first visit to Quebec since 1964, when separatist demonstrators had been charged at by police wielding riot sticks. That visit was remembered as *le samedi de la matraque*, the Saturday of the riot sticks.

This time, the Queen came on the royal yacht *Britannia*, so that she could go directly from federal territory, the river, to the Expo site, without having to travel through Quebec. The grounds had been cleared in anticipation of the visit of Her Majesty and Prince Philip. Seven hundred and fifty police officers guarded the site as she toured the pavilions.

I did not recognize her as my Queen, but saw her as the queen of French Canadians only by right of conquest, making her throne here precarious indeed. When she came to Quebec — rarely — she had to be protected from her subjects.

That same July, Charles de Gaulle came to Quebec and to Expo. He, too, came by boat, aboard the warship *Colbert*, but for very different reasons from those of the Queen. De Gaulle came by boat because the Canadian government was afraid of the effect he would have on people in Quebec. Officials wanted to make sure that the French president stopped first in Ottawa to render homage to Canadian federalism before he set foot in Quebec, but the general outwitted the Canadian government. He came in a big ship that could not sail past Montreal, and so he stepped first on Quebec's soil.

What an irony of history! The *Colbert* stopped at Quebec City at the Anse au Foulon, where James Wolfe had landed his troops by stealth in 1759. The cannon boomed a salute to the French general from the Plains of Abraham where the Marquis de Montcalm had been defeated. De Gaulle, in uniform, travelled from Quebec City to Montreal along the ancient Chemin du Roy, the highway of New France. Everywhere, he was acclaimed as a hero, almost as a liberator. Every few feet along the road he saw painted the blue fleur-de-lys, heraldic emblem of the kings of France.

France returned triumphantly to the children it had abandoned centuries before. English Canadians could not understand the delirium of the people along the Chemin du Roy. At Sainte Anne de la Pérade, the flags of France and of Quebec adorned the houses. My grandfather, eighty-two years old, had tears running down his cheeks when the General appeared at the town hall. There were banners announcing, "The Dusablons who originated from Auvergne salute you, *mon Général!*" "The Duvals who came from Poitou salute *mon Général!*" The descendants saluted in de Gaulle the kings of ancient France, returned after a long absence. My Uncle Jules also cried. In Quebec that day, no one was ashamed to cry.

That night, de Gaulle was in Montreal, and he spoke to the people from the balcony of City Hall: "*Vive le Québec! Vive le Québec libre!*"

I was watching television with a friend in her garden, that evening of July 24, 1967. I saw those upraised arms, heard the cry that would go right to the heart of the people of Quebec. "*Vive le Québec libre!*" A shiver went down my spine. We threw our arms around each other, we danced and hugged. My friend ran for a bottle of French wine and we drank to the health of the General and to a free Quebec.

We knew what the cry meant. De Gaulle was telling us to take our future into our own hands. His words also said we had a right to a place in the sun. He was telling us to throw off the domination of the English. He had come to avenge Jeanne d'Arc and Montcalm.

The next day, all of Quebec was excited, though reactions varied, depending on whether your name was Lafleur or Smith. Most of the *Anglais* were outraged. One of the executives at Steinberg criticized de Gaulle in front of his secretary. She retorted: "I'm telling you, if we go to war with the Canadians, I'll kill you myself." He was astounded at her vehemence.

I think that all French-speaking Quebeckers held their heads a little higher that day. I had gone to the French pavilion after work with a friend named Judee. We hoped to see de Gaulle when he visited the pavilion. Jean Causse helped us out. He told us that the building was to be closed to the public, but that the foreign press would be allowed to remain. So Judee and I took out steno pads and pretended to be journalists. Someone came and told us we had to leave. When we said that we were journalists, he asked us to show our press cards. We claimed that we had left them downstairs in the press room, but he led us down so that he could see them. At the door, we thought our game was up, but a young French journalist came out, sized up the situation and called out: "Ah, there you are, my *cocottes*, we've been waiting for you." So we were allowed into the press room, in the company of the journalist from *France-Soir*.

A few minutes later, I saw Charles de Gaulle walk in with the Premier of Quebec. With excitement and admiration, I stood a few feet away from the greatest Frenchman of our day, who had come to Quebec to make up for the past and to urge French-speaking Quebeckers to prepare for their future in a free Quebec.

CHAPTER 5
June 24, 1968

— �֍ —

I hadn't expected to find myself caught up in a riot when I went to the Saint Jean Baptiste parade on June 24, 1968. I only went as a favour to a friend. In fact, I had always avoided the parade celebrating the patron saint of French Canadians. I found it *quetaine*, corny. The Saint was usually represented by a curly-haired little boy resting on a walking stick, with a lamb at his side.

For generations, Jean Baptiste was the very symbol of the French Canadian. If you didn't know someone's name, you referred to him as *Jean Baptiste*. He represented the old French Canadian society that my generation rejected. Innocent, ignorant, and rustic, knowing nothing about the modern world, he symbolized a traditional Catholic people who had remained unchanged since the days of New France. The lamb too, seemed to me and my friends to represent the simple, docile French Canadians who had always been shorn for the benefit of the English.

My generation defined itself as Quebecois, no longer as French Canadian. For us, to be Quebecois meant to belong to a modern society that had turned its back on Canada. We placed our hopes in an independent Quebec, not in a submissive and colonized French Canada.

On that 24th day of June, a friend who worked at the front desk of the Queen Elizabeth Hotel called me up. She asked me if I would escort to the parade a young German by the name of Gunther. He was studying hotel management and had been spending a few months in training at the hotel. He had heard about the parade on the holiday of the patron saint of French Canadians, and he didn't want to return to his country without seeing this authentic example of folk tradition.

I agreed. Gunther came to the phone and we arranged to meet at a restaurant downtown. He described himself: six foot two inches, fair, thin, and he would be wearing a navy blue blazer with gold buttons and grey flannel slacks. I told him I was five foot four inches tall, had long brown hair and would be wearing a yellow blouse, a lemon-yellow miniskirt, yellow net stockings and yellow shoes with low heels. I recognized him immediately in the restaurant because he looked so German. Over coffee, he explained how he had acquired his flawless French. He was born during the Second World War and never knew his father, an officer in the German army killed by the French. His embittered mother sent him to a French school in Switzerland so that someday he would be able to tell the French in their own language how they had murdered his father. Later, he studied hotel management at Lugano in southern Switzerland, where Italian is the dominant language. Besides French and German, he spoke Italian and some English.

I told him how the Queen Elizabeth Hotel got its name. In the early 1960s, the Canadian National Railway decided to build a hotel near Central Station and name it for the Queen. For the Quebecois, the Queen is a symbol of imperialism, so we protested; we wanted the hotel to be named after the founder of Montreal, de Maisonneuve, and thus respect the French character of Montreal. The president of the CNR, Donald Gordon, had said that there were no French Canadians holding top positions in the railway because French Canadians don't have a head for business. We were insulted. The demonstration which followed was the first I had ever attended. There were speeches, anti-English chants, and Donald Gordon was burned in effigy.

After coffee, we began a leisurely walk east along Sherbrooke Street towards Lafontaine Park. I warned Gunther not to expect too much, that these parades had become dull and commercial. The tradition of lighting bonfires on both banks of the Saint Lawrence on the eve of June 24 goes back to the earliest days of the colony, and has come down to the present. The communal bonfires are called *feux de joie*, fires of joy, and the parade was added more recently, with floats sponsored by large department store chains who wanted to show that they thought of the French Canadians once a year, in the hope that *Jean Baptiste* would spend his money with them the rest of the year.

But Gunther wanted to see the parade. He also hoped to see the next Prime Minister of Canada, who was to be the guest of honour at the parade despite the objections of the nationalists. The next day was election day throughout Canada, and Pierre Trudeau's presence at the parade was to be his last appearance of the campaign.

Like many people on that warm summer evening, Gunther was intrigued by Trudeau. The election campaign now ending had been unlike any other in Canadian history. A new word, Trudeaumania, described the sometimes hysterical reaction he provoked in crowds.

As we walked along Sherbrooke Street, the crowds got thicker. Women pushing buggies and tugging children hurried to see the parade. The posts along the street were decked with fleur-de-lys flags, and since it was a warm night, the balconies were full of people. It was a rather poor district in east Montreal, and those who lived in flats overlooking the parade route had invited their relatives and friends to share the occasion. Children played on the wrought-iron outdoor stairways.

We reached the park opposite the still-empty reviewing stand. It was a wooden structure decorated in bright colours, built on the great steps leading to the doors of Montreal's municipal library, with its grey Doric columns. Before taking up our positions along the street, we walked on the grass of Lafontaine Park, an oasis amid the hot streets of east-end Montreal. As always in the summer, lovers were stretched out on the grass, indifferent to the coming parade, and people rowed boats under the curved bridges of the large central pond.

Darkness was falling when we finally rejoined the crowd massed on the sidewalk and at the edge of the park across from the reviewing stand. There were people of all ages, some in their summer best in honour of Saint Jean Baptiste, others in their everyday jeans.

Vendors with bicycle stands sold hot dogs, French fries, hamburgers, soft drinks, and ice cream. Some sold little Quebec flags. The smell of grease was on the summer air. The empty bottles from the soft drinks began accumulating underfoot. Good-humoured policemen kept the crowd from spilling over onto the street where the parade was to pass. Now and then, a patrol car drove slowly by, its wheels a few inches from the curb.

Clusters of young people carrying protest banners began the rhythmic chants heard in all the demonstrations of those days: *"Le Québec aux Québécois! Le Québec aux Québécois! Trudeau au poteau."* Over and over: "Quebec for the Quebecois! Trudeau to the gallows!" There were also choruses of a chant that had come down from revolutionary France. The call for beheading the aristocrats had been adapted to fit the nationalist passions of the 1960s.

Gunther was surprised to hear the anti-English chants around us. This wasn't how he had imagined the celebration.

"Les Anglais dehors! Les Anglais dehors!" Out with the English!

It was getting darker. The crowd was swelling. Policemen rolled by in front of the reviewing stand on motorcycles, the sidecar occupied by a second policeman. Behind us, police on horseback appeared, gentling their mounts on the grass, waiting. The chants were getting louder. Children, piggyback on their father's shoulders, craned their necks, looking down the street for the first sight of the parade.

Gunther and I discussed the election campaign. He could not

understand why so many were angry at Trudeau, the philosopher-king, the man who had studied law at the University of Montreal, then politics at Harvard, Paris, and the University of London; the rich man who had set out on foot, a pack on his back, to explore the world, who had been thrown in jail, interrogated as a spy, who was a brown belt in judo, who could do flawless double somersaults from a diving board, who could as gracefully quote Machiavelli, Locke and Lord Acton.

I had mixed feelings about Trudeau. He did seem a new kind of ruler, one who put reason above passion, who thought it more important to ask the right questions than to pretend to have all the answers. His encounters with students outside Quebec during the spring campaign were teach-ins and love-ins promising new involvement by young people in the political process and participatory democracy.

No person from Quebec could escape a feeling of pride that this man was one of us. For too long, we had been considered the hewers of wood and drawers of water. He was one of us, but there lay the danger. He had emerged as a kind of pied piper. But where was he leading us, this new-style leader who had become a symbol of youth, this utter individualist?

He offered a new vision of Canada, one in which French and English accepted each other, as his father Charles-Emile Trudeau had accepted Grace Elliott. He had mastered even the slang of both English and French, and spoke both languages across the country in that 1968 campaign, running on a platform of one Canada with two official languages.

One Canada, although the thrust of Quebec during the Quiet Revolution was towards two Canadas. Many of us had lost faith in English Canada. We had waited too long. For a century, English Canada had tried to suppress the French language, French institutions and the French population in every province but Quebec. Even in Quebec, the English treated French Canadians as inferior, superstitious, priest-ridden people who needed to be guided for their own good by those who spoke English. When our legendary birth rate plummeted during the Quiet Revolution, we knew that we would never achieve our fondest wish — recognition of French from ocean to ocean.

Was Trudeau not leading us into a trap, as the pied piper of the folk tale had led the children into a mountain, never to be seen again? He left the university in 1965 to fight the rise of Quebecois nationalism. He stood for the counter-revolution, for resistance to Quebec's sovereignty, and even against special powers for Quebec. He rejected the concept of an independent Quebec to provide a homeland for those who speak French in Canada. He offered instead some acceptance for French across the country.

Those of us who dreamed of a sovereign Quebec saw in Trudeau our most dangerous adversary, all the more dangerous because he was from Quebec. His election campaign was an attempt to put Quebec back into line, to make it just another province like nine others.

There was movement on the reviewing stand: the guests of honour took up their positions, to a chorus of a few cheers and loud boos. You could make out Montreal's Mayor Jean Drapeau, and the Premier of Quebec, Daniel Johnson — French-speaking, despite his name — who had promised the people equality within Canada or independence. And, at last, Pierre Trudeau arrived.

The chants became a roar. What was happening? Now there was something hysterical about the mood of the night. Down the street came the sounds of an approaching band. The rhythm of the drums played counterpoint to the insults hurled at Trudeau: *"Trudeau au poteau! Trudeau vendu! Trudeau traître!"* Trudeau to the gallows! Trudeau sold out! Trudeau traitor!

Bottles flew through the air, aimed at the reviewing stand. They crashed on the street, sending shards of glass along the asphalt.

I heard screams, cries of fear and pain. The crowd began moving. I felt gripped by panic. I have never liked crowds and the feeling of being caught amid thousands of people, unable to move outside the mass.

Behind us in the park a fire was burning, but we could not make out what was happening. We saw the police on horseback raise their riot sticks and charge at the crowd. People screamed trying to get away. We heard firecrackers. The parade passed by under the bottles that showered on the reviewing stand. Sirens wailed over the sound of the marching bands. Gilles Vigneault passed by on a float, singing "Mon Pays."

Gunther had grabbed my hand and was pulling me backwards, shouting German words that I couldn't understand. I saw a bottle arc high in the air, glittering in the bright lights before it crashed into the reviewing stand. There was a commotion, Trudeau disappeared under his bodyguards, and the dignitaries fled from the bottles into the library. Then Trudeau reappeared, with only his guards. He waved at the crowd as though the shouts of hatred and pain were cheers.

The sound of sirens was deafening. We began to run. I held on to Gunther's hand. In front of me I saw a policeman on a horse, his riot stick poised in the air. I felt pain.

People around us were screaming, falling. Children and adults tried to scramble away from the charge of the police. I ran blindly, trying to escape from the park, to get away from the crowd.

A restaurant! We went in. My face was bloody from a cut over my left eye. My head throbbed. A girl sat at a nearby table, holding her one remaining shoe. There were people with torn clothing, bleeding noses, and clotted hair. Some were crying hysterically.

I cleaned myself up in the washroom. My cut didn't seem serious — though I carry a scar to this day over my left eye — and I didn't want to go to a hospital. I just wanted to get away from there as soon as possible. The violence had upset me terribly.

I was full of anger. What had I done to deserve being hit? I felt an overwhelming resentment towards the police for using indiscriminate violence, towards Trudeau for coming to the parade when his presence was a provocation, and towards the crowd for throwing bottles, firecrackers, stones, and bags of paint. This was not the way for a civilized society to express its opposition.

About forty-five minutes later, somewhat recovered, we left. When I got home, I took a couple of Aspirins for the pain in my head. Since that night, I've been overwhelmed with anxiety whenever I've been in a large crowd, especially at a demonstration.

The newspapers the next morning drew up a tally sheet of the night: 292 people arrested, 123 treated in hospital, including 80 civilians and 43 policemen; 6 horses injured, 12 police cars damaged. Among those arrested in the violence of the night were Jacques Lanctôt and Paul Rose.

For Pierre Trudeau, the outcome was a political triumph. In the last hours before voting day, he was seen on television sets across Canada shaking off his bodyguards and sitting defiantly in the reviewing stand under the barrage of bottles, while the others ran for cover. He appeared as a fearless champion who stood up to the separatists. He even grinned and waved at the crowd, a hand shielding his eyes from the glare of floodlights, as though he was enjoying the parade and had never seen a June 24 quite like it.

When the votes were counted, Trudeau was Prime Minister with a majority government, the first in four general elections. He had his chance to put his pledge of One Canada into practice.

A few days later, I received a card from Gunther. He thanked me for bringing him to the Saint Jean Baptiste celebration, and added with irony: "You had told me that the parade would be dull. If that is what you call dull, I would like to see you when you are excited."

CHAPTER 6
Noel

❧

At long last, it seemed, I had found a purpose. It was high time. For the first two years after I left college, I seemed to drift. My work in Steinberg's public relations department hardly offered a lifetime career. Then, in 1967, I began first year law at the University of Montreal, but without interest. I often skipped lectures and did not write the final exams. It seemed too lifeless.

In the fall of 1968, I registered in history at the Université du Québec à Montréal (UQAM). Here, in a manner of speaking, I fell in love. From almost the first lecture in my international relations course, I decided that this was what I had been waiting for. My future became clear. I would concentrate on international relations, complete a doctorate, take up university teaching and lead a quiet, studious life, passing my time in archives and libraries.

The course was given by Noel Vallerand. He would walk in late, a styrofoam cup of coffee in his right hand, a folder full of notes and a pack of Gitanes in his left. He was quite an ordinary-looking man in his mid-thirties, below average height, paunchy, his fair hair receding. But what superb lectures! You could have heard a pin drop in his class.

History had always fascinated me, particularly European history, but I had always looked at the history of one country at a time. Now I discovered that international relations was history between countries, a story of naked power beyond the rule of law, of intrigue, diplomacy, coalitions, treachery, assassinations, agents and double agents, war, victory, and defeat.

At the first lecture, Noel Vallerand, smoking incessantly, spoke for three hours without ever referring to the notes before him. He gave us an outline of the course, then launched into a description of Europe in 1871, with an evaluation of each of the five Great Powers.

After the lecture, I went out and bought all the books he had recommended and began reading them through, like novels. In bed at night, I fell asleep reading Pierre Renouvin's *Histoire des relations internationales*.

I took other courses: the history of Russia, the United States, human geography, methodology, and anthropology. But the lecture in international relations made my week.

In time, I came to know Noel Vallerand better without ever losing my regard for his brilliant mind, so superbly organized. His personal life, however, was something else. Although he had been married, his wife had left him and taken the children to South America. Noel sometimes came to lectures barely able to keep his eyes open after being up all night. He was always broke, and would borrow cigarettes or a couple of dollars from students, or more from his fellow instructors. He ate badly: hamburgers, fried chicken, and pizza, often on the run. He dressed in abominable taste. He might appear in a canary-yellow sweater and red corduroy trousers, but almost never in tie, shirt, or jacket.

He took a personal interest in the brighter students, but had little time for the others, and could be cruel in putting down someone who didn't know that when he said "The Gate," he was referring to the Ottoman Empire, or that Camillo Benzo was the name of the Italian patriot usually known as "Cavour." He loved to roll off his tongue German words we had never heard of, then wait for a student to ask him to write it on the board. Someone asked one day if he could speak German. "Yes," he replied. It was years before I discovered that he couldn't.

One day Noel asked us to submit a fifteen-page essay on some topic in international relations between 1871 and 1914. Most of the students picked Bismarck's Second Reich or the Triple Alliance. We had to get his approval of the topic chosen, and most of the students left his office crestfallen after hearing his criticisms. I submitted my proposal: the relations between Alexander von Battenberg of Bulgaria and Czar Alexander III of Russia. He brought his fist down on the table.

"Brilliant!" When I turned the essay in, he gave me a grade of 88 percent. That was high praise from him.

He often joined us in the cafeteria or in a bar two blocks from the university called the Ratz Keller, where you could eat a lunch at noon, or have a drink and dance. In the evening it was a gathering place for lesbians.

About five o'clock one evening, my friend Denise and I went to the Ratz for a drink. We had known each other at Collège Saint Denis, where she was a year behind me. She was now studying philosophy at the UQAM. A professor from the history department came by and sat at out table. Then Noel Vallerand joined us. We drank, chatted, and got up sometimes to dance, when Noel suddenly remembered he had to give a lecture. He thought of skipping it, but changed his mind and gave us the keys to his house where he would meet us later, saying, "We can't just end the evening like this. It has started too well."

We drove to his place in the north end of Montreal, ordered Chinese food from a restaurant, and put Noel's portion in the oven. When he arrived, we went down to the basement, where he had a fine stereo system and about 3,000 classical records.

We chatted and listened to music. Noel was a great connoisseur. He had every piece by Johann Sebastian Bach ever recorded. He played the same concerto recorded by different performers, Martha Argerich, Claudio Arrau, Vladimir Ashkenazy or Arthur Rubenstein. He would play a symphony conducted by von Karajan, and the same symphony conducted by Solti.

We talked of music, history, and personalities. Noel enjoyed gossip and mimicking his students or fellow faculty members. He loved to laugh, holding his bulging stomach in both hands, shaking, sometimes until the tears ran down his cheeks. He drank beer and gin, but could not stand coloured alcohol such as scotch or rye, which gave him cramps.

"My life is dominated by three liquids," he would say. "Ink, gasoline, and sperm."

I don't know why he didn't include alcohol. Without being an alcoholic, he drank copiously. One day he came to his lecture with a split lip. The story went around that he had had an altercation with a bouncer in a nightclub while under the influence. Another time he had a car accident late at night.

We sipped gin in Noel's basement and occasionally danced. About four o'clock, Denise and the other professor left us for a nearby room. We heard a crash, and then giggling. Noel wondered what had happened, but was not about to investigate. We listened to music and chatted until about five o'clock, when we both stretched out on the couch fully dressed and fell asleep.

The alarm woke us two hours later. Noel had a lecture to give at eight — the course I was taking. In the car on the way to the university, Denise explained what had happened. She and her companion had gone into the room without turning on the light. She tripped over something and fell flat on the floor: it was a large stuffed animal left behind by one of Noel's children.

We grabbed some coffee in the cafeteria and went to the lecture room. Noel was bleary-eyed. He leaned against a pillar, a styrofoam cup of coffee in one hand, while the other elbow pressed against the pillar and his head rested in his hand.

Tired or not, he gave a wonderful lecture.

Noel was one of the great influences on my life. Through him, I learned about international relations, which I thought I would choose for a career. He set in motion a chain of events that led me to become a police informer.

CHAPTER 7
Quebec

—————————————— ❧ ——————————————

Quebec had changed. Everyone knew that something important had happened here during the 1960s, but no one could say where it would end.

We lived through that period day by day and we called it the Quiet Revolution. Our society, so long ultra-stable, suddenly was changing faster than any other area in North America. Previously, anthropologists had come to Quebec to study it as an example of a "folk society." Now, a revolutionary ferment was working in us, undermining our commitment to the past. The future had become a matter of wild surmise.

One event stands out in my memory from the year 1969 which catches the mood of the time. During that year's Saint Jean Baptiste parade, a group of protestors stormed the float carrying a large statue of the patron saint of French Canadians. The statue fell to the street, and its detached head rolled away.

The symbolism was accurate. French-speaking Quebeckers no longer recognized themselves in the saint who had fled to the desert to avoid the world. During the 1960s, the curly-haired little boy with a lamb was replaced by a statue of the saint as a powerful man. The religious symbol had been inflated. But as the decade came to an end, no religious symbol would do. The old social order based on reactionary Catholicism had been overturned. Yet the new order had not clearly emerged.

You could see the change by walking the streets. You no longer encountered the black-soutaned priests and brothers, or the nuns in black, brown, grey, or white robes with outlandish coronettes. Gone were the parish processions with crosses, banners, statues, canopies, and incense. You no longer heard the litanies chanted in the streets, you didn't see people pause three times a day at the toll of the bell to recite the *Angelus*, or bow their heads each time they passed in front of a church.

The liturgy disappeared from the rhythm of our daily lives. Many religious institutions — seminaries, novitiates, convents, and monasteries were emptied, as young men and women ceased to think religious life was the highest calling. Many of those who had been ordained or had taken vows of poverty, chastity, and obedience reconsidered and answered the new call of the world.

Everyone had a sister, brother, cousin, uncle or aunt who had left a religious order. Those returning to the secular life they had fled in adolescence came face-to-face with the customs, conventions, dishonesty, competitiveness, conflicts, and brutality of life in the world. They often had severe problems of adjustment.

Only the old-fashioned continued to take communion on the first Friday of the month, to make novenas to obtain miraculous favours, or to go up the steps of Saint Joseph's Oratory on their knees.

In a sense, all of Quebec was leaving the religious life for the secular. All of Quebec was living through a crisis of faith. When I was a child, nuns and priests accompanied us through much of our lives. The nuns ran the hospitals where we were born and the orphanages for children without parents. They ran the convents and colleges for boys and girls of prosperous families, and the ordinary Catholic schools for average families. Priests baptized us, taught us our catechism, heard our confessions and absolved us of our sins, gave us Holy Eucharist, married us, counselled us on our marital problems, warned us against birth control, comforted us in our misfortunes, anointed us when we were dying, and led us to the grave.

But in the 1960s, the clergy gave up its control of the schools, hospitals, colleges, universities, the mass-circulation newspapers, the trade unions, the parish organizations, and leisure activities. The clergy stopped being the shepherds and became, like us, stray sheep.

There was a pervasive challenge to authority. Suddenly, we saw ourselves as others had always seen us and, instead of being amused, we were outraged. History had made fools of us. We resented above all the humility we had always shown before the priest, the demagogue, the business establishment, the English.

Quebec had been the land of cheap labour and a docile work force. The Catholic unions had been forbidden a strike fund for fear it would encourage class warfare. But during the 1960s, the Catholic unions became the Confederation of National Trade Unions, the most militant in Canada. Quebec soon had more workdays lost through strikes than any other Canadian province. The encyclicals of Leo XIII and Pius XI, *Rerum Novarum* and *Quadrigesimo Anno*, ceased to be the inspired charters of labour relations. Instead, astonished, workers discovered Karl Marx.

The student movement in the 1950s had been totally dominated by the clergy. It was respectful of all authority, especially when it came dressed in religious garb. During the 1960s, a new movement, the Union Générale des Etudiants du Québec, took over the universities, inspired by the student movement in France. In UGEQ, students became intellectual workers who had rights and responsibilities that they were ready to fight for; they were committed to the struggle for social justice in Quebec. UGEQ worked enthusiastically with the Quebec government at the start of the Quiet Revolution, but it soon lost faith in the honesty of the political system and withdrew from the consultative bodies where government and students met.

"To participate is to be screwed," became the students' cry as the movement radicalized. By the fall of 1968, students had occupied just about every college and university campus across Quebec in the name of student power. By 1969, undermined by debts and dissension, too pure to live in this imperfect world, the student movement went out of existence, executed by its own firing squads.

Quebec society was divided, the unanimity of the past shattered. The reform of the educational system had opened up a vast generation gap. Many parents were happy that their children would receive the education they had been denied, but soon wondered if it was worth the price. Taxes shot up to support the new multidisciplinary high schools. Children in rural areas were bused long distances to the new regional schools, and many parents worried about boys and girls riding together. Teachers no longer illustrated their arithmetic lessons with angels or rosaries. They spoke of sex and pot and were often on strike. The strict discipline in the schools of the past had disappeared with the strap. The teachers were studying Marx.

Quebec began the decade with a convert's faith in liberalism. People decided that the long period of conservatism had been based on moral pessimism, on a distrust of human nature. Suddenly in the 1960s, Quebec plunged into reform. *Rattrapage*, catching up, was the slogan of the day. Quebec, catching up with North America, would become like North America, only it would speak French. It all seemed so easy.

By the end of the decade, however, pessimism had returned to Quebec. People felt betrayed by the broken promises of reform. To many, it seemed that only revolution could guarantee the future. We became aware of class warfare, of long-repressed hatreds, and of the dog-eat-dog mentality of the society.

Could we survive our collective crisis of faith? It was a serious question by 1969. Counter-revolutionary Catholicism had been at the heart of our culture, the inner logic integrating our institutions. We had made faith the guarantor of our identity. *Qui perd sa langue, perd sa foi*, we had often heard repeated. If you lose the French language, you will lose the Catholic faith. But now the question had become: could you lose your faith without losing your language? Had we lost our identity? If God was dying, terrible things became possible. Were those our nightmares in the tortured poems of Anne Hébert, the novels of Marie-Claire Blais? By 1969, we had begun to fear that our nightmares might come to pass.

The Church had encouraged us to have large families to populate both heaven and French Canada. But in the 1960s, the Quebecois took to birth control with such enthusiasm that Quebec's birthrate plunged to the lowest in Canada. How could a small society based on French survive in North America, where English tends to assimilate all languages?

During the 1960s, French Canadians across the country came to realize that it would only be a matter of time before the French language disappeared from one province after another, except in Quebec. Canada had become less hostile towards French at the very moment when hostility was no longer needed to repress the French minority. In 1969 Canada passed the Official Languages Act, making French, in theory, the equal of English in the federal government. But a law passed in Ottawa could not make French flourish in British Columbia, in Newfoundland, or in Nova Scotia, which had once been Acadia.

Only Quebec could survive as a French society, and even Quebec seemed threatened. Command of the economy was in the hands of English-speaking North Americans. In Quebec, economic pressures forced French-speaking Quebeckers to learn English in order to hold a job, and immigrants adopted English as the language of their future. Could a French Quebec survive?

By 1969, Quebec had experienced a crisis of confidence as well as a crisis of faith. The serenity of the first years of the Quiet Revolution was gone. A sense of urgency, even of panic, expressed itself in public discussions about the future. Where were we going? Reform might not be enough. It might have come too late. The year 1969 was one of violence in a society used to peaceful ways. The violence came sporadically, without obvious pattern, disturbing our peace, undermining our sense of security.

We had been used to the occasional explosion of FLQ bombs since the first in 1963. They came in waves. About once a year, a new group would go into action, and after a few months the police would swoop down, arrest and charge a few terrorists, and the bombs would cease until the next wave a few months later.

In early 1969, however, the bombs came with a freqency we had never seen before. We were shocked on February 13 when a powerful bomb exploded at the Montreal Stock Exchange in the afternoon, when there were about 300 people in the galleries. Twenty-three people were injured, three of them seriously. This disregard for human life was something new. Had the FLQ changed its tactics?

On March 4, the police arrested a twenty-four-year-old student, Pierre-Paul Geoffroy, who was sentenced to 124 terms of life imprisonment. An accomplice, Pierre Charette, fled to New York where the Blank Panthers sheltered him for two months. He then made his way to Cuba by hijacking at gunpoint a Boeing 727 belonging to National Airlines.

In February, students occupied a computer centre at Montreal's Sir George Williams University and destroyed it, with damage estimated at $2 million.

In March, McGill became the target of the nationalists. We considered McGill a tool of the English-speaking establishment of Montreal, a university aloof from the French-speaking majority, in Quebec but not of Quebec. We wanted it to become a part of the society it was supposed to serve, and to operate as a French-language institution. One night we marched 10,000 strong against McGill, with shouts of "McGill in French! McGill for the Quebecois!"

One of the organizers of the march was Mario Bachand, a veteran of the FLQ of 1963. Many demonstrators carried posters showing the FLQ martyrs Pierre-Paul Geoffroy, Pierre Vallières and Charles Gagnon, then in prison. It was a peaceful march, but the English establishment shuddered. Was this the beginning of a revolt by the long-submissive Quebecois?

During the summer bombs went off again in Montreal, and even in Quebec City there were seven bomb blasts.

The language issue was also explosive that year. A nasty quarrel began in Saint Léonard, an Italian suburb of Montreal, and spread to the whole province. At first, the issue was the unhappiness of French-speaking parents over losing their local school. It was to be converted to an English school, mainly to serve the children of Italian immigrants. Soon, however, it turned into a matter of principle: why should immigrant children have the right to attend English school in Quebec where the majority speaks French? This systematic preference for English threatened the very foundations of Quebec as a French society. People from all over Montreal took sides, and the school board finally reversed its stand and ordered the Italian children to go to the French school.

There were demonstrations and counter-demonstrations. On September 10, a crowd of 2,500 came to blows. The mayor of Saint Léonard read the riot act. Eighteen people were injured in the mêlée.

Saint Léonard was a warning of violence building below the surface of Quebec society, which had until then been freely expressed only by the FLQ. It was the ordinary citizenry who came to violence in Saint Léonard, even though Paul Rose was among those arrested. The language issue, thanks to Saint Léonard, polarized people right across Quebec.

Along with ethnic tensions, we experienced class tensions. On October 7, an unprecedented event occurred: the Montreal police went on strike, along with the Montreal firemen. The strike was illegal. The police met in a study session, several thousand strong, while shops across the city were being looted and burned. The police strike gave us a new picture of ourselves. We saw what we would be like if sheer brute force did not restrain us. The destruction in those hours before emergency legislation sent the police back to work required us to reassess our self-image. We had to face the violence and the hatred which had been there all along but had been kept in check by the guardians of law and order.

The peak of the violence came that evening, during a demonstration organized by taxi drivers resentful of the monopoly enjoyed by Murray Hill Limousine Service for the transportation of passengers to and from Montreal International Airport. About 400 cabs paraded noisily to the company's garage. There, the demonstrators began by throwing Molotov cocktails at the buses, then sent one crashing into the locked doors of the headquarters. From the roof, employees of the company fired shotgun blasts at the demonstrators. One person was killed, an undercover policeman of the provincial police, the Sûreté du Québec. Several were wounded by the buckshot blasts, including Jacques Lanctôt and Marc Carbonneau, both of whom were to take part the next year in the kidnapping of James Cross.

The police strike was over by midnight, but it left the faith of Quebeckers in themselves profoundly shaken. We could no longer depend on the police, whose commitment to protect society came second to their own interests. Some of us — and we did not know how many — had murderous hatreds that awaited only the right moment to burst out.

It was in this climate of unease that Premier Jean-Jacques Bertrand brought forward legislation that many of us saw as a betrayal. The conflict in Saint Léonard had exposed a Quebec-wide problem. Our whole future would depend on whether enough immigrants decided to learn French as their first language. Instead of legislating to compel immigrant children to attend French schools, Premier Bertrand proposed in Bill 63 to give parents a choice between French and English schooling.

Protests broke out across Quebec on a scale never seen before. Opposition to Bill 63 was widespread, articulate, and passionate.

In Montreal, by the end of October, just about every French school had closed its doors to allow students to demonstrate against the unpopular bill. On October 29, I was one of 25,000 people marching in the streets of Montreal and chanting: "*Le Québec aux Québécois! Québec français! Au Québec tout en français! Bertrand traître! Bertrand au poteau.*"

Various organizations had come together in opposition to Bill 63, calling themselves the Front du Québec français. It included teachers, the labour movement and patriotic organizations, like the Saint Jean Baptiste Society and the League for Educational Integration. Protest demonstrations were held in Hull, in Trois Rivières, in Rimouski, in Sherbrooke. The high point of the campaign would be a giant demonstration against the bill in front of the Quebec National Assembly on Friday, October 30.

The evening before the demonstrations, about a dozen of us who gave guided tours of the Steinberg bakery had decided to go to Quebec to participate. We would leave after work.

One of the guides was the daughter of the head of public relations at Steinberg. She knew her father would disapprove, so she phoned an aunt who was also against the language bill and asked her to say that she would be spending the next night at her place.

We were to leave for Quebec at five in the evening. Some of the guides showed up for work with picket signs on which were written: "In Quebec, everything in French!" That was hardly a message to please the management at Steinberg, and one executive came to tell us to put "those things" away in an office where they wouldn't offend the eyes of the visitors.

During the day, we went through the usual paean to the bakery, then we climbed into our cars and headed for Quebec City. Along Route 2, cars were decked out with the fleur-de-lys flag of Quebec. They honked their greeting to one another while passengers rolled down windows, thrust out clenched fists and shouted: "*En français! En français!*" Sometimes a car would stop and a passenger would get out to leave beside the road a little pile of pamphlets denouncing Bill 63. Hundreds of tracts littered the ground among the multicoloured fall leaves. They invited everyone to go to Quebec City to demonstrate their opposition to Bill 63, which threatened the extinction of French in Quebec.

Townspeople in the villages that we drove through and farmers in their fields held up clenched fists as we passed in a show of solidarity; some shouted that they would join us. It was as though the whole province was mobilized to defend its language.

It was cold in Quebec City. Someone set fire to some old tires and, in the midst of the black, billowing smoke, Premier Bertrand was burned in effigy while thousands shouted: "Bertrand traitor! Bertrand to the gallows! Bertrand sell-out! March or die! No to Bill 63!" Speakers climbed on the roofs of trucks to denounce Bill 63 through bullhorns, and they read aloud the telegrams of support that were coming from every corner of Quebec.

Despite the protests, Bill 63 was adopted by the National Assembly with the support of both major political parties: the governing Union Nationale and the opposition Liberal Party of Quebec. Only four elected members voted against it, including René Lévesque, who was then sitting as an independent. The Union Nationale would soon pay for its treachery: the people drove it from power a few months later and the party that had ruled Quebec for most of the years since the Second World War soon became an empty shell.

The people's confidence in their government and in their political institutions was shaken. Quebec, now carried a wound that would not heal.

On the Tuesday following the demonstration in Quebec City, I received a letter telling me that Steinberg had fired me from my part-time job. The reason given was that I performed my duties badly. Yet I had received a raise only the week before. It seemed likely to me that my firing had more to do with the language demonstrations than with my work.

No one doubted, at the close of 1969, that Quebec was in a state of crisis. How would it end? At what price, and after what trials? Those were the questions we asked ourselves at the end of the decade which had begun bravely with the Quiet Revolution.

CHAPTER 8
Working for the Parti Quebecois
❧

One Saturday in the fall of 1969, while I was eating my lunch in front of my telephone at Steinberg, my eyes fell on an advertisement in the newspaper which urged people to join the Parti Quebecois. I cut out the ad and wrote down my name, address, age, and occupation, and the name of my riding, Ahuntsic. I dropped the envelope in the mail with a cheque for $3. A few months later, my example was followed by my mother, my sister, my uncle and my aunt. We all joined the party of René Lévesque.

April 29, 1970, the day of the Quebec general elections, was a beautiful spring day. At eight o'clock, I took a taxi to the Parti Quebecois headquarters in Ahuntsic. I judged it a good omen when the taxi driver confided that he was going to vote for the Parti Quebecois because he liked its leader, René Lévesque.

I was to be in charge of telephone communications. It was my first experience in an election campaign. For months, I had spent every spare moment at party headquarters, doing the humdrum tasks that make up a campaign. I answered the phone, helped organize kitchen parties, filled out membership cards, drew up lists of voters with their supposed party preference, sold party badges, distributed pamphlets at church doors on Sunday, and answered calls from people who wanted election signs to display on their homes.

Now, after the months of work, it was voting day. The campaign headquarters were quieter than they had been in a long time, with most of our people driving supporters to the polls or acting as scrutineers in each of the hundreds of polls.

We were a team of five women on the telephones. Our task was to receive all incoming calls during the day until the polls closed. Then we were to receive the results as they were counted in each poll.

The phones rang constantly all day. "We need a car here to drive a voter to the poll. How soon can you send one?"

"Would you please send a babysitter so Mrs. Forest can go and vote?"

Someone called to have coffee sent to our people in the polls, "because the Liberals served some to their people." Another caller, over the noon hour, requested fried chicken. One of our workers called to describe a suspicious individual driving a grey Chevrolet. He could be impersonating somebody on the voters' list in order to vote illegally. We suspected the Liberals of having many such people.

Voter turnout was high. That could be a good sign, but what a day of suspense! Our candidate was Jacques Parizeau, one of the most prestigious figures in the Parti Quebecois. He was an economist, who had studied in England, had worked in Ottawa for the Bank of Canada, and had been chief economic adviser to three successive premiers of Quebec. His decision to support the Parti Quebecois had heightened the credibility of the new nationalist party. If this brilliant economist believed in an independent Quebec, he was a powerful rebuttal to the pessimists who warned that the PQ would lead Quebec to ruin.

I had come to know Jacques Parizeau in the months leading up to the election. One January night, shortly after I became a volunteer, I was about to leave the party offices and asked the receptionist to call me a cab. A man's voice spoke behind me: "Never mind, I'll share my cab with the young lady." I turned and saw a man with brown hair, luminous, large brown eyes, and a moustache. He was about forty, heavy-set, but not the huge man who was later to be Quebec's Minister of Finance. He wore a dark three-piece suit, and had a remarkably dignified bearing. That was my first impression of Jacques Parizeau. We shared a taxi and he dropped me off at home.

Over the following months, I saw him regularly. After the evening's work was done, the members of the Ahuntsic riding association executive and Parizeau sometimes went for a drink, and I joined them. On one occasion, he invited me to have a cognac with him and we talked politics. I admired him immensely, and thought he was the most interesting man I had ever met. I wanted desperately to see him elected in Ahuntsic and to see the Parti Quebecois win the elections across Quebec.

The party in power, the Union Nationale, had betrayed Quebec by passing Bill 63. The Parti Quebecois, if allowed to form the government, would make French the official language of Quebec, bring in social-democratic policies and, we hoped, declare Quebec's independence.

For a party that had only been founded two years earlier, the Parti Quebecois was doing well. Public opinion polls showed the sharp decline in popularity of the Union Nationale. Either the Parti Quebecois or the Liberals would form the government. The Liberals had chosen a new leader a few months before, the young economist Robert Bourassa. He was a colourless man who campaigned on a promise to provide "100,000 new jobs" in his first year, as though all Quebec needed was more jobs, more bread and more butter.

The Parti Quebecois held the most enthusiastic rallies and drew the biggest crowds. It was the party of style, ideals, spirit, and hope. Hearing the thousands of young people chanting *"Oui! Oui! Oui!"* with such passion, we believed in a miracle: the Parti Quebecois, which alone offered a prophetic vision of Quebec, was bound to win.

It had been a dirty campaign. The other three political parties concentrated their attacks on the Parti Quebecois, portraying it as a party of radicals and fanatics.

Premier Jean-Jacques Bertrand said shamelessly in one of his speeches: "A dictatorship would be the logical outcome of the coming to power of the Parti Quebecois." He predicted the end of democracy, a revolution in Quebec.

Réal Caouette, leader of the federal Social Credit Party, stumped the province using scare tactics against the Parti Quebecois: "Do you want a revolution within a year? If not, don't vote for the PQ. Don't vote for socialism, communism, revolution, for blood running in the streets of Quebec."

A Liberal candidate, who was elected that year, published an ad which had a picture of Saint Jean Baptiste overturned and decapitated, against the background of a riot. "The Parti Quebecois is the party of the terrorists," the ad stated. "Saint Jean Baptiste was decapitated: his was the first head to roll. Will the next be yours? Your wife's? Your child's?"

Liberal leader Bourassa went about warning of an economic catastrophe if the PQ were elected. The United States would impose a blockade against the importation of Bombardier snowmobiles, and thousands of jobs would be lost.

Pierre Laporte distributed "the Lévesque buck," a mock dollar bill with the head of René Lévesque instead of the Queen. One-third of the bill was missing, to suggest that the dollar in an independent Quebec would depreciate by one-third.

Private interests also took up the campaign of economic terrorism. The Royal Trust Company sent a caravan of Brink's armoured trucks to Ontario, supposedly containing the securities of their customers. The implication was that if the PQ were elected, all wealth would flee Quebec. This *coup de la Brink's*, as it was called, was carried out a couple of days before the election and was meant to back up the alarmist predictions that a PQ government would mean the end of old age pensions, prosperity, democracy, and peace. It was a memorable campaign!

At noon on election day, I received a sad phone call from my sister. She told me of the death of my grandmother, who had been a mother to me in my early years. My sister and my mother had already gone up to Sainte Anne de la Pérade because my grandmother had suffered a heart attack. I had not gone because I had wanted to work for the PQ on election day, and because I did not want to see her die. Now she was gone. I kept my grief to myself and turned my mind to the stream of phone calls that came in from all parts of the riding.

At long last the polls closed and the counting started. Everyone was in suspense. The campaign headquarters, empty during the day, now quickly filled up with the campaign workers who had been scattered throughout the riding. The room buzzed with happy conversations. Everyone had stories to tell about the day's events and the perfidy of the Liberals. All our people were confident that our candidate was going to win.

The phones rang steadily as each poll in the riding sent in its vote count. I tallied the votes. Jacques Parizeau kept pacing back and forth, his hands clasped behind his back, one hand holding a cigarette with the burning end turned inward toward his palm.

It was close, but he was ahead most of the time as the results came in. There was jubilation in the hall about our victory in Ahuntsic, though everyone was saddened as the news came in of losses almost everywhere in the province.

Finally, there was only one sector left to report, Saint Simon parish in the western part of the riding. It is a mostly Italian area, and we expected a poor showing there, but not a disaster. For some reason, the results from Saint Simon were slow in coming. Finally the call came, and I jotted down the figures, added them to the previous numbers, and found out that we had lost by a few hundred votes.

How sadly I looked at Jacques Parizeau, still pacing nervously. I went to him and, without a word, put in his hand the sheet of paper with the results. I then told the others working on the telephones that there was no point in taking any more calls; we had lost.

Some burst into tears. One member of the executive took a chair, smashed it on the table and began to cry. Some swore at the Italian immigrants whose massive Liberal vote had defeated our candidate. Jacques Parizeau himself remained stoic.

We went to a restaurant where a buffet had been prepared for us. What a sad meal! Afterwards, we headed down to the Paul Sauvé Arena where Parti Quebecois candidates and supporters from all over Montreal were gathering.

Together, we tasted the bitterness of defeat. René Lévesque, who had been elected as a Liberal in 1960, 1962, and 1966, went down to defeat as did the party's principal figures. Of the 108 members elected that night to the National Assembly, only 7 were from the Parti Quebecois. The Liberals had won 70 seats. The Parti Quebecois was second in popular vote, but fourth in number of elected numbers.

How disillusioning it was. Our hopes had been so high; even in our worst moments, we had never expected such a cruel setback. What would happen now to the movement for Quebec's independence?

That night, at the Paul Sauvé Arena, I burst into tears in the arms of a friend. I cried for Quebec. I cried for Jacques Parizeau, and I cried for my grandmother who had died. The next morning, dressed in black, I took the train to Sainte Anne de la Pérade to attend her funeral.

Campaign headquarters are a sad place a few days after a lost election. Silence has replaced the frenzy of election day. The useless posters, still displaying the confident, smiling face of the candidate, seem depressingly ironic. After my grandmother's funeral, I returned two or three times to the Parti Quebecois office to help tidy the papers, put away the posters, bring the files up to date, and clean up the mess we had left behind on the fateful night. The broom had the last word, and all our hopes were swept into the trash can.

I didn't expect to do any more work for the Parti Quebecois in Ahuntsic, but the phone rang a few days later at my mother's, where I was then living. It was Jacques Parizeau.

"Miss de Vault? I have put you in charge of challenging the election results in Ahuntsic. Will you do it?"

I didn't know what it meant to challenge election results. But Jacques Parizeau asked, so I agreed. Soon I discovered that it involved a lot of work.

"I can accept losing elections, but I don't like having them stolen," Parizeau said. He was convinced that his Liberal opponent had won by irregular means. Many of our campaign workers had stories about Italian immigrants who were not yet citizens, yet had been registered on the voters' list and had voted on election day. Of course, they had voted massively against the "separatists" and in favour of the federalist Liberals.

We were convinced that many people impersonating others on the voters' list had cast their votes on election day. There were rumours of a network of people who had voted several times under different names, both in our riding and in the next one over.

Five of the defeated PQ candidates, including Réne Lévesque, set out to prove that irregularities could have tipped the results against them. If they succeeded, the courts might order new elections in those ridings. My assignment was to gather evidence that the irregularities were numerous enough to have altered the outcome in Ahuntsic.

This meant carrying out an enumeration of the riding. Our lists from each poll on election day told us who had voted. If someone on the list told me they had not voted, it meant that someone had voted in his or her place. I was also to check on the citizenship of those who had voted.

It was an enormous undertaking to go to each of the thousands of households in the riding and ask people whether or not they had voted and if they had, to ask them to produce proof of citizenship. And I soon found that I could expect little cooperation from the members of the Ahuntsic riding executive.

In part, it was a matter of envy. Preparing the election challenge was a major responsibility, and the members of the executive were resentful that Parizeau had entrusted it to a newcomer who was not even on the executive. From that day on they saw me as Parizeau's pet, and held it against me.

He had made enemies with his abrasive style. He was very demanding and sometimes temperamental. When someone disappointed him, he would have nothing further to do with the person.

I remember when one of the volunteers prepared a biography of the candidate for a campaign pamphlet. Parizeau didn't like the biography, and made a terrible scene over it. Later he entrusted the task to his own wife, Alice, a novelist as well as a criminologist.

During the campaign, there had been differences of opinion over strategy. Parizeau insisted the campaign be run his way and it was. But some on the executive thought he was a poor strategist, and even held him responsible for the defeat. They did not dare take him to task directly, but they showed their resentment through their treatment of me.

Politics and flirtations go together, as I had discovered when I began my volunteer work. It amused me that several members of the executive in turn made passes at the new recruit.

One member of the executive was a professor at the University of Quebec, where I was a student. He had a car and we lived in the same district, so we travelled together every day from the university to the PQ office, and he drove me home. Sometimes, after an evening's work, we went out for a drink with the other members of the executive. Our relationship soon became close, though hardly intense.

Soon another member of the executive confided to my friend that he was smitten with me. Through my friend, I sent back word that he could invite me to dinner. He did. We had a hurried hamburger at a fast-food outlet. My would-be lover was dumbstruck and couldn't find a word to say during our snack.

And so it went. A third invited me to spend the weekend with him in Quebec City. I declined. A fourth invited me to his place for the evening, confiding that his wife would be absent. I refused. A fifth drove me home, took my hand, and told me soulfully how much he would like to know me better. A sixth threw his arms around me, called me his ray of sunshine, and kept inviting me, despite all refusals to the cinema. Fortunately, a seventh preferred men and didn't press his attentions on me.

I took it all lightly, concluding that politics is an aphrodisiac, at least in the Parti Quebecois. However, it became more serious after the elections when Jacques Parizeau asked me to take charge of the election challenge and I was thought to be his favourite. The pillars of the PQ, their vanity wounded, showed no interest in helping me. They were too busy painting the party offices. They wouldn't speak to me. I asked for paper to keep records of our work. I was told there was no paper available.

One day Pothier Ferland called — he was the legal adviser for the election challenge — and asked me how things were going. Badly, I told him, and explained why. He spoke to Jacques Parizeau.

That evening there was a meeting of the riding executive, which Parizeau attended. I was in another office with Pothier Ferland when I was sent for. I walked in and saw that Parizeau was flushed with anger, his hands trembling. He had removed his jacket and rolled up his sleeves to the elbow. He kept bringing his fist down on the table. The members of the executive sat around in silence, with long faces.

"Is it not true, Miss de Vault, that these people on the executive refused to supply you with paper?"

"Yes."

His voice rose.

"So it's true? You refused her paper?"

No one replied.

"Well, if you want to act like babies, you'll be treated like babies. From now on, each time Miss de Vault asks you for an eraser, you will give her an eraser and you will write on a sheet of paper: 'Five cents for an eraser.' And if she asks you for a pencil, you will give her a pencil and you will write down: 'Fifteen cents for a pencil.' At the end of the month you will send the bill to party headquarters with the note: 'Election challenge in Ahuntsic,' and we will reimburse you."

Some of the people around that table are now in prominent

positions in the Parti Quebecois government. I wonder if they will blush when they remember their pettiness in 1970.

My invaluable helper during the challenge was a member of the executive who taught dramatic arts at a junior college. His name was Michel Frankland and I will describe him at length because our lives were to be fatefully intertwined for a few years. We were to be together in the FLQ.

I chose Michel Frankland as my partner in the election challenge for two good reasons. I had noticed that he was a tireless worker during the election campaign. Then, too, his job as a college teacher left him a lot of free time. Another recommendation: Michel was one of the two or three riding workers who had not tried to flirt with me.

He turned out to be an agreeable companion as well as a devoted worker. He was thirty-two years old, and had spent a few years in a religious order. He had a passion for dramatic arts and did not always make a distinction between the stage and the real world.

Michel had brown hair, grey eyes which he sometimes covered with dark horn-rimmed glasses, and even features. He wore, indoors and outdoors, fall, winter and spring, a grey workman's cap. Around his neck hung a full grey woolen scarf, which hung down to the waist in front, while the other end was tossed back over his left shoulder. You could hear him approach: on his feet were long, droopy woolen socks, under unzippered aviator's boots that made a plodding sound as he moved.

How we walked the streets of Ahuntsic that summer! I did not yet have a summer job and Michel was through teaching for the academic year. From early morning until evening we went from door to door. Then we headed to the party offices to compile the day's information. A seventeen-year-old student helped us with the clerical work. She had shown herself to be able and willing during the election campaign. The three of us were the entire team, and we sometimes worked until two in the morning.

We concentrated first on Saint Simon parish, because 90 percent of the population there was Italian in origin, and many could speak neither French nor English. Or so it appeared. We were not popular with the Italian community.

When we rang or knocked at a door, someone would answer and look suspiciously at the two of us standing there, lists in hand.

"Good day, we are from the Parti Quebecois, and we are coming by for the election challenge. Did you vote on April twenty-ninth?"

"*Si.*"

"Could we see your proof of Canadian citizenship?"

At that moment the person ceased to understand.

"Pequese?" That is how the Pequistes were known.
"Oui, Pequese."
Often the door was closed in our face.

It was discouraging work. Perhaps two people in ten agreed to show their citizenship cards. Our impression was that each family we visited phoned the next to warn that the *Pequese* were on the way. When we arrived, there was no one at home, or no one who could speak French or English.

We knew, of course, that the Italians considered us to be nationalist fanatics, traitors to Canada, the country they had chosen. We could not expect a cordial greeting, since we were at the door to prove that hundreds of them had broken the law by voting when they were not citizens. Many of them held the state in awe, and feared what would happen if it were proven they had acted illegally. Some even feared deportation.

Their paranoia touched off ours. Michel, who always had a vivid imagination, began peopling Saint Simon parish with members of the Mafia. We would come to an ordinary house with two black Cadillacs in the driveway. Our list showed that six people lived in those cramped quarters.

"That looks very suspicious! How can they afford Cadillacs? They must be in the Mafia. Let's not ring at that door."

Soon we imagined another sign of danger. We noticed that many houses had a carved wooden bull's head over the door. The horns were unusually large. These heads came in all sizes, and some of them were huge.

Michel was convinced, for reasons I don't know, that the wooden animal head over a door was the sign of membership in a Sicilian secret criminal society. Soon we trembled when we knocked at a door guarded by a bull's head. Only Italian families had them. When we encountered a house that had both a bull's head and a black Cadillac in the driveway, we were thrown into a panic.

We were friends, trudging the streets together, sharing the same fear. But the hard work didn't keep Michel from thinking about women.

Soon after leaving the religious order, he had married an unpretentious dietician. "I am a *seigneur*, she is a peasant," he would pronounce.

When we were back at the party office he would take out his little black book and he would dial.

"Bonsoir, princesse," he would say gravely, "it is I."

He would ask his princess whether she was free to see him.

"Ah! you're not free. Too bad. Another time, then. *Bonsoir, princesse."*

It could take him five, six, or seven phone calls until he found a princess ready to meet him. Then he would drive off in his red Barracuda.

Our long hours of work did not produce the results we had hoped for. We did discover some Italians who had voted and were astonished to learn that you had to be a citizen to cast a ballot. We also came up with about fifty people who said they had not voted on election day but whose names were ticked off on the voters' list.

But, without greater cooperation, we could not produce evidence that the number of irregularities was sufficient to have swung the election. What could we do about all the people who refused to produce their proof of citizenship? Were they non-citizens, or merely citizens exercising their right to privacy?

One way of telling was to go to Ottawa with our lists of names and addresses and check through the records of the federal Department of Immigration, so four of us drove to Ottawa one day. There, we learned that it would cost 25 cents per name to make the check. We had a list of thousands. We phoned our lawyer, Pothier Ferland, who told us to stand by until we heard from him. That evening we received a call from Jacques Parizeau, who asked us to meet him at the Ottawa airport.

The decision was that we would take a small sample of names and have them checked, to see if it was worth pursuing. We picked twenty-five names. Most of them, it turned out, belonged to non-citizens. Parizeau was jubilant. We might yet get the court to overturn the election. We returned more determined than every to do a complete canvass of the riding. Where we suspected that a non-citizen had voted, we would have Pothier Ferland take a statement from the person under oath.

Our hopes were premature. We had chosen the names of people who had particularly aroused our suspicions. The full list was not nearly as rewarding. When all the work was done, we did not have sufficient evidence of irregularities to apply to the court. Our time had been spent for nothing.

It was during those couple of days in the capital region that Jacques Parizeau showed that he was attracted to me. It happened not only in the ugly little city of Hull, but at a run-down motel called La Dolce Vita. What was a fastidious patrician like Jacques Parizeau doing there?

We four party workers — two men and two women — had refused to take a room in Ottawa, the federal capital, so we went across the river to Hull, Quebec, and took two rooms in the first motel we came across. Hull is a rather dreary town, but at least it was in Quebec.

When Jacques Parizeau phoned from the airport, the other three went out by car to pick him up. I was washing my hair, so I stayed behind. When he arrived, I went out to meet him with my hair wrapped in a turban.

Whenever he was in Ottawa, Parizeau always stayed at the Chateau Laurier. A female party worker had phoned to reserve a room for him there, but she was told that the hotel was fully booked. Parizeau thought she might have received that answer because she spoke in French, so he called himself, speaking English in his best Oxford accent. He received the same answer.

He resigned himself to spending the night at La Dolce Vita. That night the five of us met in the bar where there was a dance floor, and soon we were all dancing. Jacques Parizeau gyrated with me, sweating profusely. His teeth gleamed under the green and violet rays of a turning strobe light. As we headed for our rooms, he warned us that he would be around to wake us early the next morning.

At seven o'clock he rapped at the door of the room where the two men slept. One of them, in only his undershorts stumbled to answer. He opened the door and saw the dignified Mr. Parizeau in a pinstriped suit, carrying an umbrella.

"Excuse me," he mumbled, "I thought it was one of the girls."

Our patrician soon announced that he was going across the river for breakfast at the Chateau Laurier with Miss de Vault, and that the others could eat in Hull. During our tête-à-tête he amused me with his anecdotes from the great world of politics.

We were kept busy most of the day with our citizenship inquiries, but at one point realized we needed a document that had been left behind at the motel. I offered to go for it in a taxi.

I had just arrived at my room and noticed that my undergarments were strewn about when there was a knock at the door. It was Jacques Parizeau. I let him in, and offered him an armchair and a glass of scotch, while doing my best to slip the undies under the mattress unnoticed.

Suddenly he reached over and swept me onto his knee.

"You know that I have a weakness for you?"

"No, I didn't."

"You can't be serious. Have you not been told, and often, that you are a very beautiful woman?"

It could have been the prelude to a romantic scene. But just then the door opened and one of the men entered. Flustered, I sprang to my feet. It was time to return to Montreal.

Jacques Parizeau was considerably older than I was — forty to my twenty-four — and married. But neither fact seemed important to me. He was so much more sophisticated, so much more experienced. How I admired his intelligence and knowledge of the world!

I had met his wife during the election campaign, a stout woman a few years older than Jacques: by now, their marriage seemed to be one of reason and friendship rather than passion.

In my reading of novels and of history, great men and great women always took mistresses or lovers. It seemed natural to me, and I thought of Jacques Parizeau as a great man.

He impressed me as the most intelligent person I had ever met. I loved to hear him talk about politics, about history, about going to Paris with Premier Daniel Johnson. How he laughed when he told his stories! And he could just as easily evoke a revolt of the serfs in czarist Russia, or the revolutions in Germany in 1848.

I was awed by the man, by his personal qualities, and by a sense that he would play an historic role in Quebec's nationalist evolution. And yet, he reminded me of a stuffed bear that I hugged at night in my childhood. I called Jacques "Coco," the name of the bear.

The days that we spent together as lovers, in Montreal, in Ottawa, and in Toronto, were probably part of a passing adventure for him. But for me, he was the first real love of my life. I was still very naïve.

PART TWO

CHAPTER 9
The October Crisis

─────────────────── �֍ ───────────────────

All my generation remembers the kidnapping of James Cross and the events that followed. We refer to it as the October Crisis. There is only one October, that of 1970.

At first, no one paid much attention. It was a strange occurrence, this kidnapping of a British diplomat, but it concerned us very little.

The police, notified by a radio station called by the kidnappers, had found a communiqué with a political manifesto, both signed by the FLQ.

The representative of Great Britain in Quebec, Mr. J. Cross, is in the hands of the Front de Libération du Québec. Here are the conditions that the ruling authorities must fulfill in order to save the life of the representative of the ancient racist and colonialist British system.

There followed seven conditions for the release of the hostage. Then the threat.

All these conditions must be dealt with within forty-eight hours from the release of this communiqué. All these conditions are irrevocable. The life of the diplomat depends therefore on the good-will of the ruling authorities.

The main condition was the freeing of twenty-one "political prisoners," members of the FLQ in jail for bombings, armed robbery, manslaughter, and other crimes linked to terrorist activity since 1963. An airplane was to be put at their disposal to send them with their families to Cuba or Algeria. The Front also demanded "a voluntary tax" of $500,000 be contributed by the government to the terrorists. The police were warned to make no attempt to find the kidnapped diplomat. The political manifesto of the FLQ was to be read on CBC television and published on the front pages of Quebec's main daily newspapers.

Two days went by, and public interest began to increase. Would the kidnappers execute their hostage at the end of the forty-eight hour period? The government stalled. Macabre suspense. Would a corpse show up? Where?

Cross was out there somewhere, but no one knew where. Mysterious messages were picked up in trash cans, in telephone booths, under a door mat. Sometimes a laconic call to a radio station told where to find the latest communiqué. Journalists would rush over. The public got caught up in the suspense, little by little.

The kidnapping took on a deeper significance with the reading of the FLQ's manifesto on television. To play for time, to fulfill one of the kidnapper's conditions without giving in to the main one, the government had the CBC read the manifesto on the evening of October 8.

Now I and many other Quebeckers began to feel involved. The manifesto spoke a language that everyone recognized, but that had never before been spoken on television. It was the same mocking language, crude and irreverent, that is heard on the street and at work — the way real people talk. Newscaster Gaétan Montreuil read the text with the countenance of an undertaker and the solemnity of a preacher at a funeral.

The Front de Libération du Québec is not a Messiah, nor a modern-day Robin Hood. It is a group of Quebec workers who have decided to use every means to make sure that the people of Quebec take control of their destiny.

The Front de Libération du Québec wants the total independence of all Quebecois united in a free society purged forever of the clique of voracious sharks, the patronizing "big bosses," and their henchmen who have made Quebec their hunting preserve for cheap labour and unscrupulous exploitation.

A breath of populism gave life to the sentences of the manifesto. The FLQ took the side of the poor against the rich. It denounced the powerful, and especially the political leaders of Quebec and Canada. And in what language! Business leaders and financiers were ridiculed. From the unsmiling mouth of Gaétan Montreuil, we heard Prime Minister Trudeau called "Trudeau the fruit." Premier Robert Bourassa was solemnly dubbed "the mincing queen of the Simards." Montreal's Mayor Jean Drapeau was "Drapeau the dog." The rectors of the University of Montreal and the Université du Québec à Montréal (UQAM) became "the monkey directors." All the elements of the Quebec establishment were scorned, and only the unions and the people were spared.

The manifesto ended in a flight of rhetoric.

*We are the workers of Quebec and we will continue to the bitter end.
We want to replace the slave society with a free society, functioning by
itself and for itself; a society open to the world.
   Our struggle can only lead to victory. You cannot hold an awaken-
ing people in misery and contempt indefinitely.*
   Vive le Québec libre! *Long live free Quebec!*
   Vive our imprisoned political comrades.
   Vive the Quebec revolution!
   Vive le Front de Libération du Québec.

   Everyone was discussing the manifesto the next morning. Everyone now felt involved. Some were for, some against, but no one
remained neutral. The populist tone had touched a responsive chord
among the Quebecois. It seemed to many that the FLQ had just
spoken the plain truth — expressed in bold language what everyone privately thought.
   I spent the weekend at Sainte Anne de la Pérade, where discussion of the manifesto occupied every meal. My Uncle Jules railed
against those who kidnapped Cross as mere thugs, as criminals
who needed to be kept in prison for a good while to give them time
to think. He feared as I did that the FLQ would harm the Parti
Quebecois.
   "It's hard enough as it is to make people understand that the PQ
is not dangerous, and now those idiots have to kidnap an Englishman
in the name of liberating the Quebec people. Bloody band of criminals! That's all the FLQ is!"
   My Aunt Jacqueline, a nurse, choked on a piece of pork. She
dropped her fork, gasped for breath, and red with anger and blue
from choking, she took a sip of water and cried out:
   "Jules, you should be ashamed to speak like that! Did you even
read the manifesto? I read it, and I'd like to know what you have
against it. I agree with the FLQ. The PQ is fine, I voted for the PQ,
too, but it does nothing for the people, for the poor who have no
money because companies are closing down one after another, or
because those big companies remaining pay a pittance to their employees. The people are going to have to get tough with the multi-
nationals. Why can't you see it? Honestly, there are times you
really disappoint me. I wonder what world you're living in. When I
see a woman arrive at the hospital at Cap de la Madeleine to give
birth to her seventh baby, and she doesn't even have a bathrobe to
put on because her husband has lost his job, I can only think that
the child will never be fed properly, and it is high time that people
rise up in protest. Read the manifesto!"

There was the same split between my parents. My father hated the FLQ.

"They deserve to hang! Those damned Felquistes, those bomb setters, that neurotic bunch of birdbrains, think they're so smart, but you'll see — they'll come to a bad end. Just wait till the police get their hands on them. I wouldn't want to be in their shoes, then."

My mother backed the FLQ. She disliked the English, and thought it not a bad idea that the FLQ had kidnapped an Englishman. She approved of the fact that the FLQ were fighting for Quebec.

I also supported the manifesto.

I endorsed the FLQ denunciation of the capitalists and approved of their solidarity with the workers in all the recent labour conflicts. I, too, wanted to see an end to American control of our economy. I didn't much like the street language, though, the vulgar words used to describe our political leaders. I liked the manifesto but was against the kidnapping.

At the university, all the professors and students I encountered also seemed to approve of the manifesto. A professor of economic history, a Marxist, thought that it might trigger a socialist revolution in Quebec. The students saw in the manifesto the logical extension of their own recent causes. For some, it was the student revolt of 1968 and 1969 carried on by other means. They declared themselves disgusted with the society that their elders were preparing for them. "I am not for violence, but . . ." How often I heard that phrase, followed by approval of the manifesto.

The language of the manifesto came up again and again in conversations among students. In the cafeteria, the director of a department would be referred to as "Monkey so-and-so." An amateur artist drew a caricature of Prime Minister Trudeau with a rose in his lapel and a snake's tongue on a pillar of the Saint Marie pavilion. Written underneath: "Monkey Trudeau the fruit."

For the five days that followed the kidnapping of Cross, all Quebec was wrapped up in it. If the truth be known, they even joked about it. There was no crisis yet, merely suspense. But it all changed suddenly at 6:18 in the evening of October 10. The Quebec Minister of Justice, Jerôme Choquette, gave a press conference at which he rejected the conditions set by the kidnappers. His only concession would be to allow the kidnappers a safe-conduct out of the country if they surrendered their hostage. No freeing of political prisoners, no ransom money, no divulging the name of the informer who, the FLQ believed, had enabled the police to foil a kidnapping plot in June. In a word, nothing. Free your hostage and beat it.

The answer from the FLQ was swift and brutal. The Minister of Justice had barely finished speaking on the six o'clock news when the FLQ kidnapped the Acting Premier, Pierre Laporte. He was the strong man of the Bourassa regime, the Minister of Labour and Immigration. This time the FLQ had kidnapped a Quebecois. Shock! Disbelief! Consternation! Was the FLQ everywhere? Could the FLQ do anything it wanted? The population began to rethink its assessment of the FLQ. Until now, its members had been considered rash young idealists, perhaps impractical, but likeable overall. You couldn't help but feel sorry for all those young people who had caused a commotion for a while before ending up in prison. How many times had the FLQ surfaced since 1963? All the cells had been discovered sooner or later by the police.

Could it be that a large and powerful movement had been building in the shadows while no one was watching? For some years now, everything had been changing at a frantic pace in Quebec. Could it be that the most threatening change of all had escaped notice? Could this be revolution?

The impression of power was confirmed when the new cell delivered its message. Like the Liberation Cell that had kidnapped Cross, the Chénier Cell hid its communiqués in trash cans and made mysterious calls to a radio station to tell the location of the latest message. Here is part of the Chénier Cell's first communiqué:

The minister will be executed Sunday evening at 10 p.m. if between now and then the ruling authorities have not responded favourably to the seven demands set forth following the kidnapping of Mr. James Cross.

Any partial acceptance will be considered as a refusal.

In the meantime, the Liberation Cell will make known the technical details of the whole operation.

What an inflexible tone! The FLQ sounded so self-assured, so confident of bending the government to its will. A pathetic, pleading letter from Pierre Laporte to Premier Bourassa was found in a trash can following a call to a radio station. In it, he begged Bourassa to free the political prisoners before the FLQ carried out its threat to kill him.

Panic spread through the population. Premier Bourassa returned from New York and called an emergency session of the Cabinet, to be held in Montreal. Ministers and officials from Quebec City formed an armed convoy on the highway and sped to Montreal, all in line, under the protection of the provincial police. Political figures left their houses only under escort.

At the Cabinet meeting on October 11, Mr. Bourassa received the letter from Pierre Laporte addressed to him. He began to read it aloud but couldn't continue. His voice faltered; he handed the letter to an official, Paul Tellier, who read it to the end.

The FLQ was everywhere. The FLQ was nowhere. Rumours abounded. Thousands of excited calls flooded the police switchboard. Someone had seen Cross in a car. Laporte had been glimpsed in a garage. The Felquistes were hiding out in a neighbour's basement. Ordinary citizens, their imaginations aflame, explored fields and woods, quarries, and abandoned shacks. They spotted Felquistes by the score. The police were kept running everywhere, day and night.

According to rumour, Ottawa and Quebec were at loggerheads. The Premier of Quebec wanted to exchange the political prisoners to save the lives of the two hostages, but the Prime Minister of Canada refused: no concessions! Robert Bourassa was said to have bowed before the determination of Pierre Trudeau. Leading figures in Quebec were becoming concerned. Did Quebec have its own government, or was it run from Ottawa?

Jacques Parizeau arrived at my apartment about seven o'clock in the evening, on, I think, October 13. He seemed excited.

"Carole, do you have anything to drink?"

I brought him a glass of Chivas Regal, his favourite scotch.

"You know, Carole, the Bourassa government is no longer capable of making decisions."

He sat down on the couch beside the telephone and took a notebook out of his pocket. I was seated on the carpet at his feet. He told me that there were people ready to take over from the government, to set up what he called either a parallel government or a provisional government.

"You know, your apartment will be historic, because you will be able to say that the parallel government began here."

Using my telephone, he tried to reach Claude Ryan, publisher of *Le Devoir*, and Marcel Pépin, president of the Confederation of National Trade Unions. Neither was available. He left after an hour, telling me that I would soon hear more about the subject of our conversation. And adding that I must not talk about it to anyone.

I recall this incident because there was later much talk about a supposed "parallel government" under consideration by Claude Ryan, René Lévesque and others. I cannot say what meaning Jacques Parizeau gave to these words when he came to my place nor the scope of the responsibility he anticipated for this body. But I can affirm that Jacques Parizeau spoke about it to me, and very seriously. It is up to him to explain what role he played.

The newspapers of October 14 quoted the fierce words of Ontario Premier John Robarts. He said that terrorism in Quebec was turning into "total war" and that the time had come to "stand and fight."

Prime Minister Trudeau, challenged by journalist Tim Ralfe, who was disturbed by the presence of the army in Ottawa, answered that only "bleeding hearts" would take offence at the helmets and guns.

Before the television cameras, Ralfe asked the Prime Minister how far he was prepared to go to maintain law and order.

"Just watch me," was the reply.

"I think the society must take every means at its disposal to defend itself against the emergence of a parallel power which defies the elected power in this country and I think that goes to any distance...."

On the same day, prominent Quebeckers came forward to encourage the Premier of Quebec to stand firm against actions and pressures from outside. They called a press conference chaired by Claude Ryan, while René Lévesque read their common statement.

The Cross-Laporte affair is primarily a Quebec drama....

Certain attitudes outside Quebec, the last and most unbelievable of which was that of Premier Robarts of Ontario, plus the rigid—almost military—atmosphere we see in Ottawa runs the risk of reducing Quebec and its government to a tragic ineffectualness....

Particularly in certain non-Quebec quarters, we fear the terrible temptation of the worst type of politics, in other words the idea that Quebec in chaos and disorder would at last be easy to control by any available means.

This is why, forgetting the difference of opinion we have on a number of subjects, solely conscious for the moment of being Quebecois and therefore totally involved, we wish to give our ... strongest support for negotiating an exchange of the two hostages for the political prisoners. This must be accomplished despite and against any obstruction from outside Quebec...."

The joint statement was signed by sixteen people, including René Lévesque, Jacques Parizeau and Camille Laurin of the Parti Quebecois; union leaders Marcel Pépin, Louis Laberge, Yvon Charbonneau, Fernand Daoust, Mathias Rioux and Raymond Laliberté; the journalist Claude Ryan; university professors Guy Rocher, Fernand Dumont, Paul Bélanger and Marcel Rioux; Alfred Rouleau, president of l'Assurance-vie Desjardins; and Jean-Marc Kirouac, president of the Catholic Farmers Union. It was the voice of the moderate left in Quebec.

The FLQ had the initiative. It had kidnapped a diplomat, set conditions for his release, given ultimatums, postponed them, dropped some of the demands, kidnapped a minister, restored the original demands, threatened and mocked the authorities. The government seemed to have lost control over events. It could only react. It couldn't even guarantee the protection of its citizens. The event was unprecedented: a group was defying and insulting the authorities and they, helpless, were answering politely.

Journalists rushed out every time the FLQ showed itself. In the surrealistic atmosphere of the time, the FLQ imposed its logic. The Front, invisible and anonymous, was calling the tune, and leading the *danse macabre*.

Then the FLQ, little by little, acquired a face, that of a twenty-nine-year-old lawyer with a moustache and d'Artagnan curls, daring in manner and with a splendid insolence towards the authorities. His name was Robert Lemieux. He was equally at ease in French or English, being French on his father's side, and English on his mother's. He had studied law at McGill. He favoured the independence of Quebec and for the previous three years had defended, for a pittance, Felquistes charged with criminal offences. As bohemian as he was revolutionary, he had a small room on the third floor of an aging, shabby hotel on Place Jacques Cartier, for which he paid $16 a week.

His role, at first, was minor. When the FLQ demanded the release of the political prisoners, it was he who hurried to the jails to get their agreement to flight to Cuba or Algeria.

He made no secret of his sympathy for the FLQ and his solidarity with the kidnappers of the diplomat. "I see in this new breed of Felquistes a deepening of their ideology, their character, and their revolutionary fervour," he said.

At his press conferences, all well attended, he addressed himself to the Felquistes and gave them advice and warnings. "The federal government, through Mitchell Sharp, pretends to be willing to negotiate with the Front de Libération du Québec. That is really just another gambit to trick the FLQ and to gain as much time as possible so that the police can discover the hideout of Cross and his kidnappers, and so provoke a shoot-out and an execution."

He warned the kidnappers that Mr. Cross's letters, which accompanied the communiqués to authenticate them, contained a secret code whereby the hostage tried to give the authorities clues to his whereabouts.

There was some indignation at the sight of this lawyer helping the Felquistes. He was arrested the day after Laporte's kidnapping and detained, charged with having by his statements "obstructed peace officers in the execution of their duty." The police seized his files, hoping in vain to find there some information that could help them to locate Cross or Laporte.

The second kidnapping had shaken the Premier of Quebec. The next night, Robert Bourassa addressed the kidnappers on television and now seemed to be disposed to release the Felquiste prisoners. He even called them "political prisoners," a term previously shunned by the authorities. The Felquistes were in prison for criminal acts, and not for the political dimension of their undertaking.

Mr. Bourassa asked the kidnappers to get in touch with the government. The two cells named Robert Lemieux as their intermediary in the negotiations. The government then named its negotiator, who visited Mr. Lemieux in jail to begin the talks. Mr. Lemieux was released after two days of incarceration.

Three times a day, he went back before the television cameras to give the kidnappers an account of the negotiations. Here was the strange sight of a lawyer speaking to his clients through the media. The journalists concentrated their attention on him: they had come from all over America and Europe to cover the kidnappings in Quebec, and the only person they could interview, film, and tape record was Mr. Lemieux, who had now become the public face, the non-clandestine voice, of the FLQ. Mr. Lemieux repeated over and over that he feared for the lives of the hostages, that the FLQ meant business, that the government must act quickly.

But the Quebec government stalled. Its negotiator, Robert Demers, wanted the Liberation and Chénier cells each to leave one of their members as hostage in the hands of the authorities until Cross and Laporte had been liberated. Mr. Lemieux replied that he had no mandate to discuss such a possibility. On television, he spoke again to the invisible kidnappers to ask for instructions.

"*Chers patriotes,*" he said to the camera, "I address myself to those who gave me a mandate to negotiate. My mandate covers the means of applying the six conditions, but now a precondition has been raised with respect to guaranteeing the release of the hostages. The mandate you gave me does not authorize me to discuss such a precondition. Given the government's refusal to budge, I cannot continue without receiving a new mandate."

The next day, the answer to Mr. Lemieux came by the usual route. Pierre Pascau, a journalist at radio station CKLM, found a communiqué in a trash can, a joint message from the two cells. They refused to hand over one of their members as a hostage.

We accept, however, as an ultimate solution, the proposal of Mr. Lemieux, namely that the country which receives the political prisoners keep them in detention (as well as the $500,000) until we have surrendered unharmed J. Cross and P. Laporte.

We have serious doubts about the good faith of the authorities. What "guarantees" can they give us with respect to the cessation of searches, raids, and arrests by their fascist political police? For more than eight

*days now, the repressive police forces, under the command of Choquette
the dog, have multiplied their illegal raids and arrests despite the fact
that it is one of the chief conditions for the release (unharmed) of
J. Cross and Pierre Laporte. . . .*

On October 15, the Canadian army entered Montreal and Quebec
and soldiers took up positions before public buildings. For the
first time in my life, I saw soldiers in my city, wearing steel helmets
and carrying rifles. I had the feeling that my country had been
occupied.

Towards the end of the afternoon, I decided to attend a Robert
Lemieux press conference. I climbed the steps behind City Hall
and crossed Place Vauquelin to reach Place Jacques Cartier. The
headquarters of the Montreal police, as I passed it, were barricaded
on all sides and soldiers were standing guard.

There was a crowd at the door of the Nelson Hotel where Robert
Lemieux lived and where he held his press conferences. I tried to
go in, but it was impossible to push through the crowd.

A rumour drifted back that only those with press cards would
be admitted. I did not give up, but decided to grab the first journalist
I came across. I turned to my neighbour and saw to my joy, that he
had a press card hanging from his neck. I asked him: "Is it true
that only journalists are allowed in?"

He answered almost in a shout, because it was hard to hear over
the noise of the crowd. "Yes. You want to go in?" He took my hand
and drew me through the crowd. They had finally opened the door.

Someone asked for our press identification. My journalist showed
his card and shouted: "Toto Gingras from *Le Journal de Montréal*,
and she is with me." We pushed in, and no one asked to see my
press card.

The press conference was to be held on the ground floor, in a hall
at the far end. In the hall, the tables were placed in a semi-circle.
We rushed to grab a chair. Gingras, who was a photographer, led
me to a seat by the wall, about fifteen feet from where Lemieux
was to speak.

There was a commotion and the famous lawyer swept in. The
cameras rolled, the lights flashed like strobes. Then Lemieux went
up to a microphone, lit a cigarette, took a sip of beer and began to
speak.

He warned the Front that the police had discovered the hiding
place of the Chénier Cell. A Montreal businessman with connec-
tions in the government had come to him to say that the police
knew where Laporte was being held, but that they would not act
until they had found Cross.

The journalists interrupted him, all trying to ask questions at the same time. He became impatient, and called for silence. It was clear that he aimed his message at the people who were holding Laporte rather than the journalists.

There was tension in the smoke-filled hall. Everyone had a sense of the drama of the moment. Would the police appear? I felt that they must be in the room looking for a clue that would lead them to the kidnappers, but how were they disguised?

There must also have been Felquistes in the room. But who were they? I didn't recognize them. From the back of the room, the well-known union leader Michel Chartrand denounced "the fascist Prime Minister of Canada." The neighbour on my left asked me for a cigarette. I recognized him, René Mailhot, a CBC reporter. When the press conference was over he invited me to have a drink with him. I accepted, thinking that I might learn more from a reporter than a photographer. We went to a bar in Old Montreal, and drank a half-bottle of wine. René Mailhot questioned me about what was happening among the students at UQAM.

For, as he had heard, the students were mobilizing to back the action of the FLQ. The previous evening, Robert Lemieux had gone to a meeting of the University of Montreal teachers' union. He had asked the 400 professors and students in attendance to "suspend their courses for a few hours in order to reflect on the problem." His proposal had been accepted with enthusiasm. "Operation Strike" had begun.

That morning, October 15, the students in arts and social sciences at the University of Montreal had held a study session on the FLQ manifesto. About 1,000 students had voted to boycott classes until the political prisoners were freed. The students had come out in favour of the manifesto and against the police action to find the hostages.

The students had scheduled a mass meeting for the afternoon, in order that all faculties could vote for a general strike in support of the FLQ. But the university authorities had closed the sports centre where the meeting was to have been held.

At the UQAM, we had been summoned over the noon hour to the Gésu hall. About 800 students had attended. As I arrived, I ran into a young history professor, Robert Comeau, who had never spoken to me before. He greeted me: "Hi, participationist!"

The hall was full of smoke and of students. About 10 were seated on the stage. The atmosphere was solemn and there was a sense in the air that this was a momentous occasion. The organizers of the meeting spoke first, and asked us to support the FLQ. I don't recall a single voice urging an opposing viewpoint. After the opening

speeches, the audience expressed itself, more or less in the following words:

"I agree with the FLQ. We should strike. But I would also urge
that we take advantage of the strike to make known the ideals of
the FLQ. People are frightened. They don't know the FLQ. We have
to help people get rid of their fear, to educate them. That's how you
make a revolution. So I move this motion."

Each speaker was applauded. "*Bravo! Bravo! Vive le FLQ!*"

Resolutions were adopted. The students voted for a general strike
until such time as the government had complied with the six conditions of the kidnappers. We set up an action committee which
was to support the FLQ, and an information secretariat.

Among the proposals discussed at the meeting were the following: to distribute the manifesto from door to door, to distribute the
Patriote flag, to talk to people on the street about the objectives of
the FLQ, to honk car horns to the rhythm of the chant of the students in France in 1968: "*Ce n'est qu'un début, continuons le com-
bat.*" This is just the beginning, let's continue to fight.

The UQAM went on strike; all of its 6,000 students left their classes,
although it would be a mistake to think that all had a political
motive. I could hear them talking around me.

"I'm behind in my assignments. It will give me a chance to catch
up."

"Me, too. Do you think the strike will last very long?"

"Tomorrow I'm going up to Saint Donat in the Laurentians. The
weather is beautiful and I'm going to have a rest."

As we left the meeting, Noel Vallerand had fallen in beside me.
He was unhappy.

"What a bunch of idiots. This doesn't make the least bit of sense."
Some other professors had been of the same opinion.

While sipping wine, I explained to René Mailhot my perception
of the students' attitudes toward the FLQ. The Front was all the
rage at the moment, and so the students had come out in its favour.
But most of them gave it superficial support. I myself was in favour of the manifesto, but I couldn't take too seriously the decision
we had just made to go on strike. I believed that only a small minority felt entrusted with an historic mission or believed that the
hour for revolution had come. We finished our wine, and René Mailhot
drove me home.

That evening, I decided not to go to the meeting at the Paul Sauvé
Arena. Some students, mostly those from the University of Montreal
who had been unable to hold their meeting at the university sports
centre, went down to a meeting that included an auction sale to
raise money for the Front d'Action politique (FRAP), the municipal
political party. The preceding Sunday, the permanent council of

FRAP had come out in favour of the objectives of the manifesto, but not in favour of the terrorist acts of the FLQ. At the same time, FRAP condemned "the violence of the system." On the evening of October 15, the FRAP meeting soon turned into a celebration of the FLQ. Playwright Michel Garneau solemnly read the manifesto. Pierre Vallières spoke to the 2,000 young people and told them: "You are the FLQ, you and all the people's groups who fight for the liberation of Quebec."

The students, their fists raised, chanted: "FLQ! FLQ! FLQ!"

At nine o'clock in the evening, Premier Bourassa issued a communiqué in which he rejected all the demands made by the kidnappers. His one concession was to promise to "recommend firmly the parole" of five prisoners who were already eligible, if the kidnappers freed their hostages. He also promised them safe-conduct and a plane to take them to the country of their choice. He gave them six hours to reply.

Earlier that day, the chief of the Montreal police department had written a letter to Mayor Jean Drapeau and to the Chairman of the city's Executive Council, Lucien Saulnier, saying that the police could no longer control events. Chief Marcel Saint-Pierre wrote:

An extremely dangerous subversive movement has progressively developed in Quebec in recent years with the objective of overthrowing the legitimate state by means of sedition and eventually armed insurrection.

The recent kidnappings of a foreign diplomat and a Crown minister of the province have signalled the launching by this movement of their seditious projects and acts leading directly to the insurrection and the overthrow of the state. . . .

Considering how extremely urgent it is to achieve concrete results and unmask all the ramifications of this movement and its seditious activities, considering the volume and complexity of the proofs which must be collected and preserved, considering, finally, the enormity of the task we must accomplish, without moving into a repression which would be neither healthy nor desirable, the help of higher governments is essential to the completion of our job.

The slowness of procedures and the restraints imposed by the legal methods and mechanisms now at our disposal do not allow us at this time to cope with the situation.

Consequently, I recommend that the executive committee of the city request that the higher governments give us all the means they think appropriate and useful, so as to allow us to collect and present the proofs needed to protect society from the seditious and insurrectional manoeuvres unleashed by the kidnappings. . . .

When Mayor Drapeau and Mr. Saulnier received this letter, whose analysis of events supported their own alarmist perceptions, they immediately sent a letter similar in tone to the Prime Minister of Canada.

Mr. Prime Minister,

The chief of the Montreal Police Service has informed us that the means available to him are proving inadequate and that the assistance of higher levels of government has become essential for the protection of society against the seditious plot and the apprehended insurrection in which the recent kidnappings were the first step.

We are forwarding as a matter of the utmost urgency the report describing the scope of the threat and the urgent need to reinforce the machinery to cope with it.

We ask for every measure of assistance the federal government may deem useful and desirable in order to carry out the task of protecting society and the lives of citizens in this difficult period.

Lucien Saulnier	*Jean Drapeau*
Chairman of the	*Mayor of Montreal*
Executive Committee	

Finally, on that same October 15, the Premier of Quebec signed a letter in which he asked the Prime Minister of Canada for emergency powers. The letter was actually signed that evening, but dated October 16, no doubt because Mr. Bourassa had given the kidnappers six hours to respond. The expiry of his ultimatum coincided pretty well with the moment the letter reached the federal government in Ottawa.

Quebec City, October 16, 1970

Mr. Prime Minister,

During the last few days the people of Quebec have been greatly shocked by the kidnapping of Mr. James R. Cross, representative of the British Government in Montreal, and the Hon. Pierre Laporte, Minister of Labour and Manpower and Minister of Immigration of Quebec, as well as by the threats to the security of the state and individuals expressed in communiqués issued by the Front de Libération du Québec or on its behalf, and finally by all the circumstances surrounding these events.

After consultation with authorities directly responsible for the administration of justice in Quebec, the Quebec Government is convinced that the law, as it stands now, is inadequate to meet this situation satisfactorily.

Under the circumstances, on behalf of the Government of Quebec, I request that emergency powers be provided as soon as possible so that more effective steps may be taken. I request particularly that such powers encompass the authority to apprehend and keep in custody individuals who, the Attorney General of Quebec has valid reasons to believe, are determined to overthrow the government through violence and illegal means. . . .

The Quebec Government is convinced that such powers are necessary to meet the present emergency. Not only are two completely innocent men threatened with death, but we are also faced with an attempt by a minority to destroy social order through criminal action; it is for those reasons that our government is making the present request.

The government is confident that, through such powers, it will be able to put an immediate stop to intimidation and terror and to ensure peace and security for all citizens. . . .

Robert Bourassa

At four in the morning, the federal Cabinet proclaimed the War Measures Act. The FLQ became an illegal association. It also became illegal for any group to advocate the use of force or of crime to obtain a change in government. The proclamation suspended civil liberties and gave to the police the power to arrest without a warrant, to detain without laying a charge. Because of the *apprehended insurrection*, the federal government suspended freedom, supposedly across Canada, but in fact only in Quebec.

By five o'clock in the morning, the police had begun their mass arrests. They picked up 242 people in the first few hours. Robert Lemieux, the two leaders of the 1965 FLQ, Pierre Vallières and Charles Gagnon, union leader Michel Chartrand, singer Pauline Julien and her companion, and many others known as radicals were rounded up and taken to the cells of the provincial police on Parthenais Street.

When I heard the news of the War Measures Act on October 16, I burst into tears. "Poor Quebec!" I kept repeating as I wept. Yesterday, the army, and today, the mass arrests. I had always had a certain admiration for Pierre Trudeau, even if I did not share his views on federalism. But I've never forgiven him the War Measures Act of October 16, 1970.

That noon, the UQAM students met in the Gésu hall. A jittery mood pervaded the room where only the previous day we had voted to strike in such a mood of euphoria. There was a lot of talk about going underground to support the FLQ, but I don't recall that we adopted a single resolution. The savage action of the government had completely changed the situation. It was too late, now, to play at revolution. This was serious business. We felt certain that there were plainclothes officers in the hall. The students were now afraid of speaking too openly in favour of the FLQ — it was now illegal to do so — lest the police take them away on the spot. To avoid announcing openly that this was a pro-FLQ meeting, it had been billed as an assembly for "the study of green mice." A great number of students — including me — left the meeting before the end. Our hearts were no longer in it.

We teased the soldiers on guard near the UQAM at the door to the Black Watch regiment. "Quebec is beautiful, isn't it? But be careful, we're having a revolution here."

It was the beginning of a strange period. Everyone recounted the raid at the home of someone or other that we knew, with a description of where the police had searched and what books they had carted off. Sometimes, we would notice the absence of two or even three students in one of our classes. We would say, "They are taking their holidays at Parthenais Beach." When they showed up again, they would confirm that they had a period of leisure at the expense of the government.

One night, a girl from my class arrived at my place about midnight with her husband. They asked me to take them in for the night because their friends had been arrested earlier in the evening. I put them up on the carpet in the living room and we all went to sleep. They left the next morning and disappeared. When I saw them four days later, they told me that they had been arrested.

On the evening of the 17th, at seven o'clock, radio station CKAC received a phone call. A voice said that Pierre Laporte had been executed and that his corpse would be found in the trunk of a car parked near the military airport at Saint Hubert. The station did not take the call seriously. Another call came at nine-thirty, with directions for finding a communiqué at Place des Arts. This time, journalist Michel Saint-Louis went there, found the communiqué, and read it.

In face of the arrogance of the federal government and of its lackey Bourassa, in the face of their obvious bad faith, the FLQ has therefore decided to act.

Pierre Laporte, Minister of Unemployment and Assimilation, was executed at 6:18 tonight by the Dieppe Cell (Royal 22nd).

You will find the body in the trunk of a green Chevrolet (9J-2420) at the Saint Hubert base. . . .

Nous vaincrons.

FLQ

P.S. The exploiters of the Quebec people had better watch out.

The provincial police and soldiers went to the scene, found the car, and opened the trunk. They discovered the corpse of Pierre Laporte.

On October 5, when he learned of the kidnapping of James Cross, Pierre Laporte's reaction had been: "It is a wind of madness that blows temporarily over Canada and which will be extinguished." But it was Pierre Laporte's life that was extinguished.

CHAPTER 10
Caught in the Works

❊

It all began with a simple phone call. One morning towards the end of October, I was working at the Parti Quebecois office in Ahuntsic, with Michel Frankland beside me. I had a message for Noel Vallerand, who had been my teacher and was now a friend. I dialed his number. Michel Frankland heard the name and thought he recognized it. When he had been a student at Collège Jean de Brébeuf there was someone by that name in his class.

"Ask him if his nickname was Biglaise at college," Frankland said.

I passed on the question. Yes, it was Biglaise. Frankland took the receiver and the two former classmates greeted each other. Noel invited Michel and me to drop by his place that evening.

Vallerand was still the professor I most admired, and we shared a taste for classical music. Sometimes I went to his place with Yves Brossard, a professor of international relations, for an evening of Bach or of Brahms. For several hours, Noel would play records while we listened intently, holding glasses of gin. We called these evenings our musical orgies.

So Frankland and I arrived at his apartment on Troie Avenue. The two alumni of Brébeuf exchanged college memories. They named their professors and the students they knew, recalled the pranks they had played, and questioned each other about the fate of former companions.

After a few hours of reminiscences, the conversation turned to the FLQ, the War Measures Act, the searches, and the arrests. Suddenly Michel Frankland expressed his admiration for the FLQ and its actions. He said, as nearly as I can remember:

"I agree with the people in the FLQ. I would really like to meet them. I'd like to belong to the FLQ."

My recollection is that Noel replied, "I know those people. When they go to set their bombs, they come here first to ask my advice."

These words left us flabbergasted. Was Noel serious? Had he simply drunk too much gin? Michel and I were a bit embarrassed, and no one pursued the subject. We talked about other things. Shortly afterwards, Michel and I left. Even when we were together, we did not speak of it.

A few days later, on Saturday, October 31, I had my coat on and was just about to leave my apartment when the telephone rang. I answered, and the line went dead. I thought nothing of it; it must have been a wrong number. I took my keys out of my handbag and was about to lock the door to my apartment when I saw a man walking towards me down the corridor. It was Robert Comeau, a professor in the history department at l'Université du Québec à Montréal where I was a student.*

"Are you going out?"

"Yes."

"I was the one who called you a moment ago. I know that people don't like having someone hang up on them, but I had good reasons for doing it. Can I come in for a moment?"

We went inside. He looked over the apartment as though he were looking for something.

"Do you live here alone?"

"Yes."

He seemed to be pleased with what he saw. He turned to me: "Would you be willing to hide someone here, or keep a mimeograph machine?"

I was astonished. Was he joking? He was a man of about twenty-six, not much older than I, thin, with short hair and black, horn-rimmed glasses, a studious young professor dressed in navy-blue blazer, turtleneck sweater, and grey trousers.

"FLQ?"

He nodded. I wanted to leave, to have time to think. I got up and looked at my watch.

"I have to go."

"Fine, I'll drive you."

We walked in silence to a blue Volvo parked in front of my apartment on Saint Joseph Boulevard. I told him that I was on my way to see a lawyer, Pothier Ferland, about something that had to do with the Parti Quebecois. Once in the car, I asked him about his strange approach.

---

*Testifying before the Keable Commission, Robert Comeau first denied ever having come to my place. Then he changed his testimony. According to the Keable Commission report, "he acknowledged having met Madame Devault [sic] frequently. He said she invited him to her home on Saint Joseph Boulevard after meeting him in a bar. His relations with Madame Devault [sic] following this first meeting had nothing to do with activities of a terrorist nature." (Report of the Keable Commission, p. 190). His recollection was completely different from mine.

"Do you make a habit of talking like that to people you don't know?"

I had often encountered Robert Comeau in the corridors of the history department, but I couldn't remember ever speaking to him. "No, Noel Vallerand spoke to me about you. It seems you were at his place this week with a friend. You spoke about the FLQ and your friend said he wanted to join the ranks of the Front. Noel told me you are okay, and so I came to see you."

Noel! Was Noel in the FLQ?* Noel had sent Comeau to me! And now they were asking me if I was prepared to hide someone in my apartment or keep an FLQ mimeograph machine. I didn't know what to do.

Robert Comeau waited in the car while I was with the lawyer. Then he drove me home but stayed only a few minutes. He had an important errand to run; he had to deliver a message from Marc Carbonneau to his mistress. The message was hidden in the heel of his shoe. I looked at the shoe, intrigued. So he was in contact with Marc Carbonneau, wanted in connection with the kidnapping of James Cross and Pierre Laporte, and the assassination of Laporte. His picture had appeared in all the newspapers.

Robert told me about his first visit to this woman.

"The first time I had to bring her a message from Carbonneau, I went to the address given to me and a woman came to the door. We recognized each other immediately, and we both said at the same time: 'You are in it too?', and we burst out laughing."

Robert then asked me if I was free that evening. He invited me to accompany him to a party given by another history professor, and I accepted. He went off to deliver his message and I prepared my supper.

---

*Noel Vallerand denied ever having been in the FLQ in his in camera testimony of March 18, 1980. He said ". . . I have never been a member of the FLQ, I have never been associated, directly or indirectly, with any activity whatsoever of the FLQ, and particularly, I have never been the head of the FLQ, not even in the sense of being an adviser, a counsellor . . . all that is not true." (Keable Commission, p. 189).

I believe that he was never formally a member of the FLQ. But my recruitment into the FLQ did take place in the way I described, after my visit with Michel Frankland to Noel Vallerand's home. I think, too, that the now associate deputy minister of cultural affairs lacked candour when he testified before the Keable Commission. He said, for instance: ". . . the image that I had of people who were part of the FLQ, and whose participation in it I happened to know about, through reading newspapers following their arrests, did not correspond at all to the face presented by my colleague, Robert Comeau." (Keable Commission, p. 188).

Noel Vallerand did not know the Felquistes only by the newspapers, as he has tried to lead people to believe. At one time or another, he was the professor of some well-known Felquistes, including Pierre-Paul Geoffroy, Michel Lambert, Alain Allard, Robert Comeau, and others who were never convicted.

At nine-thirty, he returned to pick me up. We went to a suburb south of Montreal, across the Saint Lawrence River. As we were driving across the Jacques Cartier bridge, Robert became nervous. "It's possible that we will be stopped by the police. There is something happening in this area. If they stop us, stay calm." I looked around me, in front, behind, beside the bridge, on the river. What was it? I didn't dare ask. He said no more about it.

I almost expected to find myself in a meeting of Felquistes plotting their next coup. But no, nothing could have been more petit-bourgeois. Robert was quite the serious young professor among all these suburbanites. We chatted about various inconsequential things with our host: it was an evening for young couples in the suburbs.

On the way back, Robert was once again nervous when we crossed the bridge. Again I looked everywhere, but I could see nothing.

It was after midnight when we arrived at my apartment. Robert was feeling particularly talkative. We were having a cup of tea when he suddenly stared at the golden chain I was wearing around my neck.

"As long as I live, I'll never be able to wear a chain around my neck," he said, putting a hand to his neck.

I asked him why.

"Because that's how Pierre Laporte was killed. Usually, he was chained to a bed by a dog leash. Sometimes they removed the leash and let him walk around. One day, he took his pillow between his teeth for protection and jumped at the window. He got stuck there and cut himself. Later, Laporte heard a siren in the street and tried to escape by the front door. One of the kidnappers took him by the chain he wore around his neck and strangled him."

I was horrified, but intrigued. The whole country wanted to know the circumstances surrounding the death of the minister, and here was someone describing it to me over a cup of tea. Robert added that he knew in advance that Laporte would be kidnapped.

"I was talking to my father," he continued, "and I said: 'It would be funny if the FLQ kidnapped someone today.' My father looked at me and said: 'Don't talk nonsense.' A few hours later we were having supper when they reported on television that the FLQ had kidnapped Pierre Laporte. My father looked at me and said: 'How did you know about that?' "

Naturally, I found all of this fascinating. I didn't want to seem indiscreet and I asked no questions, but he apparently had a need to talk. He treated me like a friend. Perhaps he saw in me a future co-conspirator? I was too interested by what he was telling me to correct his mistake.

He told me that the FLQ would soon publish another communiqué, printed at Saint Hyacinthe on a Gestetner machine which he'd heard had been stolen from an office of the Parti Quebecois. For some reason, he found it very funny that the FLQ had stolen a mimeograph machine from the PQ. I did not. Our Gestetner in Ahuntsic had been stolen the previous month. Now I knew where it had gone!

Robert added that 400 to 500 copies of the communiqué would be run off, but that the Front would tell the public that 50,000 copies had been printed. It was one way of conveying an impression of strength to the police, the politicians, and the public. The communiqué would be sent to the newspapers, to Prime Minister Trudeau, to René Lévesque, and to union leaders.

At last we fell asleep. When I woke up the next morning, he was gone.

I was still thinking over what was happening to me when, about noon, Robert Comeau returned. He wanted to meet Michel Frankland. Since it was Sunday, he gave me his home telephone number to pass on to Michel. Michel was to ask for "Robert." Robert knew only Michel's first name, and he didn't want Michel to know his full name either.

He soon left and I called Michel. I told him that I had an important message for him. Would he please come over to my place?

Half an hour later, Michel arrived.

"Listen, Michel, do you remember that last week when we were at Noel Vallerand's, you said you wanted to join the FLQ? Were you serious or joking?"

"I was serious."

"Because someone from the FLQ just left here. Noel Vallerand told him about our conversation. This man wants to get in touch with you."

Michel was delighted. When he was pleased, he had a habit of slapping his head with the palm of his hand and exclaiming: "Ah! Ah! We are wonderful! We are wonderful!" This time he tapped his head with particular zest.

"Ah! Carole, you have been keeping something from me!"

He seemed to think that I was an FLQ veteran who had just tipped her hand.

"But Michel, have you really thought of the consequences? You don't know what it all could lead to. We are under the War Measures Act. You could be involved in placing bombs, you might be asked to take part in a kidnapping, you could end up in jail. Have you thought about Jeannine and Isabelle?"

The thought of his family did not seem to deter him at all.

"Jeannine has a job and a good salary. Even if I went to prison, she could look after Isabelle. I really want to join the FLQ. I believe in what they're doing. The most important thing in my life is to liberate Quebec. I used to believe the PQ could do it, but since the last elections I don't believe that any more. Now, I think that Quebec's last hope lies with the FLQ."

I gave him Robert's number. He started to use my telephone but I told him that I would rather he use a public telephone. Since Robert's first visit, it had seemed to me that the FLQ was everywhere, and the police, too. I was afraid that when Robert had come to my place, he might have been followed. The police might have put a tap on my telephone. I was filled with anxiety.

Michel left, coming back a few hours later with Robert Comeau. Michel was exultant, and Robert seemed happy too. We sat around the table and Robert told me, "Michel has passed the political test and he is accepted into the FLQ."

I looked at Michel, who was wearing a satisfied smile. As usual, he had on his grey cap, his black horn-rimmed glasses, with a long wool scarf tied around his neck.

"They will be proud of me," he promised.

Robert Comeau began to give us instructions. Michel's first mission would be to create a new FLQ cell with three or four people, no more. The recruits must have no criminal record and must not be known to the anti-terrorist squad. Ideally, the new members would never even have taken part in a demonstration.

"The only thing the police have on me is that I was arrested during a demonstration. Carole will be the contact between the Viger Cell and your cell. She will have a foot in each cell," Robert announced, to my astonishment.

"You'll see, it won't take long. Within a week, my cell will be formed," said Michel.

Robert advised Michel to get out of the Parti Quebecois. Most of the Felquistes had been in the PQ, but they had not renewed their membership. It would be embarrassing for the PQ if the police arrested terrorists and they turned out to belong to the party.

Michel left first. Robert remained a few minutes longer. He told me that he had gone with Michel to a restaurant and discussed politics with him. He was delighted with the political attitudes he had discovered in his new recruit.

"He seems like the right person, determined to go all the way."

He asked me for my opinion. I told him that I had only known Michel since January, but that we had worked together on the election challenge in Ahuntsic: I could truthfully say that Michel had never hesitated to work long hours, sometimes until two or three in the morning. Robert seemed satisfied. He also talked a bit more about himself.

Once, he said, he had just placed a bomb near a federal Manpower building and was leaving when, turning back, he saw someone at a window. So as not to risk a human life, he went back and defused the bomb.*

"You can see that the FLQ doesn't want to kill people for no reason."

He also knew about several bombs that had been set off in Westmount in the summer of 1970.**

With some trepidation, I began to wonder where all this would lead. I was learning more and more about the FLQ: I had just seen the creation of a new cell. Robert's visit had plunged me into a drama that appealed to my natural romanticism. Would I collaborate with the FLQ or not? Robert Comeau assumed that I would; after his conversation with Noel Vallerand, he seemed to take for granted my commitment to the struggle. But so far, it had been nothing but talk.

The situation changed the next day, when Robert came by in the evening. We talked about my part-time job at the Caloil Company. I told him that, each day, I accompanied a Commissionnaire as he deposited money at a number of banks on behalf of the firm. At each bank, while I waited in the car, the man would deposit part of the money, while I kept watch over the rest. Robert was quite interested. Did he already know about this part of my job from his conversation with Noel Vallerand? Or did he hear about it for the first time from me? He asked me for details of our itinerary, our stops, the amount of money we carried.

Robert, in great spirits, told me of an aborted hold-up a few days earlier. The film *Quiet Days in Clichy* was then playing at two theatres in Montreal. At that time, sex films drew long lineups of people. The Viger Cell had planned to hold up one of the theatres. The gunman wore a toque, and was short and fat. According to Robert, if he put powder in his hair, he looked fifty.

When the gunman got to the cinema, he found the place almost deserted. The Montreal police had seized the film on grounds of obscenity. The theatre had replaced it with a western and there were few paying customers. The hold-up failed.

But the cell still needed money.

I didn't know whether I was going to be held up. The next day, I became certain of it beyond a doubt. At noon hour, as I left the

---

*On May 12, 1969, the police found a bomb made up of four sticks of dynamite each weighing two pounds, and fourteen inches long. This bomb, set at the federal Manpower Centre, had not exploded.

**Between May and August 1970, the police dealt with twelve bombs, nine of them placed somewhere in Westmount.

office with the Commissionnaire, I noticed two men on the sidewalk checking out everyone who came through the door. They showed a particular interest in me. They were waiting for me, I was sure of it: they stared at me as I passed. One of them, rather good-looking, had dark hair and looked to be about twenty-five years old. The other had brown hair. When they had looked me over thoroughly, they walked away. I got into the car with Mr. Lavoie, the Commissionnaire. He was carrying a large bag that contained other bags holding the bundles of money to be deposited. We went off on our daily rounds.

At Metropolitan News, downtown, we made a last stop: I used to buy newspapers from across the country to scan them for any item on Caloil. As I was turning around between two tall stacks of newspapers, I suddenly saw the man with the dark hair again. There, in front of me. He flipped through the pages of a pornographic magazine without looking at them. I froze. We stared at each other for a fraction of a second, then I turned to pay for my newspapers, shaken. Now I knew that it was more than a fantasy.

It was from that moment that I began to consider going to the police.

Robert Comeau returned to my apartment that evening. I asked him about the two men I had seen on the sidewalk in front of Caloil. Usually there were no pedestrians in that neighbourhood, since the company was located in an area of refineries and petroleum storage tanks, with no private residences.

"I mentioned you to the others and they decided to rob you. They'll probably have help from a hired thug. The FLQ is not a money-maker, but it needs the money. If it comes off, you'll probably be given 20 percent of the take."

I felt cornered. What had I got myself into?

The next day, after supper, I was chatting with my Aunt Jacqueline, who was visiting me, when the doorbell rang. It was Robert Comeau. I put a finger to my lips to let him know that I was not alone. I started to close the door, when he said:

"Could you come out for a moment? There is someone who wants to talk to you."

I put on a coat and he directed me to the car parked on the side-street. Someone was in the back seat: he was wearing a white turtle-neck, pulled up to cover the lower part of his face. It was the dark man I had seen the day before.

His eyes were unsmiling, his speech terse. Without introduction, he asked me to describe the route that we followed and he wanted to know how much money we carried. I described our daily round, but about the money I could only say, "I don't know. Sometimes there is a lot of money, sometimes there are only cheques."

He told me to try and find out how much money we would be carrying the next day. He would be armed and the hold-up would take place at our first stop. Right before the robbery, I was to give him a signal. If there was money in the bags, I was to lower my head. If I didn't know, I would sit still, and if there was no money, I was to light a cigarette.

He spoke in staccato bursts of words. I told him that I had seen him the day before at Metropolitan News. He replied that he had followed us on our run. At last his face disappeared into the darkness of the back seat of the car. The interview was over.

Returning home, I said nothing about what had happened to my aunt, but I was preoccupied. This adventure was becoming all too real. I had made up my mind, though, that there would not be a hold-up and I knew what I would do: he had told me to light a cigarette if there was no money in the bag. Tomorrow, I would have my lighter ready.

I felt very nervous when I went out to the car with Mr. Lavoie for our daily round of the banks the next day. We stopped at the corner of Bossuet and Hochelaga. The Commissionnaire went into the bank to make the deposit while I waited in the car my heart pounding.

Suddenly, in front of me, I saw the dark-haired man on the sidewalk, coming toward the car. He was about fifty feet away, staring at me as he walked. Looking straight at him, I put my right hand in my pocket, pulled out the cigarette and put it in my mouth. I lit it with a trembling hand. What if he didn't recognize the signal? He looked at me intently. Then he passed by me and kept on walking.

I sank back against the seat, weak with relief. Mr. Lavoie returned and we continued on. Back at the office, I received a call from Robert Comeau. He asked me to meet him at the entrance of the university. I had a course at seven-thirty that evening, so I agreed to meet him shortly before.

On arrival at the university, I was looking around for Robert when someone tapped me on the shoulder. I whirled around: it was my robber.

He spoke rapidly, in a tone that frightened me:

"Listen, signal or no signal, the robbery is tomorrow. And don't forget to unlock the door!" He disappeared.

I was appalled. How could I avoid the hold-up? I went to my lecture in economic history, but I couldn't take in a word of what the professor said. I kept casting around in my mind for a way out, or for someone who could help me. I decided to discuss my problem with Jacques Parizeau.

During the break after the first fifty minutes of the lecture, I dialed Parizeau's number. His wife, Alice, answered. I had met her during her visits to the Ahuntsic office of the PQ and I recognized her voice. She told me that Jacques was not home and was not expected until midnight, or even later.

"Madame Parizeau?"

"Yes."

"This is Carole speaking. I really must meet with you. I have something very important to tell you."

We agreed to meet near the university, after the second hour of my class.

She picked me up in her beaten-up old car.

"What I have to tell you is about the FLQ!"

She stopped me, put a finger to her lips, and then pointed to various parts of the car, to let me know that listening devices might be planted there. We drove in silence to a nearby restaurant.

Over a scotch, I told her how I had been contacted by the FLQ, and that two of its members intended to rob Caloil the next day. She was alarmed: Parizeau was a consultant for Caloil and it was he who had got me my job in public relations there.

"You can't be involved in such a thing! Remember, Carole, that you are very close to a public figure."

She was a large women, Polish by birth, about twenty years older than I. She spoke French with an accent, rolling the "rs" in her throat. She insisted that the hold-up must not take place, that it could implicate Jacques in a scandal.

She talked on, smoking her unfiltered Player's cigarettes. She suggested that I leave town, that I take the train and escape to the country. Or that I go to the police.

After about fifteen minutes, we left the restaurant and she drove me to a subway station. I returned home, where my Aunt Jacqueline was waiting for me. I told her about the imminent hold-up. The finality of the words spoken by the dark man had left me frantic. She, too, thought that I should get in touch with the police. She remembered seeing in the paper the provincial police number for people who had information on the FLQ, and she offered to call for me.

"My niece has information about the FLQ," she said on the phone.

They took down my address and phone number and said they would come by. I waited up, far too tense to go to bed. I kept my aunt awake talking as long as I could. At last, about one o'clock, she went to bed and I soon followed her.

But I couldn't sleep. I tossed restlessly in my bed. Should I go to the police? I changed my mind five times. I was tormented by uncertainty. Yet, I had to decide soon because the hold-up was tomorrow and, this time, I couldn't call it off by lighting a cigarette. I had to go to the police, but how could I inform on my friends? If I didn't go, where would it all end? Would I become a terrorist in earnest? If I went to the police, I would become a traitor. Everyone I knew was in sympathy with the FLQ, not the police. It would be considered a disgrace to cooperate with the police.

Whatever I did, the consequences would be serious. I remembered what Robert Comeau had said when he was telling me about the FLQ's attempts to discover who the informer was when the FLQ plot to kidnap American Consul Harrison Burgess was uncovered by the police. The suspect was the boyfriend of one of the Lanctôt women.

"Informers. One day we will pay them a visit. We will put a bullet through their heart and pin a note to their body saying 'This is what happens to those who betray the FLQ!'"

I had become involved with the FLQ by accident, but now I didn't know how to get out of it. I, too, wanted to see Quebec break its colonial bonds with Canada, but I didn't approve of the methods of the FLQ. I didn't believe in violence. I thought that the FLQ, by its excesses, was a threat to the Parti Quebecois. And the life of a man was at stake. I didn't want to see James Cross assassinated as Pierre Laporte had been. I didn't want to see the independence movement compromised by the irresponsibility of Robert Comeau and his ilk. I preferred to see Quebec's future in the hands of Jacques Parizeau and René Lévesque.

I knew I should go to the police, but could I face the consequences? I had a terrible fear for my future, no matter what decision I made. How could I live with myself if I allowed the hold-up to take place, if I let James Cross die? But if I went to the police, how could I live with myself knowing that I was an informer? No matter what I did, my whole future seemed threatened.

It was five-thirty when I decided to get up. No point in trying to sleep, I was too upset. I took a shower. My mind was made up. I would go to the police.

At six-thirty I went out the door, wearing my dark glasses, with a large silk scarf covering my head. I was afraid the FLQ might be watching me. I looked around. The police station was close by, just a short diagonal walk across a park. There was no one around. It was still dark, and the street lights shone dimly in the morning mist. I began walking across the park toward the police station. From that walk, there was no going back.

CHAPTER 11
No. 17 Police Station

❖

No. 17 Police Station had the gloomy look of a Victorian castle. The morning mist half hid its corner towers in the early hours of November 6, 1970. A soldier paced before the grey stone front of the building. We looked at each other without a word. I climbed the stone steps leading to the main entrance.

At the reception desk, a constable in uniform came to the counter. "Can I help you?"

"I have information about the FLQ."

He looked me over carefully. "You will have to see the officer in charge. He is not in yet. You can sit down on the bench while you're waiting."

I sat down, unbuttoned my coat, threw the scarf back on my shoulders and took a book out of my handbag. The tension in me was diminishing now that it was day.

"Would you like a coffee?" The constable brought me some in a styrofoam cup and went back to his desk.

I waited an hour, an hour-and-a-half. At about eight o'clock, Detective-Sergeant Fernand Tanguay arrived and summoned me up to his office. I took a seat.

"I hear you have information on the FLQ?"

I removed my coloured glasses and blurted out, "I am going to be held up today by the FLQ!"

Sergeant Tanguay was tall, about thirty-three years old, and had a placid manner. He answered politely.

"Really? And what makes you think that you will be held up by the FLQ?"

"Listen, there's a fellow at the university who is in contact with the FLQ. He probably knows where Cross is, and he knows things about the kidnapping of Laporte. He says I'm going to be involved in a hold-up at noon today."

My elbows were on his desk and I kept gesturing. I knew that it sounded foolish, but I wanted to make him believe me.

"Wait a minute, now! This fellow at the university, what is his name?"

"Robert Comeau. I know that he lives in Longueuil with his parents on Quinn Street. I don't know his address, only his phone number." I told him the number.

Sergeant Tanguay took out a telephone book and looked under the name Comeau. He found the phone number and read out the address: it was on Quinn Street. He seemed slightly reassured and asked me my name.

"Carole de Vault. I am a student at the Université du Québec à Montréal, where Robert Comeau is a professor.

"Does he have a car?"

"Yes, a blue Volvo."

"Do you know its licence number?"

"No."

Sergeant Tanguay began to take notes. I told him my story: Robert Comeau had asked me if I would be willing to hide someone for the FLQ in my apartment. The next thing I knew, I was to be both accomplice and victim in a hold-up. I explained that I worked part-time for an oil company in the east end of Montreal, and that every day I went by car with a Commissionnaire to convey several thousand dollars in deposits to a number of banks.

Sergeant Tanguay took down the details. It was only later that I was to see his report, from which I quote a few passages.

> For the presumed hold-up, the men will be armed and at the corner of Hochelaga and Bossuet; the hold-up will take place between 1:15 and 1:30 in the afternoon. Miss de Vault is to stay in the car and leave the right front door unlocked. The only description that I get of the two suspects who will carry out the hold-up: the first is fair, measures five foot seven inches, is of medium build, no age provided. The second has black hair, measures about five foot six inches, weighs 160 pounds, no description provided. They will be in an unknown car. These two are said to have followed Miss de Vault on the day of Tuesday, November 3; she noticed them.
>
> They are said to have asked Miss de Vault, to signal to them at the moment of the robbery, by lowering her head forward if she did not think that there was money in the bags. If she did not know, she was not to move, and if she was certain that there was no money, she was to light a cigarette.

In his shirtsleeves, he continued writing on his pad, his face expressionless, although my impression was that he did not take me too seriously. He wrote:

> There are said to be *Anglais* from McGill in the FLQ, including an engineer and an electrician. Their names are unknown. Dur-

ing the kidnapping of Mr. Cross, there is said to have been an *Anglais* involved.

Tanguay kept his eyes on his note pad, only occasionally looking up to interrupt my account, to ask me to repeat something, or to ask for more details.

According to the informer, Cross has no more pills and he refuses to eat lest his food be poisoned . . . One of the guards of Mr. Cross is presently disguised as Chinese. The guards take turns guarding Mr. Cross. The kidnappers don't want to kill Mr. Cross and they are said to have a kindly feeling for him. They are afraid he will die, for he hardly eats any more, he has been without his pills for about five days, and he won't sleep.

Since the safe-conduct has been withdrawn, the kidnappers no longer know what to do with Mr. Cross; however, they want to neither kill him or release him.

Sergeant Tanguay wrote it all down as calmly as if I were reporting the loss of my cat or my bicycle.

According to the informer, as soon as the soldiers leave Montreal there will be a third kidnapping, probably of the journalist Mr. Jean Pellerin.

(Jean Pellerin was an editorial writer with the newspaper *La Presse*, and a long-time friend of Prime Minister Trudeau. Robert Comeau had told me that the FLQ was considering kidnapping Jean Pellerin. Becaue he was a friend of Trudeau, his kidnapping was more likely to force the Prime Minister to give in to the FLQ's demands.) From time to time, Sergeant Tanguay stopped to light a cigarette or order another coffee. He took it with cream and sugar. I took mine black.

Comeau is said to have carried a letter from Carbonneau to his mistress, who is said to have been questioned for six hours recently. She is a former student of Collège Sainte Marie.
A fellow by the name of Campeau, who is under arrest, is said to be an active member of the FLQ.

At last, about ten o'clock, Sergeant Tanguay closed his notebook. He picked up a telephone book, looked for the anti-terrorist section, dialed the number and made an appointment with Detective-Lieutenant Julien Giguère. He explained to me that the anti-terrorist section handled this kind of information.
"I will drive you to work."
He rose, put on his navy-blue jacket, and then a grey trench coat.

I put on my smoked glasses and tied the silk scarf over my head. As we were leaving, I said to him: "Listen, I'm pretty nervous about the hold-up this afternoon. Those guys are going to be armed. Will the police be there? What's going to happen?"

"I'm going to the anti-terrorist office and I'll drop you off at work on the way. Now that you have let us know, we will look after it. Don't worry. Someone will get in touch with you. Here is my card. Call me if there is anything new."

We went down the stone stairway leading to the sidewalk. Now, the sun was shining. I felt a great relief. I pulled the scarf around so that it hid half my face. We entered the parking lot and got into Sergeant Tanguay's unmarked car. We were soon driving toward the east end, with the radio broadcasting its coded messages all the way. It was a new experience for me to ride in a police car.

He dropped me off three blocks from the Caloil building, then headed north to where the anti-terrorist section was located.

Julien Giguère told me later about his meeting with Sergeant Tanguay. The sergeant gave him an account of the visit of a young woman and read aloud from his notes. Julien Giguère, unimpressed, repeated "Yeah, yeah, yeah," at the end of each paragraph.

"One of the cells of the FLQ is supposed to be printing 500 copies of a communiqué that will soon be released. Since the police have forbidden the broadcasting of the communiqué, it will include photos of Mr. Cross, and Comeau is supposed to have seen the photos. In the photo, Cross is said to be seated on a bed with a white sheet behind him. In the communiqué there is also a message from Cross or a sentence ending with *shocking Mr. Trudeau.*"

Julien Giguère listened, his eyes closed. Since October 5, he had often worked all night. But that phrase, *shocking Mr. Trudeau*, remained lodged in his memory.

"The communiqué suggests a distribution of 50,000 copies; in reality there will be only 400 to 500 printed."

Julien Giguère listened to the end of the report. There were thirty-nine paragraphs. Then, he asked Sergeant Tanguay for his impression of the woman. The detective avoided making a categorical judgment.

"Listen, what do you make of her?"

"I don't know."

"Is she a crackpot, or not?"

"Time will tell."

"Listen, aren't you able to evaluate someone after such a long interview? You must have formed some opinion of her. You were with her quite a while."

"Oh, yes, a good while. I took a lot of notes."

"Well, is she a crackpot, or what? Is she a nut? Was she stoned? Did she seem to be having a nervous breakdown? What impression did she make on you?"

"I don't know. Time will tell. We'll see what happens. Let's wait."

Sergeant Tanguay dictated his notes to a secretary and signed the report. Then he left.

Julien Giguère had two stacks of files on his desk, one with leads that were felt to be promising; the other, much larger, with all the crackpot messages and crank calls.

He took the report on Carole de Vault and placed it on the bottom of the crackpot pile.

CHAPTER 12
Decoy for a Hold-up

❊

After I arrived at the office, I tried to work normally, but I kept thinking of my meeting that morning with the police, and my rendezvous in a couple of hours at the corner of Hochelaga and Bossuet. Quite clearly, I didn't have the right nerves to be a terrorist!

About eleven-thirty, I took some apples from my bag and ate them outside where the smell of oil was always present. I sat in the sunshine, on a step at the back of the building. Then I went back inside.

The building was deserted. Everyone had gone out for lunch. At the top of the stairway, I saw Jacques Parizeau seated at the receptionist's desk. He was scribbling something on a piece of paper. Seeing me, he motioned for me to come over and he whispered:

"What did you do? My wife told me all about it this morning."

I started to answer in a normal voice, but he put a finger to his lips as a sign of silence, then pointed several times at the light fixture, rolling his eyes. Be careful, there might be a listening device, he seemed to be saying. Decidedly the Parizeaus saw listening devices everywhere.

I whispered: "I went to the police this morning and told them everything."

"You did the right thing. Really, there was nothing else you could do," he murmured back.

There was the sound of steps in the hallway. Parizeau turned back to his papers and I pushed open the door leading into my office.

Mr. Lavoie, the Commissionnaire, was not back yet from his rounds. We finally left for the bank an hour later than usual. The bag with the money for the deposits was on the front seat of the car. In big white letters, across the middle it said, *"Banque de Montréal."*

I got into Mr. Lavoie's yellow Chrysler. We were about to go through our usual little routine. I found it strange to be carrying on normally despite the tension of a sleepless night and the stress of the past week. Poor Mr. Lavoie had no idea we were heading for a hold-up.

"Bonjour, Madame la journaliste. Are you well?"

He always called me the journalist, perhaps because I prepared the press releases for the company.

"Yes, very well, Mr. Lavoie. And you?"

"Ah, if you knew, if you only knew. Everyone thinks that Mr. Lavoie is just fine. But he is not fine. He is poor. Mr. Lavoie is even very poor."

On the sidewalk, as I had walked towards the car, I had looked quickly to see if anyone was watching. No one: neither the two men who had been there on Tuesday, nor the police.

Mr. Lavoie changed his glasses before starting the car. He wore tinted glasses to drive that he kept on the dashboard in front of the steering wheel. Then he put his ordinary glasses in a case on the seat beside us, between a mystery novel and the money.

"Mr. Lavoie is reduced to eating baloney. Baloney the day before yesterday. Baloney yesterday, and baloney today. Baloney sandwiches, baloney fried in the pan."

We were on our way. Mr. Lavoie was a garrulous man, fat and jovial. He had been with the company forever. He was about fifty and balding. He giggled a lot, making limp gestures with his right hand to illustrate his conversation while he drove with the left. He lived with his mother and gave me lengthy accounts of the special care she required. To hear him talk, he lived in penury, though he drove a big car of the current year. The company persecuted him, he said, though he obviously adored his job. He was always in the middle of reading a mystery novel, which he would relate to me in minute detail during the ninety minutes of our daily run.

"Apart from that, are you well, Mr. Lavoie?"

I kept glancing over my shoulder to see if we were being followed. Would the police keep us under surveillance? Would the hold-up men drive along behind us? I tried to seem casual.

"Boy, that Sénécal is a dreadful man!" exclaimed Mr. Lavoie. Mr. Sénécal was president of the company. "Boy, that Sénécal! He is always saying, 'Mr. Lavoie, come here, Mr. Lavoie, go there.' It's always here, there, and everywhere."

We drove east on Notre Dame, then north to Hochelaga where we made the first stop on our route.

"Mr. Lavoie never has time to go out at night, he must look after his old mother. Hee, hee, hee!"

He had a habit of giggling at almost any time during a conversation. His chuckles seemed to well up from some permanent source of humour inside him rather than to be triggered by anything that was said.

My nervousness increased as we got closer to the bank. But I didn't want Mr. Lavoie to notice it. I looked at the title of the book he was reading, *Do You Remember Paco?*

"How is your mystery, Mr. Lavoie?"

"Ah, *Madame la journaliste*, I haven't finished it, but I think it's the best mystery I have ever read. You really should read it."

He always recommended his current mystery, but to this day I have not read one. On the dashboard, he always had the last one he had finished and the one he would read next. The book he was currently reading was lying on the seat beside the money.

He told me the story. It was about Paco, a handsome young tough in Spain who becomes a police informer. The gang finds out about him, cuts off his head and sends it in a box through the mail to the police inspector. The inspector's wife opens the parcel and sees Paco's head. She faints, for he was her secret lover.

"It was horrible! You can just imagine it. A head in a box, completely white, no more blood, and that poor woman opened the box and fainted. No wonder! Hee, hee, hee!"

Was I really on my way to a hold-up? It seemed so melodramatic, just like the story that Mr. Lavoie was telling me with such relish. "This is my first hold-up." That thought kept running absurdly through my head.

He parked in front of the bank, changed his glasses, and took a canvas bag full of money from the larger vinyl bag.

"Here, why don't you read my book while you're waiting, my journalist friend. It's exceptionally good, as you will find out. It won the prize for the best adventure story in France in 1958. It's really something, you'll see."

He walked with his bag towards the bank. I looked at the sidewalk ahead. It was from this direction that the man had come yesterday. Women passed by carrying brown parcels from the grocery store. On my left, across the street, there was another bank. If the police had set a trap they might be in there now, waiting. And what if the police and the robbers started shooting? I wasn't afraid that the robber would want to kill me — he thought I was his accomplice. But what if a police car passed and saw the robbery? What if the police came rushing out of the bank? The man, cornered, might duck behind the car door and start shooting, and I might be caught in the cross-fire.

I glanced at the door where Mr. Lavoie had disappeared. No sign of him or of the dark man. Everything looked so normal on this corner of Hochelaga and Bossuet. Hochelaga is the business street of Montreal's east end. There are little shops run by families next to the warehouses of Steinberg and Coca-Cola. The banks don't look like Greek temples here. The bank that Mr. Lavoie had gone into was a light-coloured brick building with double glass doors at the entrance. It was Friday. It always took longer on a Friday because it was payday for many workers.

The seconds went by. I could see neither Mr. Lavoie, nor the robber, nor the police. I looked straight ahead, not daring to turn my head. My stomach was knotted. When I am under great stress, even now the old convent training takes hold of me. That day I sat up properly in my seat, back straight, one hand resting on the other. I could hear the street sounds, the passing cars and buses, the people walking by with their purchases.

Still no hold-up. Would he speak? Would he say something like "hands up"? Would he grab the bag without a word? Would I scream?

I began almost to fear that the hold-up would not take place. I had gone to the police that morning with a dramatic tale about the FLQ. I had claimed the hold-up would take place over the noon hour. If the police were watching, they would surely think that I was simply an hysterical woman who imagined things.

The car door opened on the street side. I jumped. Mr. Lavoie, smiling, had returned from the bank, an empty canvas bag in his hand.

"Ah, *Madame la journaliste*. Did you pick up the book while you were waiting? If you start reading it, I guarantee that you won't be able to put it down."

He changed his glasses and we continued on our round without incident. What had happened to the two robbers? Had they given up their idea of a hold-up? Had they simply decided to put it off because we had left for the bank an hour later than usual?

The police would surely take me for a nut.

CHAPTER 13
An Intriguing Birthday Present

❊

Sunday, November 8, was my birthday: I turned 25. In the evening I was at home on Saint Joseph Boulevard when my doorbell rang. I answered, and there was Robert Comeau, all smiles, relaxed, as neat as a pin in his navy-blue blazer. He looked so pleased with himself! He gave me a big smile and reached into the inside pocket of his blazer.

"Today is your birthday, so I have brought you something."

He handed me sheets of paper stapled together and folded twice. I wondered what it could be. On the top of the first page I saw the words *Front de Libération du Québec*.

Smiling from ear to ear, Robert told me, "It is a copy of the communiqué of the Viger Cell, to which I belong. You know — the pictures of Cross that I told you about accompany this communiqué."

Of course! He had told me about a communiqué printed at Saint Hyacinthe, and the day before yesterday I had told Sergeant Tanguay about it. I was excited. I was holding in my hands an authentic communiqué of the FLQ! It was the best birthday present Robert could possibly have given me. I began reading the first paragraph.

The present authorities have declared war on the Quebec patriots. After having pretended to negotiate for several days, they have finally revealed their true faces as hypocrites and terrorists.

Robert Comeau could hardly contain himself. "Look at the last sentence!"

I turned the pages, of which there were four. My eyes fell on the last lines.

The day is coming when all the Westmounts of Quebec will disappear from the map!"

I read it aloud, and Robert repeated the sentence after me.

"That's good, isn't it? It's my own addition to the communiqué. I think it reads well, that it has impact. Don't you think so?"

Robert was delighted with himself. He kept repeating his sentence. Never had I seen him so happy. He was clearly proud. I was anxious to read the whole communiqué, but this was not the right time. I just read a few more sentences.

The colonial army came to lend its strongarm support to the "bouncers" of Choquette and Drapeau-the-dog. Their aim is to terrorize the population by the mass arrests and the countless raids, by massive police deployments, by weighty pronouncements on the state of emergency in Quebec. Remember the demagogic words of Trudeau-the-monkey ("the FLQ could kidnap the manager of a caisse populaire, a farmer, a child, you or me . . .") and of his under-monkey-Marchand about the affiliation between FRAP and the FLQ, lies taken up and embellished a few hours before the municipal elections by the dictator Drapeau-the-dog, who even added the lie of a vague plot for a coup d'Etat! The Front de Libération du Québec does not covet political power. We are determined to bring about a revolution, the only true way for Quebec workers to achieve and exercise power.

I folded the paper and hid it on my bookshelf inside a novel. I would wait until I was alone and without distractions to enjoy reading my communiqué. I had a communiqué of the FLQ in my hands! Not a copy, a real one! And it had been given to me as a present by a member of the cell that issued it!

I put on my coat, because Robert was taking me out to dinner. In the car he asked me whether I liked crêpes bretonnes. Of course I liked crêpes bretonnes! I would have liked anything that night. And especially crêpes stuffed with cheese and asparagus! We drove west, Robert parked, and we walked to the Crêperie Bretonne on Mountain Street. We went up to the restaurant on the second floor, where we were led to a table for two.

We ordered apéritifs, Robert a beer and I a dry martini. Robert was still preoccupied with the communiqué.

"You know, we picked out names randomly from the Montreal telephone book, and we mailed out hundreds of communiqués. I can just imagine the look on the faces of the people when they receive one. We also sent a copy to René Lévesque with a personal letter. Isn't that something?"

Robert was laughing as he probably had not since the start of the October Crisis. We ate our crêpes — he had ham and béchamel sauce, I had asparagus and cheese — with a bottle of red wine. We shared another crêpe stuffed with strawberries and ice cream for dessert. Then we lingered over coffee.

For most of the meal, Robert could not hide his pleasure at the thought of the communiqué. I expressed surprise at the way the communiqué had been mailed out.

"Just like that! To people you don't even know?"

"Of course, it's the best way of spreading the ideas of the FLQ now that they can't publish our communiqués."

"But you only mailed out 500 copies."

"Yes, as I told you, 50,000 was just impossible. It would have taken too much time. But you know, 400 to 500 copies is an awful lot. Just think. If just 300 people notify the police that they have received a communiqué from the FLQ in the mail, it will really shake them. They will easily believe that we sent out 50,000. That's great, isn't it?"

After the coffee, Robert drove me home. As soon as I was alone, I undressed and got into bed, holding my communiqué.

I picked up reading where I had left off before supper.

The Revolution will not be brought about by one hundred people, as the authorities in their self-interest will have everyone believe, but by the whole population of Quebec. The true people's power will be exercised by the people and for the people. The Front de Libération du Québec leaves coups d'Etat to three governments, who are past masters at them.

The authorities have decided to destroy at all cost that "dangerous" sympathy that a great number of Quebeckers feel for the patriots of the Front de Libération du Québec, since the kidnapping of J. Cross and Pierre Laporte, since the publication of the Front's manifesto.

They decreed that all information concerning the FLQ be censored. They arrested close to five hundred citizens, in the first place to gag those who might be inclined to favor the Front, then to terrorize and frighten all those, intellectuals or workers, who might be tempted to sympathize with the patriots of the Front de Libération du Québec. The "democracy" of the Bronfmans, Thomsons, Hershorns, Neapoles, Simards, cannot allow the Quebec people to threaten its power directly.

We want to say to Choquette-the-dog and to his filthy judges that we plead guilty to high treason:

treason against the Dominion of Canada;

treason against the Trudeau-Bourassa-Drapeau puppets;

treason against the financial power of the big bosses,* the money-makers* and of all of their little lackeys;

treason against the "democracy canadian"* and its institutions, the Montreal Stock Exchange, Royal Trust, Brink's, Power Corp., etc.

treason against the real Canadian government, the one that sits in Washington.

---

*Written in English in the original.

By their refusal to negotiate, by their concern to defend above all their privileges and those of their class, the authorities assassinated Pierre Laporte. Laporte is the victim of those who thirst for power, of those who want to govern at all costs, who are ready to resort to any dirty trick to screw the Quebec people. The authorities reacted in the manner that a boss reacts when he sees the increasing powers of his employees, by flouting every humanitarian feeling. So the sole responsibility is theirs.

We have faith in the people of Quebec. We know that they will not be fooled by the demagogic machinations of the petty fascists like Drapeau. The exploited, the scorned, the humiliated know very well that the army is not here to protect them, as the authorities keep repeating. . . .

It is up to each citizen, each group of citizens, to find the most effective weapon against all these opponents of justice and of liberty.

The day is coming when all the Westmounts of Quebec will disappear from the map!
Nous vaincrons
Front de Libération du Québec

I fell asleep reading these rolling sentences, these vibrant appeals to resistance. I wasn't impressed. I did not know it, but Julien Giguère of the anti-terrorist section had read the same manifesto on the same day. It had been sent to newspapers with pictures of James Cross. You could see Mr. Cross seated on a bed, with a white sheet in the background. That reminded Julien Giguère of something. Where had he heard about this picture before seeing it? Then he read the short communiqué that accompanied the long message from the Viger Information Cell. Here is what it said, in square letters written with a pen:

Saturday, November 7, 1970
Herewith, the proof of the authenticity of the 50,000 communiqués sent out by the "Viger Information Cell."

Nous vaincrons
FLQ

This wasn't the first time he had seen the figure of 50,000 communiqués. Where had he heard it? In the background of one of the pictures, he saw the words, *"Shocking Mr. Trudeau."*

Julien Giguère started to search through the piles of folders on his desk, beginning with the pile of serious leads. Nothing. Then he worked his way through the stack of crackpot files. The last file at the bottom was the one that was brought to him by Sergeant Tanguay.

The one about the woman who had arrived at the police station saying she had information on the FLQ.

He read the report and immediately dialed my telephone number. But I was not at home, I was out with Robert Comeau, celebrating my birthday and the communiqué of the Viger Cell. Then he dialed my mother's phone number. I was not there either. Much later, he told me how he had put my report at the bottom of the crank files.

CHAPTER 14
A Hold-up at Last

❊

Being caught between the FLQ and the police was like a continuing nightmare. I kept waiting for the hold-up to take place. It was always imminent and always postponed. I was reaching the point of hoping it would happen, so that I could stop living with a gun pointed at me.

It had been nine days since I first saw the two men lounging on the sidewalk outside the office. Once I had aborted the hold-up by a signal. The second time, it had been called off because Mr. Lavoie and I were late. The third time, the previous day, it had fallen through for a farcical reason: no one had thought of Remembrance Day.

After stopping at the bank, Mr. Lavoie took a bag of money and went to make a deposit. I saw the dark-haired man coming towards me, through the rain, wearing a trench coat. He hesitated and looked towards the bank. Mr. Lavoie was tugging at the door, but it wouldn't open. He came back to the car, passing a few feet from the robber.

"Ah, *Madame la journaliste*, the bank is closed. It's Remembrance Day. I had completely forgotten."

Expressionless, the robber walked on while Mr. Lavoie started up the car. There would be no deposits. We drove back to the company.

An hour later, I got a call from Detective-Lieutenant Roche. Now the police were taking me seriously. They had staked out the area, Lieutenant Roche said, and they had spotted the two men I described. They saw the darker of the two approaching the Chrysler in front of the bank. Where had the police been hidden? I hadn't noticed them. But Lieutenant Roche was now convinced that I was telling the truth and he expected the hold-up to take place the following day. He asked me to meet him in the morning, about eight o'clock, at the corner of Saint Joseph Boulevard and Saint Denis Street, next to the subway stop and not far from my apartment.

But in the evening, Robert Comeau came by and spent the night. He was often at my place, feeling a terrible need to talk. What a bundle of nerves he was! He couldn't stay put for more than a few minutes, he could scarcely eat. He had lost twelve pounds since the kidnapping of Cross. Our relationship was ambiguous. We had occasionally exchanged loving words and caresses, but Robert was under far too much strain to go any further. Since our meeting on October 31, I, too, had been under constant pressure. I was happy to let him speak, though: it did him good and gave me information. Sometimes, exhausted, he fell asleep on my bed or sofa. He was usually gone when I woke up in the morning.

But on the morning I was to meet Lieutenant Roche, Robert was still asleep. I woke him up, and together, we had a cup of coffee. I told him that I had to be at the office early. He walked with me to the subway. I hoped that Lieutenant Roche, seeing me with somebody, would not come up and speak to me. I had never seen him, but I knew that he had seen me before, outside the bank. At the corner of Saint Denis Street, Robert and I passed a man in dark clothes waiting there. Was it Lieutenant Roche?

I went into the Métro and waited a few moments to give Robert time to disappear. Then I came back out and crossed the street. It was the detective. He shook my hand and invited me into his car, parked nearby.

"Keep calm," he told me. "My men and I will be there."

He drove me to work, dropping me off before we reached the building.

Keep calm he had said. I wanted to, but the more I tried, the less I succeeded. I visualized the hold-up, and in my anxiety I saw myself caught in the middle of a shoot-out between the police and the gunmen of the FLQ. I didn't know which side to fear more if I got caught in their cross-fire.

At the office, I received a call from Detective-Lieutenant Julien Giguère. He, too, tried to reassure me. I told him how nervous I was, how I couldn't stand violence of any kind.

"I don't want to be turned into a sieve!"

I reminded him that the robber would be armed. He tried to comfort me by saying that the police would also be armed. That was the trouble, I'd be the only one without a gun.

Just after noon, Mr. Lavoie came by my office as usual and we left on our daily run. As always, he wore a big smile and described the poverty to which he had been reduced.

No one on the sidewalk in front of the office! Along our route, I kept watch to see if we were followed, but I saw nobody. Mr. Lavoie, with many gestures, recalled the lurid details of his current mystery. I listened with half an ear. My mind was already at the corner of Bossuet and Hochelaga, our first stop.

He parked the car, changed his glasses, opened the big bag and took out a smaller one. The money was on the seat to my left. On my right, I had a beige travel bag in which I kept my course notes and my handbag.

It was a beautiful day. I looked towards the corner to see if my robber was coming. He wasn't there. The tension in my muscles began to relax. It wasn't going to happen today.

Suddenly the door opened on my left. His dark brown eyes stared into mine. I saw the barrel of a gun sticking out from the trench coat draped over his arm. Not a word. His right hand pushed me back against the seat, he reached past me, grabbed my travel bag, and was gone.

For a moment I sat there, stunned. It had happened! It was over! And he had taken the wrong bag! There were several thousand dollars in the bag in the middle of the seat and he had made off with my notes and a purse that contained twelve dollars.

I opened the car door and ran into the bank.

"Mr. Lavoie! Mr. Lavoie! There was a hold-up! I've been robbed!"

"What? Where's the company's money?"

"Oh! I forgot it in the car."

He ran out to the car to check on the money I had left in the unlocked car. A teller called the police and led me into the office of the manager, who was away having lunch. A uniformed policeman appeared and took my statement. I made no mention of having warned Sergeant Tanguay or having spoken to Lieutenant Roche. I told the officer that I didn't know the robber. Since I had only seen him for a second, I could give only a summary description. Not a word about the FLQ.

After my deposition, which took about twenty minutes, the policeman let me go. Mr. Lavoie and I, instead of continuing on our route, returned directly to the office. I felt relieved of a great weight. It was over! Now I could return to a normal life. I could forget about the FLQ, and the police. I would concentrate on international relations. For the first time in two weeks, I felt like myself again and experienced the euphoria that follows a long period of tension.

We parked in the Caloil lot and Mr. Lavoie launched into an account of the hold-up for the other employees while I headed for my office. As I was opening the door, two men in dark suits came up to me.

"Miss de Vault?" I turned around.

"Police. Will you please follow us?"

"But why?"

"You were the victim of a hold-up today?"

"Yes, and I made a statement to a police officer at the bank."

"Follow us, please."

"Where?"

"To the police headquarters on Gosford Street."

We walked out together. I felt like a criminal walking between two guards. Their car was parked in front of the building. I got in the back; they rode silently in front. My tension was returning. Did they suspect me?

The unmarked car drove through the streets of Montreal. We were still under the War Measures Act and, through the window, I could see armed soldiers on guard in front of public buildings. The police and the army seemed to have taken over the city.

We stopped at the grey stone building that housed police headquarters. With a policeman on either side, I walked along a corridor and took an elevator that let us off after a few floors. We walked through a long room where dozens of uniformed policemen were writing at tables. This room led to a narrow corridor and they told me to go into the third door on my left. It was a tiny room with a table, three chairs, a typewriter, an ashtray, and pencils. There were bars on the window. They asked me to wait.

I was hungry. It was the middle of the afternoon and I had had nothing but a cup of coffee all day. I felt out of place in this little room — more like a cell — where I had been made to come whether I wanted to or not. I was losing control of my life.

At last the door opened. A fair-haired man with slightly wavy hair came in and introduced himself as Detective-Sergeant François Fortin of the armed robbery squad. He sat down at the typewriter, inserted a sheet of paper, and began asking the questions that I seemed to have answered so often lately. A second policeman, Detective-Sergeant Harvey, came in and sat down beside me.

Name, age, occupation. Description of the robber. Did I know him?

"No, I haven't the faintest idea who he is or what he does."

I had to tell my story all over again. He typed my answers, making occasional, brief comments.

Finally a familiar face appeared at the door, Lieutenant Roche, the man I had met that morning. I hoped that he had come to rescue me.

"It went off very well, didn't it?" He might have been talking about a hockey game.

"Yes, but what am I doing here?"

"We are trying to identify your robber."

"I'm hungry. I haven't eaten a thing all day."

It was now late afternoon. Sergeant Fortin returned, lugging two thick books of mug shots. He put them on the table and suggested I go with him to the cafeteria. Never had I seen so many policemen together at one time. They looked at me as curiously as I looked at them. I was the only woman in sight.

I ordered a chicken sandwich and a cup of coffee, which Sergeant Fortin paid for. Since the robber had made off with my handbag, I didn't have a penny. I took my food back with me to the little room. I opened the first book and, munching on my sandwich, tried to identify my robber.

As I remembered him, he was about my age, a handsome man, with piercing brown eyes. A crooked tooth on the right side gave him a slightly sinister look when he parted his lips.

Sergeant Fortin called the books of mug shots "the family albums." What a collection of cut-throats! They were faces to give a person nightmares. Some had scars on their cheeks, others were missing some teeth. They had the wild look of stranglers in their eyes as they stared at the camera with hatred. I kept turning the pages, but no one looked like my robber.

Sergeant Harvey returned, a sheet of paper in his hand.

"We have arrested your robber. No need to continue looking through the album." He glanced at my statement and looked back at me suspiciously. "Your robber is also a student at the University of Quebec. I thought you told me that you didn't know him."

The University of Quebec! There were about 10,000 students scattered on different campuses. It turned out that my robber's name was Luc Gosselin and he was a sociology student in a building located near Lafontaine Park, while all my courses were taken downtown.

The police had recovered my travel bag and I asked for it back. But they wanted to keep it as evidence. I needed my keys, my money, my ID, and my lecture notes dating back to the beginning of the semester.

Sergeant Fortin proposed a compromise. They would give me back the purse but keep the travel bag. So I could have my keys, my money and my ID, but not my lecture notes. And when the time came for the preliminary inquiry, I was to bring my purse to the Court with all its present contents.

Sergeant Fortin told me that I could go. It was about seven o'clock, and already dark. He and Sergeant Harvey dropped me off near the university, where I had an evening class.

I sat through the lecture, feeling better than I had for some time. Another student lent me his lecture notes for me to transcribe. I arrived home with a sense of relief, tired, ready to sleep.

The doorbell rang. It was Robert Comeau, coming to find out how everything went.

"Badly. That fellow has been arrested."

"What! What happened?"

I told him about the day's events: the thief's blunder, my statement to the constable at the bank, and my lengthy questioning at headquarters.

"Did they mention the FLQ?"

"Not a word. The policemen who questioned me were from the armed robbery section.

Robert was upset. He did not seem as worried about the fate of his friend as he was anxious about a mysterious suitcase* that he feared the police might find. He said that the police must not find the suitcase, because it contained incriminating FLQ material. It was somewhere in a field near a farm. His name and that of the thief were written inside the suitcase, and if the police found it, they could identify a link between the two men and the FLQ.

Finally Robert was ready to go. I walked him to the door, where he kissed me and said: "Good night, and thanks for helping us. See you tomorrow."

Exhausted, I took my laundry down to the laundry room in the basement and copied out the lecture notes while the clothes dried. It was midnight by the time I went to bed, and I soon fell into a deep sleep.

---

*In June, 1971, police found a suitcase in a field near Brownsburg, Quebec. It contained electronic gadgets, papers about the FLQ, plans for assembling a bomb, the names of Robert Comeau and Luc Gosselin, and the address of James Cross's daughter, Susan.

CHAPTER 15
Julien Giguère

⚜

It was midnight. I dialled the number of the anti-terrorist section.

"Detective-Lieutenant Giguère speaking."

I kept my voice low. I had taken the phone to my bedroom and used a pillow to cover my head and the receiver, to make sure no one could hear from the hall.

"It's Carole de Vault. You know, the one who was involved in a hold-up."

"Yes, I know who you are. What's up!"

"I have something new, Lieutenant. Did you know that the Rose brothers and Simard were in the apartment on Queen Mary Road while your men were there?"

There was silence at the other end.

"What are you talking about?"

"They were there for twenty-four hours in a hiding place in the closet. When the police went to supper, they came out and left a big hole in the closet!"

A week before, the police had carried out a raid at 3720 Queen Mary Road, and they had arrested Bernard Lortie, one of the kidnappers of Pierre Laporte. The police were proud of their coup, the first success since the Cross kidnapping on October 5. Lortie had testified at the coroner's inquest the following day, November 7. He had admitted that the Chénier Cell kidnapped and assassinated Pierre Laporte.

"Is it true, Lieutenant? If it is false, tell me now; Robert Comeau and I are going to write a communiqué in which we will reveal the whole story of the hiding place."

I was speaking almost in a whisper, but I couldn't conceal a trace of irony and of triumph.

"You and Robert Comeau are writing a communiqué? About the hiding place? When?"

"Comeau left here just now, and he will be back tomorrow morning. We've already started writing the communiqué."

Julien Giguère seemed most interested.

"I must meet you. Are you free?"

"Yes."

"Isn't there a park in front of your apartment?"

"Yes."

"And there's a church with an odd façade facing the park?"

"Yes."

"I'll meet you at the corner of Laurier and that church. I'll be alone in a car. You have never seen me, but I know you by sight. I've seen pictures of you. I'll be driving a dark blue car, I'll have on a hat, a navy-blue suit, a white shirt and a blue tie with yellow dots. Just look for a man with a tie that has yellow dots. How will you be dressed?"

"I have long brown hair. I'll wear a long brown cape that does up on the left side with four gold buttons. It looks like a military cape."

"Fine, I'll be there in an hour."

I put on my cape and my smoked glasses. I crossed the park to the north corner by the church, and waited. I kept scanning the neighbourhood, almost deserted at this time of night. Was the FLQ watching me? I didn't know how they treated new members. Now that I had seen a still unpublished communiqué, the FLQ might be keeping me under surveillance to make sure I didn't betray their secret.

Robert Comeau had rung my doorbell at about seven-thirty that evening, while I was working on an essay about the history of Russia. There he was, all smiles, acting mysterious. It was Friday, November 13, the day after the hold-up. Robert showed no sign of the nervousness he had expressed the previous day after the arrest of his comrade.

He closed the door behind him and sat down at the table. He reached into his inside pocket and drew out a folded sheet of paper.

"Carole, this is the rough draft of a communiqué that a comrade gave me. We will write it out together. You know when they arrested Lortie on Queen Mary? Well, the Roses and Francis Simard were there, hidden in a clothes closet. They stayed there the whole time the police occupied the apartment, and they escaped twenty-four hours later. They even took with them the guns that the police had left in the apartment when they went out for supper. That's a good one, isn't it?"

He laughed heartily. I could hardly believe it.

"I never heard that the Roses were there."

"You can be sure that the police didn't talk about it. They would look too stupid. But we will tell everybody about it, you and I."

He delighted in the discomfiture of the police.

"Now people will really laugh at them."

He opened out the draft of the communiqué on the table and

asked me for paper and two pens. I brought the paper that I used for my university essays, ordinary white paper, 8½ by 11 sheets. I drew up a chair and sat beside him.

He first showed me how to write a communiqué. He put on leather gloves and I went to get mine. We had to wear gloves to avoid leaving fingerprints on the paper.

"You must always write in square letters. Really square. Even the dots and the commas must be square. That way, the experts can't identify your writing."

He showed me how to write in square letters. All curves had to be eliminated, and the angles had to be as square as possible. So a "T" became a cross, and an "O," a rectangle. Robert had particular difficulty with the letter "S." He always wrote this letter bigger than the others, no matter how hard he tried.

We set about transcribing the communiqué laboriously, with our hands in leather gloves.

Saturday, Nov 14 70
Front de Libération du Québec
Viger Information Cell — Communiqué Number 2
The Viger Information Cell, in collaboration with the Chénier Financial Cell, sends you this communiqué to make clear the events surrounding the arrest of Bernard Lortie. It is of general interest to provide some particulars on the subject of various stories which have circulated in the establishment newspapers.

I felt as if I were dreaming as I bent over the paper. Last Sunday, I had been thrilled to receive a copy of an actual communiqué. Now I was writing one.

Contrary to what the present authorities want to be believed, Bernard Lortie did not squeal and did not betray.

With practice, it turned out that I could write faster than Robert in square letters. He stumbled on the letter "S," and his "2" looked more like a reversed "G."

The communiqué contained some intriguing details. It described how the four members of the Chénier Cell concealed themselves in the apartment on Queen Mary Road when the police arrived. Bernard Lortie hid in an ordinary clothes closet, but the Rose brothers and Francis Simard climbed into a hiding place they had built at the back of a doctored closet. The police found Bernard Lortie, but the Roses and Simard stayed hidden in their cubbyhole while the police searched the apartment. The next day, the two policemen guarding the apartment went off to eat in a restaurant, leaving behind their guns. The Roses and Simard escaped, taking the guns with them. We had transcribed about one-third of the communiqué when, suddenly, Robert Comeau looked at his watch. He told me he had an appointment somewhere.

"I don't have time to finish tonight, but I'll leave you the draft and we will continue tomorrow morning. It would be better if you found a place to hide these papers. The best thing is to put them inside a book, but don't choose a Marxist book!"

He went off, leaving on the table the draft, which was in someone else's writing. It was not in square letters. Who could have written it?*

I took the draft and the two partially written copies and put them in a drawer. Then I dialed the number of the anti-terrorist section that Julien Giguère had given me the previous day, a couple of hours before the robbery. I had written it on page 25 of the novel *Le Rouge et le Noir*, the hero of which is also named Julien. But I didn't have to look up the number in the novel; it had become instantly engraved on my memory.

How often I would dial that number in the months that followed!

The night of November 14 was mild and clear. We were enjoying an Indian summer. At the street corner, I looked into every car, trying to spot a man wearing a tie with yellow dots. A few cars stopped, and a man called out:

"Hey, Baby, you want a ride?"

They took me for a prostitute. I turned away with my head high, but when another car stopped for a red light (the cars all looked the same colour in the dark), I bent forward again to look at the driver's tie.

"Hey, Beautiful, what are you doing tonight?"

Then another car slowed down. The driver was wearing a hat. He beckoned to me. I looked, but I couldn't see a tie with yellow dots, so I turned away. He rolled down the window.

"Are you Carole?"

"Yes. Lieutenant Giguère?"

He pushed open the door and I got in.

"Am I ever happy to see you. While I was waiting, I was propositioned six times."

"Yes, I know the district. When I was in uniform, I worked out of No. 17 Station, right over there."

While he drove, I studied him. He was between thirty and thirty-five. He did not at all fit my image of a cop. He was rather slender

---

*It was ascertained later that the writer was Nigel Hamer, one of the kidnappers of James Cross.

in build, wore civilian clothes, had a nice profile, a mischievous smile, and pleasant manners. I always imagined policemen to be abrupt, hard, a little dumb, and untalkative. Julien Giguère, from this first meeting, gave me the impression of someone who liked to talk and joke. He soon impressed me with the quickness of his mind.

We drove to an all-night restaurant at the corner of Jean Talon and Saint Laurent. I ordered a Cinzano, he a beer. I could see that he was now studying me. He seemed in no hurry. He asked me questions about myself, but not in the way that policemen have of questioning you as though they were filling in a form. He wanted to know everything he could, and seemed interested in me as a person. He just wasn't taking the statement of a witness. In fact, he seemed more interested in the kind of person I was than in what I told him. Did he suspect a trap of the FLQ? Did he think I was there to give false information to the police? Whatever his reasons, he spent the night talking with me. He asked me about my studies at the university, my acquaintances, my relationship with Jacques Parizeau. I told him that Parizeau had been our candidate in Ahuntsic and that I had worked for him in the last election campaign.

"Yeah, but people don't usually carry a picture of their candidate in their wallets."

How did he know? He admitted that he had been there when I was questioned at police headquarters after the hold-up. In a room nearby, he had photocopied the contents of my purse, including the picture of Jacques Parizeau. I refused to answer. Julien Giguère gave me an ironic smile. He had brown eyes and a very straight nose.

He questioned me about my friends, and my love life. Robert Comeau intrigued him particularly. Was he my lover? I answered no. But Julien Giguère did not seem to believe me. He was convinced that Robert Comeau was the man I loved. I kept denying it, becoming annoyed.

"It's none of your business! It's my private life! What concern is it of yours?"

"Julien has to know everything," he replied with a little smile. Then he got around to the communiqué. Reluctantly, he admitted that the police had missed the Roses and Simard and let them get away. It made him uncomfortable to listen to me talk about the contents of the communiqué, about how the Roses and Simard fled their hiding places under the very noses of the police. And he became indignant when I said that the escapees had taken with them guns left behind by the police.

"That's a lie!"

"No, it's true."

"Oh, yeah? Well if it's true, just ask your Comeau for the serial numbers of the guns. Tell him it makes no sense, no policeman would leave his gun behind. Pretend that you don't believe him and you will see that he won't be able to give you the serial numbers, quite simply because the story's not true."

He had to admit, though, that the rest of the communiqué was accurate. The police did not discover the hiding place at the back of a closet and the Felquistes did spend twenty-four hours a few feet away from their pursuers. But he did not want the communiqué to mention the guns that the police were supposed to have left in the apartment. He told me that the FLQ would look ridiculous if it wrote such a thing.

"I can't tell Comeau that it isn't true," I objected, "I can ask him if it's true, but that's all. How could I tell him that I'm sure it's not so."

I took out of my handbag the draft of the communiqué and the two copies we had begun in square letters. Julien Giguère studied them with care.

Then I had to tell him my story from the beginning, how I had first come in contact with the FLQ. I had already told it all to Sergeant Tanguay, but the lieutenant wanted to hear the whole story. He wanted to go over even the smallest details. I had to repeat everything I knew about the FLQ, about Comeau, about the mistress of Marc Carbonneau to whom Comeau was bringing messages from her lover. He questioned me about Michel Frankland, who was supposed to be setting up a new cell, the André Ouimet cell, and about Noel Vallerand, who had sent Robert Comeau to me.

It was nearly six o'clock when we finished. He now called me Carole and I called him Julien. We used *tu*, the familiar form of address, when speaking to each other.

During those hours, I formed a very favourable impression of him, and from then on he had my full confidence. He was no longer a cop, he was someone with whom I had set out on a shared and dangerous adventure. It would be nine years before my confidence in him faltered.

We agreed on a code. When Robert Comeau had first come to me, he had asked me if I would agree to hide someone. Julien Giguère was convinced that Comeau had been looking for a new hiding place for the Roses and Simard. (Later, I became convinced that it was for Bernard Lortie, who had joined the other members of the Chénier Cell on Queen Mary Road on November 1, the day after Comeau contacted me.) If the fugitives appeared at my door I was to dial the anti-terrorist section and say:

"Could I speak to Julien, the cleaner?" And I was to leave this message: "Is my flowered dress ready? I need it today." At last we left the restaurant. Julien stopped at the offices of the anti-terrorist section to photocopy the documents I had brought him. Then he drove me back to my apartment. Robert Comeau was to come by later that morning to finish the communiqué and he mustn't find an empty apartment.

I did not know it then, but our entire conversation in the restaurant had been recorded. Julien Giguère had had a listening device hidden behind his tie. In a parking lot across the street in an unmarked car, Lieutenant-Detective Marcel Allard had been tape recording everything we said. Five hours of conversation.

I did not know it then, but I had just lost any claim to a private life.

Julien Giguère returned to the office of the anti-terrorist section to type out the notes on his first conversation with source SAT 945-171. Here is a portion of his report as the Keable Commission showed it to me, which summarizes our conversation:

November 14 1970
Re: Extra-secret source 945-171

1 This day November 14 1970 about 01:00 hours I met the above-mentioned source who informs me of these facts:

A That two communiqués of the FLQ will appear this day of November 14 1970 and more particularly Communiqué Number 2 "Viger Information Cell."

B These two communiqués will be hand-written by two different persons in square letters with a ballpoint pen and will relate the correct circumstances surrounding the arrest of Bernard Lortie and will speak of police guns left behind on the premises by the police on November 7 1970 about 18:30 hours.

C The two communiqués will be delivered to the newspapers *Québec-Presse* and *Journal de Montréal*.

D That a person known as Robert Comeau living on Quinn Street in Longueuil is the instigator of the Viger Cell.

E That another cell being formed will presently be called the Ouimet Cell.

F That the Ouimet Cell will be entrusted with the FLQ's dynamite cache and firearms.

G During the kidnapping of J. Cross, one of the kidnappers overturned or jolted a statuette or a bust [at the diplomatic residence].

H Mr. Cross is detained in an apartment for which the rent is due on Monday November 17 1970, and it is $140.00.

I   That the kidnappers of Mr. Cross obtained new pills for Mr. Cross and he had been without them for about five (5) to seven (7) days.

J   That the persons who detained Mr. Cross were six (6) in number and that at least four (4) of them worked regularly at their daily activities, but were more specially responsible for guarding Mr. Cross on weekends.

K   That Jacques Lanctôt as well as his spouse and a child of about a-year-and-a-half as well as another English-speaking individual are specially assigned to guard Mr. Cross.

L   That the kidnappers and guardians of Mr. Cross are presently taken aback by the amiability of Mr. Cross who chats with them and tells them all sorts of anecdotes, and that when he couldn't get pills, they wanted to free him rather than let him die.

M   That this same cell had considered carrying out the kidnapping of Mr. Jean Pellerin of *La Presse* newspaper (because he is a friend of Pierre Elliott Trudeau) as well as of Mr. Sam Steinberg.

N   According to the source, in the apartment where Mr. James Cross is lodged there are dynamite and firearms in rather fair number.

O   That a certain Pierre Corbeil feels strongly that he is particularly wanted in connection with the kidnappings.

P   That a person known as Michel Franklin [sic] is one of the future members of the Ouimet cell.

2   To show his good faith, the source gave us the opportunity to photocopy the drafts and the original copies of Communiqué Number 2 of the Viger Information Cell (see copies herewith obtained at about 02:00 hours on 14-11-70.)

3   The source informs us that, according to his information, the wife of "X" (a minister in the Quebec government) is the sister of "Y" and one of the FLQ has this wife as his mistress.

4   The source informs us that a member of the FLQ, Luc Gosselin lives with the daughter of a chief of police. . . .

Unaware of all this, I was in my apartment and asleep, while awaiting the return of Robert Comeau. I soon learned that an informer leading two or three lives must know how to grab some sleep whenever the opportunity presents itself. During the crisis, my best opportunities for meeting my controller would be in the middle of the night.

CHAPTER 16
Rent Money for the Kidnappers

— ❧ —

My doorbell rang at nine forty-five. I got up, barely able to open my eyes, struggled into a dressing gown, and opened the door.

It was Robert Comeau. He was wearing, under his jacket, a T-shirt with broad blue and white stripes.

"Would you like a cup of coffee? And while I'm at it I'll make breakfast. Would you like a boiled egg?"

"I'll have a cup of coffee, but I just can't eat. I'm too nervous these days."

He sat down at my table. I put on two eggs anyway, and went to my bookcase to get the draft copy of the communiqué and the two copies in square letters. I put them down in front of Robert and went back to fixing the eggs.

He took off his jacket, and seemed more relaxed. When I brought him an orange juice, he looked at me with a smile.

"You know, I've been a bundle of nerves since the kidnapping of Cross. I just can't eat anything anymore: I've lost twelve pounds in the past month. But I like it here. Everywhere else I go, they are involved in this business. Your place is really the one place where I feel at ease, where I can relax a little."

I looked at him and smiled. Yes, he really was safe here. The police would not bother him. I served his egg in a red porcelain egg cup with tiny green and yellow roosters painted on the side. He took the spoon and began to eat the egg, but he slipped and the soft-boiled egg fell on the two communiqués we had been working on.

"Oh! We'll have to start over," he said. "Otherwise the police will know that the people who wrote the communiqués had soft-boiled eggs."

I looked at him. Was he joking?

"Clean off the table. We'll have breakfast and then we'll write the communiqué afterwards."

I cooked two more eggs, we ate, and I served the coffee. With breakfast over, we started transcribing the communiqué in square

letters, each working on a copy. We did over again the section we
had written the night before, and continued on.

> *"1   Contrary to what the present authorities want to be believed,
> Bernard Lortie did not squeal and did not betray.*
>
> *He acted as he should have (this will be confirmed by what
> follows). For this reason, his name must be added to the twenty-
> three political prisoners whose release is called for by the FLQ
> demands."*

Comeau made a few changes to the text of the draft. When he wrote
that the name of Lortie must be added to that of the other political
prisoners, he noticed that the draft did not mention their number.
He began counting to himself and came up with an approximate
number.

"We'll write that there are twenty-three. Do you know how many
political prisoners there are? In any case, if we are wrong by one or
two, it won't make much difference."

We continued transcribing the communiqué:

> *"2   Here are the facts (proving the authenticity of this document)*

Comeau had an inspiration, at this point, and he added: *"Notice to
Fuhrer St-Pierre:"*

(Maurice St-Pierre, director of the provincial police, the Sureté
du Québec, had been put in charge of all the police forces in Quebec
during the October Crisis.) How Comeau relished the fine insolence
of those four words!

> *a) When the police turned up on Friday, November 6, there were
>   inside the apartment in addition to the two young women our
>   four sought-after comrades.*
> *b) The "fascist police" knocked, then smashed down the door
>   (as is their habit). The two women and Bernard Lortie (who
>   was in an ordinary clothes closet) were caught. The three oth-
>   ers had time to hide in a hiding place which they had previously
>   constructed (a hiding place which was in a closet).*
> *c) The three patriots stayed motionless for twenty-four hours.*
> *d) On Saturday evening at 6:30 the two police officers left to
>   have supper, leaving weapons in the apartment. It was at this
>   moment that our three comrades fled by the rear door of the
>   apartment, which was locked from the inside. They did not
>   forget to take with them the weapons left through a negligent
>   oversight.*

Comeau had a new idea. He added the sentence: *"The Front thanks
them for it."* He hugged himself. It was his personal contribution

to the communiqué that pleased him most. "It's marvellous, don't you think?"

I laughed. "Yes, it's very good." And we finished the communiqué.

e) Before leaving the premises, Francis Simard, Jacques Rose, and his brother Paul were careful not to reclose the entrance to their hiding place again and they left fingerprints everywhere. Despite that, the police have not disclosed the facts and preferred to make Bernard Lortie taken for a traitor to shatter the sympathy of the public for the FLQ.

f) The Chénier Cell continues to fight.

Nous vaincrons.

FLQ.

Finished! I had transcribed my first communiqué. I looked it over, I must admit, with a touch of admiration. For the first time, I had signed *Front de Libération du Québec*, all in square letters, and the communiqué contained information whose revelation would be a bombshell.

Robert showed me how to prepare a communiqué for delivery in the fashion of the FLQ. He asked me for two business size envelopes, 9½ by 4 inches. Each communiqué was folded in three and inserted into an envelope. The flaps were not sealed but tucked in, their openings covered with adhesive tape.

Robert asked me for two tabloid-sized newpapers. I was getting all the newspapers at that time, and I came back now with a copy of the *Journal de Montréal* and one of *Québec-Presse*. Still wearing gloves, Robert opened a newspaper at the centre pages, laid it down on the carpet, and placed the envelope vertically in the fold of the newspaper. He stuck it in place with strips of adhesive tape at either end of the envelope. Then, he closed the newspaper and folded it in two.

Robert put his jacket back on and, taking the two newspapers, went to the door.

"I'm going to deliver the communiqués to the *Journal de Montréal* and to *Québec-Presse*. I hope all goes well. In any case, I will come back here right after to tell you how it went."

Then, with a smile on his face, he left.

Robert always thought he was being followed by the police. He wasn't always wrong. Since the preceding Saturday, as a result of my information, he had been accompanied during all of his car rides by ten invisible guardian angels.

When he had left his place in Longueuil at half-past nine that morning, five unmarked police cars had been following him, constantly changing their formation. Sometimes, a car preceded his

Volvo, another followed it, and another took a parallel street. The cars, keeping in touch by radio, buzzed around him like a swarm of bees. Later, the surveillance cars saw him leave my place with two newspapers tucked under his arm. It was 10:34. He crossed the park, got into his Volvo and started off, accompanied by his five escorts. According to his habit, he took evasive action in case he should be followed. The surveillance team recorded all his meandering. He sped away to the north, turned east four blocks later, turned back north, again east, dipped south, again headed east, back to the north, east, again north, towards the east, then southward, he drove into a laneway, turned around, sped up, slowed down, turned in circles to shake off pursuit.

He succeeded: at 10:52 the police lost sight of him.

The five police cars spun a spider's web around the district in their search for Comeau and the blue Volvo. Where had he gone?

The air waves chattered with messages of the hunt. After five minutes, they located him. The Volvo was parked in front of a little restaurant, Steve's Snack Bar. Was he telephoning? They saw him come out two minutes later, get into his car, and drive off. They followed him on Beaubien, then south on 28th Avenue. Comeau got out of his car at precisely eleven o'clock. The policemen observed him as he walked to a STOP sign and circled it. He looked around and seemed satisfied: nothing out of the ordinary. He went back to his car, and fetched one of the newspapers. He then walked over behind the STOP sign, tossed the newspaper to the ground, and drove off.

He turned right on Bellechasse and stopped at a telephone booth. He made a brief call, no doubt one of those terse calls from the FLQ telling the media where they could find a communiqué.

A reporter from *Québec-Presse* rushed over to pick up the communiqué under the eyes of the police. *Québec-Presse* would turn it into a big scoop on the following day.

Meanwhile, Robert Comeau, still under escort, stopped on Christophe-Colomb Street, home of Luc Gosselin, my robber of the day before yesterday. He came out after five minutes carrying a big brown envelope, and returned to my place.

He was triumphant. "I have come back to reassure you. Everything went well. Can you imagine, I dropped the communiqué behind a STOP sign. Funny isn't it? Tomorrow you'll be able to read our communiqué in the newspapers. That'll cause quite a stir."

He chatted a bit over coffee and then left. Robert was very busy at that time. He was looking for money to pay the rent for the flat where the Liberation Cell was holding James Cross. He had spoken to me about it the day before when he had come by at the end of the afternoon.

"I've got to find some money for the Liberation Cell. They have to pay the rent on Monday and they have no money. They hadn't expected to keep Cross such a long time; they thought that after four or five days it would all be over! I'd lend them money myself, but I don't have any more. All my salary has gone to the Front."

I looked at him, delighted.

"So you know where Cross is kept?"

He looked me straight in the eye, with a big smile. "All I can tell you is that he is hidden, not in the City of Montreal, but somewhere on the island. He is not in a house nor in an apartment, but in a flat. And, as I told you, the rent is $140 a month. I'm sorry, but you understand that I can't tell you any more."

Still hoping to find out where James Cross was detained, I offered to lend Robert the money. It was a Friday and, after work, I had gone to the bank to cash my cheque and had withdrawn $400 to buy myself a lamb jacket. Robert could see the money, it was there in cash on the table.

"I have money right here, Robert. If you need money, take it, I want you to have it."

"Thanks a lot, but before taking your money I will approach a union I know in the Eastern Townships. It's sympathetic to the Front. If that doesn't work, I'll come back to see you."

We didn't speak of it again. The next day, after delivering the communiqué and reassuring me, Robert went off in search of money. He didn't have much luck and, towards the end of the afternoon, returned to my place looking disappointed.

"It didn't work with the union, they wouldn't do it. They refused. Does your offer still stand?"

"Of course. You need $140?"

"Yes." You know I don't like to borrow money from you, but it isn't for me. It's for the FLQ."

I went to my room and took the money out of my handbag. I handed it over to Robert.

"Thanks. Thanks a lot, in the name of the Front."

He left immediately, satisfied. And I was proud of myself: I had paid the rent for the place where James Cross was held. That might encourage Robert to tell me further secrets and perhaps, some day, to reveal where Cross was hidden. In any case, I hoped he would tell the Liberation Cell who had provided the money.

Robert went back to see Luc Gosselin at about eight o'clock and stayed with him for about a half hour. He left, made a call from a telephone booth, then drove to 3610 Hutchison Street where he met a woman in her twenties that the police were never able to identify. She was about five foot five, weighed about 115 pounds, had brown hair in a ponytail, and was dressed in a light-coloured winter coat with the hood up. She and Robert got into the car. It was 9:07 in the evening.

They drove around aimlessly, talking. After half an hour, Comeau parked the car and went into a discotheque on Maisonneuve Street, the Pom-Pom. Three minutes later he ran back out and climbed into his car. A man was following him, running towards the Volvo, but then veered off into a lane, got into a car and drove off quickly. The police never discovered who he was either.

Robert Comeau drove away still talking to the mysterious woman, and dropped her off at 9:58 at the house on Hutchison Street where he had picked her up. Then he went home.

I was never able to identify whom Robert Comeau met so mysteriously that night. But I inferred that he must have handed over my $140 to a member of the Liberation Cell, or to someone belonging to that cell's support network.

CHAPTER 17
Under Suspicion

—————————— ❊ ——————————

On November 17, I returned home earlier than usual. I walked in the main door of the apartment building and pulled out my keys to open the hall door. My apartment was the second of three located on the ground floor. As I walked around the corner to the hall leading to the three apartments, I almost bumped into two men who were coming towards me. One of them mumbled something like "Excuse me." I thought no more of it.

Robert Comeau visited me that night. He seemed cool and distant. I couldn't imagine what was bothering him. I asked him if anything was wrong. He looked at me for a while without a word. When he spoke, his voice was full of suspicion.

"Why did two policemen phone you this afternoon?"

I was thunderstruck. What had happened? What did he know? I tried to remain calm, as though I had not the faintest idea of what he was talking about. In a sense, it was true. I had received no call today from Julien Giguère or from any other policeman.

"What? What policemen are you talking about? Can you tell me what this is all about?"

He looked at me searchingly. I tried to appear innocently bewildered.

"I saw them myself. I was going to call you from the phone booth at the corner of Saint Laurent when two men entered the next booth over. I watched them and they took out a card of the Montreal police and on that card I saw your telephone number, which they dialed. I saw them!"

Fortunately for me, I had absolutely no idea what all this meant. Why would two policemen have called me from a phone booth? It all seemed very strange. I began to suspect Comeau of setting a trap for me, or of testing to see whether I had contacts in the Montreal police. Perhaps this was always done in the FLQ.

"What are you talking about Robert? I didn't get any phone calls today, and certainly none from the police. You must be mistaken."

"I saw them with my own eyes! I saw two policemen phone you. Until you can explain why those policemen called, I will tell you nothing more about the FLQ."

"Whatever you say, Robert. But I swear that I don't know what you're talking about."

He left shortly afterwards, full of distrust. I was very worried. What could have happened? I waited a few minutes, then I dialed Julien Giguère. I spoke angrily.

"Could you tell me, please, why two policemen from the City of Montreal phoned me this afternoon from a telephone booth?"

"What? What?" Julien's voice was full of innocence and surprise. I told him about Robert Comeau's visit. Julien could give no explanation. He said that he thought that Comeau had dreamed up the whole thing.

It was ten years later when I learned what had really happened that day. Julien Giguère had decided to plant a listening device at my place to monitor my telephone calls (the bug was put in the telephone) and all the conversations in my apartment. He hadn't asked for my permission, and I would never have given it. What an intrusion into my private life! I wouldn't have minded the police recording my telephone calls, but not my conversations when I was visited by friends or a lover. No, never!

Julien Giguère had sent two specialists in electronic surveillance to plant the bug. They were the men who had passed me in the corridor. If I had come home a few seconds earlier, I would have found them in my living room.

To try out their equipment, they had dialed my number from a phone booth near my apartment. That is when Robert Comeau, from the next booth, caught them phoning. Showing carelessness that could have been very costly for me, they had let a stranger spot my number on a police card.

But that night, I was aware of none of this and Robert Comeau had dark suspicions about me. I was worried, but so convinced that what Comeau said could not have happened that I was not really afraid.

Quickly, however, the atmosphere changed. Robert returned to visit me as though nothing had happened, and once again took me into his confidence. Strange man! He never forgot that those two officers had phoned me, however. He would come back to it in conversation a few months later, and it would lead to a nasty conflict between us. He soon put out the rumour that I worked for the police. The telephone incident remained etched in his memory, surfacing from time to time, but usually Robert was once again a friendly, agreeable person, as though he doubted his own suspicions.

Poor Robert! He soon began to suspect many people he knew of being on the police payroll. Such was the case with Michel Frankland. One day, Robert announced to me that Frankland had the makings of a true revolutionary. The next day he thought Frankland might be a police agent!

One evening, not long after Robert Comeau's visit, Julien Giguère asked me to get him Robert's fingerprints.

"Does Comeau drink beer? Offer him a glass of beer. Hold the glass by the base and hand it to him in such a way that his prints will remain on the glass. When he is gone, pick it up again by the base, put it in a paper bag and bring it to me."

On his next visit, Robert was in too much of a hurry to stop for a drink. No fingerprints. Better luck next time.

When he next came by, he gladly accepted a beer. As I was about to serve it, I realized that I was offering it to him in a stein. If he took the stein by the handle, his fingerprints would not be very clear. I set the beer stein aside, went to the cupboard and took down a glass. I opened the bottle and brought it to him along with the empty glass that I held by the edge. I only hoped that he would not wonder why I was holding the glass so oddly.

Robert Comeau took the glass with one hand, and with the other hand took the beer, which he poured into the glass. Before drinking he raised his glass and proposed a toast.

"To the Front!"

"To the Front!"

We both drank with satisfaction.

Later, Julien Giguère informed me that the police had obtained fingerprints of the finest quality.

CHAPTER 18
Closing in on the Cross Kidnappers
❧

The police pursuit, fumbling as it was, was getting closer and closer to the Liberation Cell that held James Cross.* It was painstaking work. They searched here, they searched there, they followed up on every clue, they chased down every lead, in the hope that one of them — no one knew which — would bring them to where the kidnappers were guarding their hostage.

On November 14, when I had first met Julien Giguère with a draft of a communiqué, he knew that the public would mock the police who had allowed three of Pierre Laporte's kidnappers to escape. And in fact, everyone did have a good laugh the next day. But by that time, Julien Giguère was asserting that the police were getting closer to the kidnappers, that, for the first time in the contemporary history of terrorist hostage-taking, a police force would succeed in finding and freeing the victim.

As a result of my information, the police had put Robert Comeau under surveillance on November 7. The net dropped over him soon caught four other members of the Viger Cell, which acted as a support network for the Liberation Cell.

Comeau, while under surveillance, met with a political science student named François Séguin. Séguin, in turn, was put under observation. Soon Jean-Pierre Piquette and Gilles Cossette were spotted in the company of Comeau and Séguin.

I had spotted Séguin, Piquette, and another student, Pierre-Louis Bourret,** without knowing who they were. I noticed them by chance while awaiting the return of one of my professors whose office was

---

* In mid-November, the heads of the anti-terrorist section (SAT) held a meeting with those of the section on organized crime. The SAT wanted help from their colleagues to keep the members of the Viger Cell under electronic and human surveillance. Their meeting took place at the Poupette Restaurant, on Mont Royal. The police decided to give this operation the code name Poupette. Soon they started calling me Poupette, and it is under this name that I was known henceforth at the SAT. Some of the officers even bought a doll (*poupée*) made of white wool which they named Poupette. For several years this mascot hung from the ceiling in the offices of the SAT.

** Robert Comeau told me during this period that Pierre-Louis Bourret was supposed to participate in the kidnapping of Cross, but couldn't make it at the last minute and was replaced. The police learned later through a tapped conversation that Bourret was one of those who guarded the hostage James Cross.

near Comeau's. Seated on a chair, I had a view of the corridor. I would not have paid any attention to the first of them except for his strange, furtive way of going into Comeau's office. He looked all around, and retraced his steps before slipping into the office. Strange. But I didn't think too much about it. I was still there waiting when a second person sidled by, repeating the furtive approach of the first. And soon a third approached. I thought: FLQ.

Of course I reported the event to Julien Giguère. He brought me photographs, some of which had been taken by the team following Robert Comeau. In one picture, Robert was speaking to a man with a receding hairline, wearing jeans and an open jacket. I recognized him as the first one who had gone into Robert Comeau's office. After checking him out, Julien Giguère told me that his name was François Séguin. He was now put under surveillance, just like Comeau. The second one I identified in the photos was curly-haired, rather slender, with the face of a choir boy. The police soon established that his name was Pierre-Louis Bourret, nineteen years old, a student at Collège Vieux Montréal. He was to die the following year in an unsuccessful robbery attempt.

The third was tall, in his early twenties, had dark wavy hair, and was wearing jeans and a black jacket. In the picture taken by the surveillance team he had his arms full of groceries from Steinberg with celery heads sticking out almost to his chin. He, too, came almost daily to Robert Comeau's office. He was Jean-Pierre Piquette, a student.

The line extending from Robert Comeau was leading closer and closer to Cross. Unfortunately, the police were not always able to see what was right before their eyes. A case in point was *l'Anglais* that the police observed meeting François Séguin on November 19. Not knowing who he was, unable to evaluate his importance, the police let him go.

This *Anglais* theme went back to my first encounters with Robert Comeau. And so, in his report of November 6 in which Sergeant Tanguay drew up his notes of our interview, he wrote: "There are said to be *Anglais* from McGill in the FLQ, including an engineer and an electrician. Their names are unknown. During the kidnapping of Mr. Cross, there is said to have been an *Anglais* involved."

The *Anglais* came up again in my first meeting with Julien Giguère. He wrote in his report of our conversation: "That Jacques Lanctôt as well as his spouse and a child of about a year-and-a-half as well as another English-speaking individual are specially assigned to guard Mr. Cross."

During the evening of November 20,* the question of the identity

---

* That is the date to the best of my memory. I could possibly be out by one day.

of the *Anglais* took on a burning urgency. Robert Comeau came to my apartment in great good humour. It was late, and I was propped up in bed wearing a dressing gown. Robert sat on the edge of the bed. He began to laugh and told me that the FLQ was sending a communiqué to U Thant, Secretary-General of the United Nations. "Don't you think that's marvellous? The FLQ writing to U Thant! I think it's fantastic!"

I can still see him seated, holding a glass of beer. He laughed, and I was just as pleased as he. I was learning about an imminent communiqué.

"But that's not all. What's really great is that it's the *Anglais* who wrote the communiqué, and it's full of mistakes. They will think that we inserted those mistakes deliberately to make them think an anglophone had written the communiqué. Isn't that a good one?"

Then, more seriously, he told me about the contents of the communiqué. "We make a plea on behalf of the other exploited peoples, you know, like Latin America, Ireland and Palestine. That's important, too, because we want the support of other revolutionaries around the world."

Then Robert gave me a knowing smile. "And you know what? The communiqué is accompanied by a letter from Cross to his wife and to the government."

I was yearning to know how Robert had gotten hold of pictures of Cross and of letters written by Cross. It seemed likely that Comeau must have gone to the house where Cross was being kept, or else he was in contact with someone who had just been there. As soon as Robert left, I hurried to phone Julien Giguère to give him the news, but he was not at the office and I couldn't reach him until the next day.

The surveillance teams, meanwhile, were at work. They saw François Séguin meet Nigel Hamer, an engineering student at McGill, on November 19. On November 20, François Séguin and Jean-Pierre Piquette met Nigel Hamer at the Select Restaurant, on Sainte Catherine Street East. It was noon hour, and Hamer was accompanied by an unknown man. The four left the restaurant and wandered on foot into Lafontaine Park.

The police were beginning to take an interest in Nigel Hamer. But they did not follow him that day, after the four men went their different ways.

The next day, November 21, in the late morning, François Séguin and Jean-Pierre Piquette left Gilles Cossette's place, each with a folded newspaper under his arm. This was the approved way of delivering a communiqué. Under the watchful eyes of the police,

Séguin and Piquette met Comeau, and the three completed the delivery. Séguin tossed the folded newspaper into a garbage can at the corner of Pie IX and Masson. Comeau made the call from a telephone booth. A reporter from *Québec-Presse* came speeding over. Another copy of the communiqué was delivered in the same way to the *Journal de Montréal*.

This new communication from the kidnappers caused quite a stir. The communiqué of the Viger Cell came with a letter handwritten by Cross to the authorities, and another letter, not for publication, from Cross to his wife. This was the first word from Cross since October 18, more than a month earlier, except for the pictures signed by him that were sent to the media. It was obvious, when one read the letter to be made public, that his kidnappers had dictated it. It was dated November 15, while the communiqué was dated November 21, the date of its delivery.

November 15
To whom it may concern
I want to assure those who are interested (if there are still some) that I am in good health and being well treated. I have heard about the treatment of the FLQ political prisonners [sic] in jail and I am quite sure that I am better treated than them [sic]. I have all the information possible: Radio-TV-Newspapers. I have "hot" dinners every day. I also have my pills. I can wash and have clean clothes and I have not been "questioned." But time drags very heavily after 6 weeks of imprisonment.

They consider me as a political prisoner [sic] and they will keep me in captivity as long as the authorities do not accept their demands.

I have heard my wife on the radio a few weeks ago. I know it must be very hard and painful for her. But it must be the same for the families of the FLQ political prisonners [sic].

What more can I say? When and how will this bad dream end?
To whom and on what depend my liberty and my life I don't know. But I am still hoping.
J. R. Cross
P.S. I join to this public letter a private letter to my wife.

Cross's letter was infinitely more interesting to the public than the political tract that accompanied it. For me, the opposite was true. I saw in the communiqué, with its obvious anglicisms, an indication that Comeau had told me the truth when he spoke of the *Anglais* who took part in the kidnapping and confinement, and of the *Anglais* who drew up the communiqué.

The day after the delivery of this communiqué, the police put

Nigel Hamer under surveillance. Henceforth they saw him meet almost daily with the members of the Viger Cell.

Robert Comeau also met another of the kidnappers. I learned of his existence little by little. First as a person who disguised himself as Chinese, then as someone by the name of Pierre Corbeil. Early in our conversations, Robert had spoken about a man who had a remarkable ability to change his appearance. This is approximately what he said:

"Yes, there is a fellow who looks Chinese! It is really funny to see him: he takes a pencil and, in front of a mirror (Robert, standing, imitated someone putting on make-up) he elongates his eyes with make-up. I swear that he looks like a real Chinese!"*

On November 6 I had mentioned him to Sergeant Tanguay, who had written in his report: "One of the guards of Mr. Cross is presently disguised as Chinese."

Later, Robert Comeau spoke mysteriously of a certain Pierre Corbeil, an important person in the FLQ, whom he used to meet. I mentioned this Pierre Corbeil during my first meeting with Julien Giguère, and he made note of it: "That a certain Pierre Corbeil feels strongly that he is wanted in connection with the kidnappings."

One day in mid-November when Robert was with me, he looked at his watch and got up quickly, saying, "Excuse me, but I have to go. I am meeting a member of the Liberation Cell at the corner of Bleury and Mont Royal. His name is Pierre Corbeil."

As soon as he was gone, I quickly phoned Julien Giguère. It was then, as I recall, about three o'clock in the afternoon. I told him that Robert had just left and that he was going to meet a member of the Liberation Cell. According to what Julien Giguère told me later, the surveillance team saw Robert Comeau pick up someone in his car, but they lost him in the traffic. This was very unfortunate, because Pierre Corbeil (an alias of Yves Langlois, as we would learn later) could have led the police straight to where Cross was detained. Corbeil was one of his kidnappers and one of his guards.

At my next meeting with Julien Giguère I became angry. I complained:

"I tell you that Comeau is meeting a member of the Liberation Cell, and you let him get away!"

"What can I say? We missed him, so we missed him."

Julien Giguère was fatalistic. The surveillance team often lost their quarry, especially when he took evasive action. Moreover, it was only after Cross was freed that we could fully appreciate the

---

* On October 5, 1970, the police took a statement from Mrs. Barbara Cross and the maid, Anna Lea Lopez. They describe one of the kidnappers as "Chinese in appearance."

importance of that meeting between Comeau and Pierre Corbeil-Yves Langlois.* The resolution of the Cross kidnapping might have come a couple of weeks earlier.

How desperately I wanted to find out where Cross was kept! I didn't dare bring up the subject directly with Robert, lest it reawaken his suspicions. But I went at it in a roundabout way. He had told me more than once about Jacques Lanctôt's wife, who lived in the house where Cross was held. Robert couldn't get over the fact that she had a child of one-and-a-half with her, and that she was pregnant besides. She was expected to give birth shortly. A pregnant woman guarding Cross!

"She is pregnant, and they want to get her out of there. You see, they hadn't anticipated that it would last so long. They thought that, after five days at the most, it would all be over and the government would have given in. They want to get her out, but they don't know where to send her. You can imagine, it wouldn't do for her to give birth where Cross is kept."

Robert had been telling me about Suzanne Lanctôt for some time, and an idea came to me. I offered to keep the Lanctôts' child. If there was one sure way of getting to the Lanctôts, it was to take care of their child at my place. So I made the offer, hoping that Robert would pass on my proposal to the Lanctôts.

"If you don't know what to do with the child, I can keep him here. There is room, and I'll look after him. At any rate, think it over, and give me your answer. But I assure you it would be no trouble at all."

On November 26, Robert brought back the reply.

"By the way, about the Lanctôt child, I talked about it with the others. They thank you, but it is no longer necessary. She and the child got out this morning at 11 o'clock."

She was out! I passed the news on to Julien Giguère, who informed the RCMP. It turned out to be of prime importance, for a reason that I could not yet appreciate.

Julien Giguère later related to me the chain of events that took place over the next few hours. During the evening of November 25, the RCMP had a stroke of luck, even though its meaning was not

---

* Journalist Marc Laurendeau has offered the theory that the FLQ cells were sealed off from each other. The theory doesn't hold up. Jacques Cossette-Trudel, of the Liberation Cell, met Paul Rose, of the Chénier Cell in October. Nigel Hamer, one of the kidnappers of Cross, met the members of the Viger Cell almost daily. Pierre Corbeil (Yves Langlois) of the Liberation Cell spent the afternoon watching television with the members of the Chénier Cell on Queen Mary Road. He also met Robert Comeau. Mr. Laurendeau repeated tales told by the Felquistes and conveyed an idealized, unreliable picture of the 1970 events.

yet clear. A surveillance team had followed two women, Denyse Quesnel and her daughter Hélène, as far as La Douce Marie Restaurant in the north end of the city.* There, under the eyes of the police, the two women met a young couple and they had a long chat together. It was Jacques Cossette-Trudel and his wife Louise, née Lanctôt. When the four left, the surveillance team followed the Cossette-Trudels to 10,945 des Récollets Street. Could Cross be there? Early in the morning of November 26, the police put the building under observation. They now were watching three different premises, but they still didn't know whether Cross was in one of the three.

At 10:55 they saw a young woman emerge with a little child in her arms. She took a taxi, which the police followed as far as Brunet Street, in Montreal North. There, they abandoned their surveillance.

Staff Sergeant Maurice Bussières of the RCMP received a field report that a young woman with a child had come out of the building on des Récollets Street. He was also told by Julien Giguère of my report from source 945-171 that the wife of Jacques Lanctôt had left the place where Cross was held at eleven o'clock. According to what Julien Giguère told me, this report confirmed for the RCMP that they had in all probability discovered the right hiding place.

Staff Sergeant Maurice Bussières phoned Julien Giguère to ask whether I was a reliable source, to which Julien replied, "Yes, unless Comeau lied to her. And her apartment is under electronic surveillance. Why do you ask?"

"Because we saw a pregnant woman come out onto des Récollets with a child in her arms five minutes before the time given by your source. It's very important, because as a result of that information, we notified Ottawa that we had just discovered the place where James R. Cross is being held."

---

* Searching for Suzanne Lanctôt, Sergeant Donald McLeery of the RCMP discovered that she had written a cheque in the name of her sister-in-law, Louise Cossette-Trudel. To track Louise down, Sergeant McLeery went to her last known address on Saint André. There, he learned that the Cossette-Trudels had moved. He found the moving company and learned from it that the furniture of the Cossette-Trudels was moved to the Laurier Street East home of Denyse Quesnel and her daughter Hélène, and of her lover Robert Dupuis. It was because the police had the Quesnel residence under surveillance that they were able to follow them to the fateful meeting with Jacques and Louise Cossette-Trudel.

CHAPTER 19
The End of the Liberation Cell
─────────────── ❀ ───────────────

The net was drawing tight around the Liberation Cell, but neither it nor the Viger Cell was aware of it. On the contrary, the Viger Cell increased its activity. The surveillance teams following the movements of its members were kept busy. On November 26, over the noon hour, Robert Comeau and François Séguin went to a Longueuil shopping centre to meet Nigel Hamer and an unidentified woman. What were they plotting? The telephone taps recorded a conversation between Nigel Hamer and Gilles Cossette. Hamer asked Cossette "Did Raoul call?" Raoul was the code name of Jean-Pierre Piquette. Nigel Hamer met Raoul and Séguin at just after six in the evening at the Poupette Restaurant on Mont Royal Street. The same night, after midnight, Hamer met Comeau again at the Verroneau Shopping Centre in Longueuil.

The police knew that something must be brewing, but they didn't know what. I continued to meet Robert Comeau, sometimes in the company of Michel Frankland. From Robert I learned that the Viger Cell was preparing to kidnap *La Presse* journalist Jean Pellerin. Robert was also putting pressure on Michel to put the Ouimet Cell on a war footing. Robert gave him a week to get the cell organized. He also asked Michel and me to buy flight bags in which to carry dynamite, since the Ouimet Cell was shortly to receive dynamite from the Viger Cell.

The hectic atmosphere at that time was expressed in a report that Julien Giguère prepared on November 26 after a telephone conversation with me on that same day.

James Richard Cross will soon be moved . . . within the next three weeks, because the place is not secure.

Michel Frankland must have his cell [the Ouimet Cell] formed by Thursday.

Friday, there is to be a meeting of the Ouimet Cell.

Individuals from the Front will bring dynamite to the Ouimet Cell and will show its members how to make bombs.

Carole Deveault [sic] will act as contact between the Viger and

161

Ouimet Cells, she will be part of the Ouimet Cell, she will have the cache of dynamite by December 5 or December 6, 1970.

The Ouimet Cell will both carry out armed robberies and plant bombs.

The Viger Cell and the Ouimet Cell will coordinate activities. The members want to blow up a police station.

The Front continues to follow Jean Pellerin, who lives in the neighbourhood of Saint Denis and Saint Joseph Boulevard.

Michel Frankland was getting his cell organized. He asked me to make a request to the Front that they give him everything necessary to carry out a kidnapping. He still took me for a veteran of the FLQ. He wanted a Polaroid camera to take pictures of the victim for the media. He wanted balaclavas, gloves, and adhesive tape to seal up the mouth of the hostage. He wanted tools, such as a crowbar, a screwdriver, and a hammer. If the Front couldn't provide all of these materials, then he wanted the money to buy them. And he wanted to get hold of some dynamite, which the Viger Cell had, as soon as possible.

I, of course, passed on these requests to Julien Giguère. He offered me $225, to be turned over to me at our next meeting, which I was to give to Michel Frankland as if it came from me.

"That way, you will make a name for yourself in the FLQ. Comeau will be impressed that you gave some more money to the FLQ."

Michel set up an interview for me with one of his recruits in the Ouimet Cell. He didn't tell me her name. But I was to meet her at eight o'clock, on the evening of November 30, in the La Lorraine Restaurant, at the corner of Mont Royal and Saint Denis. He described her, as blonde, five feet, three inches, with a good figure, and short hair. I suspected at once that Michel Frankland was sending me off to meet one of his *princesses*. I wasn't wrong.

She would be holding a copy of *Le Devoir*, and I was to carry a copy of the same newspaper.

It snowed on November 30. I went into the restaurant and looked around; there was hardly anybody there. I saw a fat blonde woman in her forties, but she was surely not Frankland's recruit. Besides, she wasn't carrying *Le Devoir*. I sat at a table and soon a woman entered, her hair covered by a racoon hat. Was she blonde? She was carrying *Le Devoir*. She approached and hesitated.

"Séverine?" That was my code name. I said yes.

She took off her coat and hat and sat down across from me. She was a woman of about twenty-five, carefully made up, dressed in the latest style. Not at all like the jeans-clad apprentice revolutionaries at the university. She spoke with a French accent.

"Are you French?"

She laughed. No, she was from Rivière-du-Loup, but she had travelled in France.

"I also spent two years in Rwanda with some French people, and that is where I acquired my accent."

I found her engaging. We chatted like two women who have met at a cocktail party and hit it off. She seemed to have forgotten the FLQ, the reason for our meeting. She told stories about her stay in Rwanda, where she ate snake steak and insects, laughing easily. She also told me about her favourite authors — she loved to read — and expressed opinions on fashion and make-up. I finally brought up the subject of politics.

"Michel told you why you are meeting me tonight?"

With a big smile, she said, "Oh, yes!"

Then, lowering her voice: "The FLQ?"

"Yes."

I asked her why she wanted to join the FLQ. The gist of her answer was: "Oh, because I think it is time that things changed. I am in the PQ, but I find that really, they don't do very much. Then Frankland spoke to me of the FLQ."

She pronounced Frankland as though it were a French name.

"Well, it doesn't surprise me that he is in it. And I agreed. But it will only be for a few months, because I am leaving for Algeria in April."

I tried to find out as much as I could about her, in part to inform Julien Giguère. With a new cell taking shape, it was important to identify each of its members. But, at the same time, I found the new recruit altogether likeable.

I learned that she taught English in a Laval elementary school. What an ironic occupation for an aspiring Felquiste! I asked for her name.

"Rose-Marie," she said with a smile. "Your real name is not Séverine, is it? Frankland told me that you use assumed names with each other."

I told her my name was Carole, that among ourselves we used our real names except when there was a stranger in the group, or when we talked on the phone, to baffle electronic surveillance. What code name would she take?

"Erème. É-RÈ-ME. When I was living in Rwanda, it was the name that the blacks gave me. In their language it means ray of sunshine. I like it a lot."

That was how I met the young woman who became my best friend. Over the years, during her many tours abroad with CUSO (Canadian University Services Overseas), we remained in contact by letter.

By mail, she shared with me her adventures in Algeria, Lebanon, Turkey, Greece, and Martinique. Until the day when my role as an informer was made known.

Meanwhile, from the morning of November 26, the RCMP had been keeping close watch on 10945 des Récollets Street. They were playing a frustrating waiting game. Was Cross in there? How could they find out without alerting his guards and provoking a panic that could be fatal to the hostage? So they observed, followed, filed reports, and scrutinized all who went in and all who came out. Even a slight movement of the window curtains was recorded in a report.

There was little enough activity that could be perceived from the outside. On November 26, Jacques Cossette-Trudel went out for a walk alone. As he ambled along, twenty-seven pairs of eyes were focused on him. He went to a little restaurant five minutes from his place, the Café Vieux-Rouet, and soon returned home, still attended by his guardian angels.

The next day, Jacques Cossette-Trudel went out four times. He walked around the block, spent a few minutes at the tavern, went to a club, and stopped by the grocery store. All his movements were noted.

On November 28, Jacques and Louise Cossette-Trudel went together to get a load of groceries at the Paul Lefebvre market.

On November 29, Jacques Cossette-Trudel went out in the afternoon to buy a newspaper. Later, the police saw silhouettes at a window of the house. They could make out the Cossette-Trudel couple and three other persons. Five. Who were the other three? The occupants looked at the street in front of the house, left the window, came back. Did they suspect something?

On November 30, Jacques Cossette-Trudel went out several times. He seemed to suspect that he was being followed.

On the evening of November 30, the Cossette-Trudel couple went by bus to the corner of Jean Talon and Pie IX, where they met Denyse Quesnel and her lover Robert Dupuis. The four, surrounded by police, spent one hour and forty-three minutes at a table of a restaurant, Le Boeuf Rouge. Then the Cossette-Trudels returned alone to 10945 des Récollets.

On December 1, Jacques and Louise Cossette-Trudel left the house in the early afternoon and went downtown. They wandered aimlessly. They browsed in three bookstores and window-shopped in the boutiques of Place Bonaventure. They returned home after an excursion of four hours and thirty-four minutes.

On December 2, a man unknown to the police, but later identified as one of the kidnappers, Yves Langlois, left the house at 10945 des Récollets at 6:39 in the morning. The police carefully described him. He was twenty-seven or twenty-eight years old, five feet seven inches tall, and weighed 150 or 160 pounds, had a long nose, a pointed chin, and long, wavy hair that was slightly greying at the temples. He was wearing black horn-rimmmed glasses, had on a light green shirt, a greenish duffel coat, black trousers, grey socks and black shoes. He had a slovenly appearance; his clothes were dirty and he was unshaven.

The man took the bus. His nerves were on edge. He bit his fingernails. He studied the faces of all the passengers, and through the bus window checked all the cars in the street. He seemed to be trying to spot a tail.

He left the bus and continued on foot, turning constantly to see if he was being followed. He boarded another bus, got off at a Métro station, and bought Export tobacco and a copy of the newspaper *Montréal-Matin*. He hailed a taxi, got out behind Place des Arts and walked to Sainte Catherine Street, turning constantly to look behind him.

It was still early in the morning. The man wandered about aimlessly in the centre of the city. He went into a tavern, and the police sat at another one of the tables. He left after ten minutes. He walked around, bought *Allô-Police*, went into another tavern, drank a draft beer, and made a telephone call from a public phone. He left, took a bus, and got off at 9:30. He lit a cigarette, walked to the corner of Sainte Catherine and Parthenais, stopped there, opened his *Allô-Police* and studied the passers-by over the top of the page. Again he boarded a bus, got off, stopped at a street corner and looked around in every direction before returning to the house and disappearing inside. It was now eleven o'clock, and the unknown person had spent five hours and fifteen minutes in his wanderings.

At noon, Jacques and Louise Cossette-Trudel left the apartment and headed north, smiling, arm in arm. They seemed particularly happy. They began to run, and caught the bus on Henri Bourassa that went to the Métro. At 12:57 they left the bus and were about to go into the subway station when the RCMP arrested them and led them away.

On the night of December 2, I was undressed, in bed, thumbing through the *Mémoires* of Georges Bonnet for an essay in the 1938 Treaty of Munich. The telephone rang at eleven o'clock. It was Julien Giguère, who wanted me to meet him immediately. I protested.

"Are you crazy? See me, at this hour? Do you know what time it is? I'm in bed!"

"Never mind the chatter. I'll pick you up in half-an-hour at the same place I met you the first time."

I was in front of the church at half-past eleven. Julien picked me up in his car. He looked very serious as we went into a bar. What he didn't tell me was that he had just come from a meeting of the three police forces at which they made the decision to close the net around the Cross kidnappers. After questioning Jacques and Louise Cossette-Trudel that afternoon, they now knew without the slightest doubt that they had surrounded the Cross kidnappers at 10945 des Récollets.

"Do you know anyone in Montreal North? Think it over. Did Comeau tell you about anyone who lives in Montreal North?"

"No. What's in Montreal North?"

"Don't ask questions. Des Récollets Street, does that mean anything to you? Did Comeau talk to you about des Récollets Street? This is important. When Comeau spoke to you about a message from Carbonneau to his mistress, did he tell you where the message came from?"

"No. Does this have something to do with Cross?"

"Yes, it has something to do with Cross."

"What is on des Récollets Street?"

"Don't ask questions. You'll soon find out."

Before leaving, he handed me the $225 that I was to give to Michel Frankland. It was the money with which he was to buy what he needed for a kidnapping.

It was 2:15 in the morning when Julien dropped me at my door. I fell asleep immediately. The next morning, when I turned on my radio, I heard the big news. The police had discovered where Cross was being held, at a house on des Récollets Street. The Canadian army had the block cordoned off. During the night, the police had the electricity cut off. The kidnappers had thrown out the window a pipe containing a message. It had been scribbled hastily, without square letters.

Front de Libération du Québec
If you attempt anything at all (gas, gunfire, etc. . .) Mr. J. Cross will be the first to die. We have several sticks of dynamite which are primed. If you want to negotiate, send us a journalist from Québec-Presse *or* Le Devoir *and Mr. B. Murgler [sic].*
Nous vaincrons.
FLQ

The occupants painted FLQ on two of the windows. The negotiations with the kidnappers were to begin as soon as Bernard Mergler, lawyer for several Felquistes, had arrived on the scene.

I rushed to the university. At a newstand near the UQAM, I bought a newspaper. Not a word yet about the news of the hour. But everyone already knew. I heard the news vendor say to a burly policeman who was parking his motorcycle:

"So you found Cross!"

"Yeah, and the damned FLQ had better not fall into our hands, because I can tell you we'll flatten them."

I went to the library. Even though the kidnappers were surrounded, I still had an assignment in international relations to hand in. All of a sudden I saw Robert Comeau, who had just come in. He hurried over to me.

"Carole," he whispered, "come over here."

He was twitching with excitement. He looked all around, his head swivelling constantly. He couldn't remain still.

"Do you know the news? They found Cross!"

He took me by the arm. "This morning I was followed by the police! I noticed it. I made all kinds of detours. At one point I went into a lane and they followed me in. Now I'm certain of it. They are going to arrest me."

He was terribly nervous. I had never seen him so wrought up.

"Listen, they are going to arrest me, and it is possible they will arrest you, too. They might have seen us together some time when they followed me. I have a plan. If they arrest me and question me about you, I will tell them a story. I will say that you are my mistress. Carole, if you are questioned, say the same thing, and our testimony will agree."

Full of fear, he soon left, saying, "I am certain that, before tonight, I will be arrested. Now I'm going. We must not be seen together."

Eventually I left the library for the cafeteria. The students and the professors could talk of nothing but the discovery of Cross. The kidnappers had negotiated a safe-conduct and a plane to fly them to Cuba in exchange for their hostage. They were now at the Cuban Pavilion at Man and his World, where Cross was to wait in the custody of the Cuban consul until the kidnappers had landed in Cuba. The names started to come out: Jacques Lanctôt, Marc Carbonneau, Jacques and Louise Cossette-Trudel, and a certain Pierre Séguin. I was astonished that there was no mention of Pierre Corbeil, nor of my *Anglais*.*

---

* Pierre Corbeil and Pierre Séguin were the same man, as the police discovered when, just before he left the Cuban Pavilion for the airport, Pierre Séguin phoned Marc Carbonneau's mistress, who had a tap on her phone. From the conversation, it became clear that Pierre Séguin, a new name to them, was the same person that they had heard of under the name of Pierre Corbeil.

A few days after the kidnappers went to Cuba, a friend who had recognized Pierre Séguin's picture in the paper phoned the police to tell them his real name was Yves Langlois.

As for Nigel Hamer, my *Anglais*, a member of the Viger Cell later revealed to the police that he was supposed to go to 10945 des Récollets on the very day the kidnappers were flushed out, to bring them money. He was saved from being caught in the net because the police had moved in on the house a few hours earlier.

The students exclaimed over the names. Some of them knew Jacques Lanctôt, others knew his sister Louise. A girl in my class was incredulous when she learned that Jacques Cossette-Trudel was in the Liberation Cell.

"He came to my place just two weeks ago, he talked about everything and nothing. I could never have imagined that he was one of the members of the Cell!"

That evening, Michel Frankland came to my door. He, too, was very nervous.

"Carole, tell me, are you afraid of the police?"

"Yes, a little." I told him that Robert Comeau had been followed by the police and expected to be arrested.

Michel was afraid that the police would arrest him, too. But he was very determined to continue the FLQ's fight. He said to me earnestly: "We will take over together where they left off, won't we?"

I served him a beer and handed him the $225 that I had received from Julien Giguère. Michel, his glass emptied dragged me out immediately to look for an apartment where we could hold the hostage that we were going to kidnap. He told me:

"Now that the police have just caught Lanctôt, we must kidnap someone else as soon as possible."

We went off in his car and criss-crossed the streets of northern Montreal.

At about that same time, a Yukon of the Canadian Armed forces took off from Dorval airport for Cuba. On board were Jacques Lanctôt, his wife Suzanne, their child named Boris, Marc Carbonneau, the Cossette-Trudels, and the mysterious Pierre Séguin.

CHAPTER 20
Michel Frankland's Plans

—————————— �֎ ——————————

François and Erème arrived at my apartment. Or, if you prefer them without their noms de guerre, Michel Frankland and Rose-Marie Parent. They were happy. The day before, on December 4, they had gone shopping, and they were now coming by to show me their purchases. Michel emptied out his bags from Miracle Mart: a Polaroid camera, two boxes of coloured film, a box of flash cubes, three canvas flight bags, an enormous *Patriote* flag, two rolls of adhesive tape, a bottle of iodine, a pair of scissors, a hammer, two white Westclock alarm clocks — a model much favoured for making bombs — batteries and copper wire for the same bombs, electrician's tape to tie the dynamite sticks into a bundle as soon as Michel had some dynamite, a screwdriver, a monkey wrench, a saw for cutting iron, gardener's gloves, a saw for wood, and heavy twine to tie up the prospective hostage.

Rose-Marie, full of delight, took out the objects one by one while Michel drank a glass of gin with a big smile. Rose-Marie laughed.

"*Voilà!* Oh, just look at those beautiful colours," she said, opening out the *Patriote* flag. "White, green, red. What a magnificent wall decoration it will make. Ah! A little bottle of iodine in case someone cuts his little pinkie. That's always practical. Ah! A little sheet of paper to write little messages to the government. Ooooh! A long rope to tie up the gentleman just like this. The gentleman-hostage will have to behave himself."

And she pretended to circle a chair with the rope.

We laughed heartily. They told me about the apartment they had rented the day before, where the hostage was to be hidden. They were as pleased as two lovers who had found a trysting place. They took me to see it.

We went out and climbed into Michel's car. Rose-Marie sat in the back, I in front. Michel went along Saint Joseph, then veered onto Saint Denis so sharply that I was thrown against the door. He turned suddenly into a lane, sped through it, and turned right. The tires squealed. I thought of the complaints of the surveillance people to Julien Giguère, who had passed them on to me.

"Lieutenant, it's terrible, he's completely crazy, he drives like a real maniac. He's going to put himself in the hospital and he's going to kill us. Lieutenant, tell Poupette to speak to Frankland so that he'll drive a little more cautiously."

In record time, and after making our way through a labyrinth of streets and lanes, we arrived at 955 Henri Bourassa East, near Saint Hubert. Michel showed us past a large glass door into a small lobby. We climbed the stairs to the second floor and turned right.

"This way."

A few doors along, Michel drew a key from his pocket and opened the door to apartment 102. We went into a small living room painted blue, with flowery wallpaper on one wall.

"Come and see the kitchen."

It was a tiny kitchenette painted yellow. Then we went on to the bathroom, which had a skylight.

"That's great," said Michel. "We can use it to make our escape."

Rose-Marie took off her shoes and climbed on the toilet. She lifted herself into the skylight and called down:

"Yes, yes, it's possible to climb through if you're not too big."

We continued our tour. "But, it has no bedroom!" I said in surprise. "No," Michel answered. "We don't need one. We'll sleep there, on the couch."

"Yes, but Michel, do you think it will be possible to live here for any length of time with whoever is our hostage? With guns and dynamite?"

"Carole, we won't keep him long. After two or three days we'll kill him. We don't need a big apartment. This is perfect."

He explained that he did not want to repeat the mistake of Jacques Lanctôt.

"He let things drag. And so the police have had time to search. The government took advantage of it to pretend to negotiate and, the first thing you know, our people were arrested and the FLQ hasn't achieved anything. But if we kill the hostage after a few days, the government will understand that it had better not play with the Front and it had better obey. I guarantee you, if we shoot our hostage, the government will jump. We have no choice. Do you understand?"

They told me that they had rented the apartment under the name of Mr. and Mrs. de Harenne. Paul de Harenne and Monique de Harenne.

"It's a French name," Rose-Marie told me. "There are not many by that name here. I am the one who picked it out."

And Michel added that they had introduced themselves as French and had spoken with a French accent.

"No one would suspect French people of being members of the FLQ and of kidnapping someone."

He was so pleased with himself that he tapped his head in an excess of joy. "Carole, now that we have an apartment, we must have dynamite and guns."

Dynamite! Michel had been demanding it for some time. Robert Comeau had promised it, but kept putting off its delivery. Michel and I decided that we would go together to speak to Robert at the first opportunity. Now that we had an apartment in which to keep a hostage, it was time that the Viger Cell gave us what we needed to make a bomb. Julien Giguère, meanwhile, had been pressing me to get hold of some dynamite. He knew through me that the Viger Cell had stolen some twenty-five cases, enough to blow up a good part of downtown Montreal. He wanted to follow the trail of the dynamite to reach the cache where the Viger Cell had hidden it.

The day after Cross was freed, Robert came by and told me about the dynamite. He had a cup of coffee, and was much more relaxed than the day before. The police hadn't yet arrested him. I talked to him about dynamite, and he told me that the FLQ had about twenty-five or thirty cases. A real arsenal! Robert told me an anecdote that I will repeat here, as nearly as I can, as he told it.

"One day a student who is in the FLQ telephoned to say he wanted to see me. I went to his place. This student lived in a tiny little room. There was just a bed and cardboard boxes. People thought they were boxes of books, but it was dynamite. So, this guy told me he couldn't live any longer with all those boxes in his apartment. We had to move them. So I left and I went to get the *Anglais* and together we moved the boxes.

"We would fill my car with boxes of dynamite, and take them elsewhere. Then we'd come back, fill up the car again, and go. Once the *Anglais* went off alone with my car while I kept watch. We had piled the boxes on the sidewalk. At that moment a girl I knew passed by and asked me if I was moving. 'No, I'm just helping out a friend.' Suddenly she took out a cigarette, which she lighted. She was talking to me and I could just see that cigarette tip getting closer and closer to the boxes of dynamite. I was terrified! I think I've never been so scared in all my life! But I couldn't tell the girl to take her hand away, and I couldn't tell her the boxes were filled with dynamite. Finally she left. What a relief!

"Then the *Anglais* came back and we loaded the boxes in the car. I put the *Anglais* in the trunk of the car to make sure he was well hidden. We went and delivered the dynamite."

They had stored it, he said, in a garage in Notre Dame de Grace, whose owner was a Scot. The *Anglais* told him that the boxes were full of books. The Scot would never suspect that an *Anglais* could be in the FLQ.

Robert Comeau spoke to me several times about the *Anglais*. He had now disappeared, he was in hiding, he was afraid of being arrested. Because the *Anglais* had been one of Cross's kidnappers.

"He is hidden at a friend's place on Edouard Montpetit. I will leave you her address, because if I am arrested, you will be able to go and see the *Anglais*. I'll give you his name, it is Nigel Hamer, and he is now at 2435 Edouard Montpetit. I will also give you his telephone number."

I got a piece of paper and wrote down the address and the phone number. Of course I passed the information on to Julien Giguère, but Nigel continued to live in hiding, and Robert told me that he was bringing him eggs to eat.

"What are you waiting for? Why don't you go and get him?" I asked Julien Giguère. "I gave you his address and phone number, use it."

My controller answered: "That's all very well, but I have no evidence that he kidnapped Cross. Even if you say that Comeau told you so, that's not proof."

I think that the fundamental reason the police did not arrest Nigel Hamer before 1980 was that the other kidnappers had been given a safe-conduct to Cuba. What use would it have been to arrest Hamer, who would have demanded a safe-conduct for himself as well? The whole kidnapping was handled in an unusual way. The political powers intervened directly to allow the kidnappers to leave the country. The normal course of justice was suspended. The police closed their books on the Cross kidnapping with the departure of the kidnappers for Cuba.

At the same time, no one knew, in December 1970, whether the FLQ had only just begun the escalation of violence. The fall of 1970 had been like no other fall. Would violence flare up again during the winter? Now, at least, the police had an important informer in position: me. I knew the identity of several Felquistes, in particular the members of the Viger Cell. The police chose to wait and see what game the FLQ would play. They were confident that they controlled the situation and could handle the terrorists' next move, if there was one.

For instance, Julien Giguère said to me of Michel Frankland's kidnapping plans more or less what follows:

"That's just fine. Let him make his plans for a kidnapping, it's fine with me. But what he doesn't realize is that we will know from Poupette when he is going to carry out his kidnapping. When he and his gang go knocking on the door one morning to kidnap their victim, Julien and his men will answer the door. There will be no kidnapping! There will never be another kidnapping!"

Michel Frankland, though, continued to dream. I went with him to Robert Comeau's office when Michel told him about the apartment he had rented on Henri Bourassa to hold a hostage. Robert asked Michel to lower his voice. Robert did not like the address.

"Oh, no! That won't do at all! The police first search the apartments without a lease. And that district is watched by the police."

Disappointed, Michel asked where the good districts were.

"The best thing is to rent the upper story of a duplex. The police don't go searching there. It's certain and secure. And it should be either in Verdun or Ville LaSalle. A suburb is better."

Robert added a piece of advice that I found strange. We were to be particularly careful of men in leather coats. They were probably cops in civilian clothes.

"Yes, they all wear leather coats. Sometimes it is black, other times brown. But beware of men dressed in leather coats!"

And so the cute little apartment on Henri Bourassa wouldn't do! Michel soon came to visit me with Rose-Marie. He did not want to go back to speak to the superintendent, to tell him that he no longer wanted the apartment. It could be risky. The police might check. He decided to terminate the rental by letter. I brought him pen and paper. He put on thick leather gloves to make sure that he would leave no fingerprints on the paper. Then he started his letter writing with his left hand, clutching his ballpoint in his glove. It looked like the writing of a four-year-old, but the police would certainly not be able to trace the author of the letter through a handwriting expert.

The planning for the kidnapping had to start all over again, but Michel wanted the world to know that the André Ouimet Cell would soon be going into action and, no doubt, into history. He dictated a long communiqué of eight pages that I transcribed slowly, in square letters on our own clumsy version of FLQ letterhead. I won't reproduce it all here because Frankland was inexhaustible. To think that poorly informed journalists were to speak later of the "false communiqués" that I was supposed to have written! Here are a few extracts:

Front de Libération du Québec
Communiqué Number 1
December 16, 1970
André Ouimet Cell

1) *This is the first communiqué of the André Ouimet Cell. It will not be the last one, nor will it be the last cell that the people of Quebec will hear about. (Notice to Fuehrer 'Choc'ette.)*
2) *Despite all the police tactics to terrorize the Quebec people and the*

active members of the FLQ, the Front de Libération du Québec continues the struggle. Despite the arrest of our 24 comrade political prisoners and the departure for Cuba of the kidnappers of James R. Cross, the fight against the oppressor only intensifies. Everywhere in Quebec, citizens standing on their own two feet take up where the others left off, and calmly organize their anger.

It was a communiqué for all seasons. It saluted our comrades who carried on the revolutionary struggle in Vietnam, in Palestine, in Latin America, in Ireland, in France. Frankland had a global, a catholic vision. The communiqué ended with a fine flourish:

We will be going into action.
Vive the Liberation struggles of all peoples!
Vive the Quebecois people!
Vive le Québec libre!
Vive le FLQ!
Nous vaincrons!
André Ouimet Cell.

As for me, I was tired. It was shortly before Christmas, and Michel drove me to the train station, where I was leaving for Sainte Anne de la Pérade. During the trip, I thought about everything that had happened to me over the past two months. My life had changed. I was now a police informer. Was it possible? I could scarcely believe it myself. At first, I had thought of continuing only until the freeing of Cross. But now I was caught in my own game. Robert Comeau and Michel Frankland were both thinking of another kidnapping. The FLQ threatened to renew itself, to continue the violent struggle.

I was in the middle of my unquiet thoughts when the train conductor came and spoke to me in a hushed voice. He was an old acquaintance. My father worked for Canadian Pacific, and all the employees of the railroad between Montreal and Quebec knew the daughter of Gérard de Vault.

"You are being followed by two men from the provincial police," he murmured. "They are seated diagonally across from you, don't turn around. They asked me where the girl carrying a telephone book was going. I saw their identification card, and I told them Sainte Anne de la Pérade."

At Trois Rivières, the two plainclothes cops got off at the station to send a telegram to their superiors, in which they said that they were following me, and that they would spend the night in La Pérade. The telegraph operator, as it happened, was my cousin, Rosario de Vault.

The cops had asked the conductor to let them off the train on the side away from the station. No doubt they wanted to go unnoticed. The conductor, of course, informed me of their request. He told me to look across the track into the field in front of the station once the train had left. The two sleuths would be there, and the snow was several feet deep.

So I got off at Sainte Anne de la Pérade, and looked back into the field. Yes, the two poor fellows were floundering about with snow right up to their hips. I continued on to my grandfather's house, laughing all the way. My Uncle Jules met me at the door, all excited.

"You were followed by the police!"

Astounded, I wondered how he could know. I had only just arrived in the village.

"They telegraphed at Trois Rivières. Your cousin Rosario telephoned your father in Montreal, and he called me."

It was not easy to arrive unnoticed in Sainte Anne de la Pérade.

I spent the Christmas holidays there. At the end of December, the police arrested Paul Rose, Jacques Rose, and Francis Simard, three members of the Chénier Cell.

CHAPTER 21
Adventures with Gasoline and Dynamite

꙼

Since his acceptance into the FLQ, Michel Frankland had been waiting impatiently to receive some dynamite. He kept asking Robert Comeau, who procrastinated and insisted that Michel must prove himself before he was given the makings of a bomb.

Michel decided to throw a Molotov cocktail at the Brink's Canada building, a good target, since the *coup de la Brink's* had gained infamy during the election campaign of spring, 1970. It was true that Brink's had only conformed to the orders of its client, Royal Trust by sending a caravan of armoured trucks to the Ontario border. It was Royal Trust, and not Brink's, that had decided to frighten the population by suggesting that capital would flee Quebec if the Parti Quebecois were elected. But never mind the facts. Michel was conscious of the dramatic possibilities: an attack with an incendiary bomb against Brink's would have a certain lustre.

I heard of the project on January 5, when I returned from spending the holidays at my grandfather's in La Pérade. Michel arrived at my apartment with another one of his *princesses*, Michèle Léger, whom I had met a few weeks previously at Noel Vallerand's, where Michel had showed up with her. She was about twenty-five, a rather attractive woman who taught sociology at Collège Bois de Boulogne, the same college Michel taught literature and theatre. She was rather shy, quiet, and agreed with everything that he said. Obviously she was much taken with him.

He had persuaded her to share his terrorist dreams. She became a member of the André Ouimet Cell of which the only other member, apart from me, was Erème, Rose-Marie Parent. Fortunately, the two rivals had not yet met.

Michel announced that he would throw a Molotov cocktail at Brink's the following night. I informed Julien and Michel was immediately placed under surveillance.

The next day, shortly before noon, he came to my apartment with Michèle Léger, in her car. At this time, he was also working on another project, that of kidnapping a businessman. I had told him of my experiences at Steinberg and he immediately thought that one of the Steinberg brothers would make a good hostage for the FLQ. So, on January 6, all three of us drove to the north end of Montreal and parked the car opposite the entrance to Steinberg's garage. We watched the cars as they entered and left over the noon hour. I was to point out the Steinbergs to Michel if I saw one of them, but I didn't.

After going to eat, we bought the materials for making a Molotov cocktail. Michel bought a jug of antifreeze, dumped out the anti-freeze and replaced it with gasoline. I went to the fabric department of Eaton's and bought some cotton to make strips for wicks.

After making our purchases, we drove to Ottawa Street to check out the Brink's building. The main door opened on the sidewalk and it would be easy to toss a Molotov cocktail at it.

Several times we passed by the front of the building, watch in hand, to see which was the quickest and the safest escape route.

Then we returned to my apartment and, in my bathtub, we prepared a Molotov cocktail. We needed the practice, because it was the first time any of us had made an incendiary bomb. We set fire to the wick to test whether the cotton flamed nicely and then we doused it under the water from the faucet. My bathtub was soon full of smoke and soot and burnt bits of cloth.

Julien warned me not to take part in the coup, so I told Michel that I had an important meeting and would not be able to go with them. I got dressed, did my hair, and left about eight-thirty in the evening. In reality, I was meeting my controller at a restaurant a few blocks from my apartment.

Michel Frankland and Michèle Léger left their supplies at my apartment and went off to his place for supper. They were followed by a provincial police surveillance team, as we had been all day. Shortly after ten o'clock, they drove back to my apartment to pick up their equipment. I was not at home, of course, but Michel got my key from the mailbox. He took the Molotov cocktail and left immediately for the Brink's headquarters.

The surveillance unit meanwhile had lost track of them. Michèle Léger had sat at the back of the car looking through the rear window to see if they were being followed. The police had to keep at a distance so as not to be spotted. When Michel was on the way to my apartment to pick up his things, they lost sight of him. After searching for him without success, they eventually drove to Ottawa Street and arrived just in time to see the door of the Brink's garage in flames.

Michel Frankland and Michèle Léger soon showed up at my apartment to which I had, meanwhile, returned. Michel tapped his head with his palm as he did when he was pleased with himself.

"We are wonderful! We are wonderful!" he repeated, chuckling. According to the story they told me, Michèle Léger tossed the cocktail while Michel Frankland was at the wheel of the car. Michel had borrowed Michèle Léger's car on the grounds that his own was too well known to the police.

Here is how *Le Devoir* described the event, under the headline: "The André Ouimet Cell Attacks Brink's."

"In the early afternoon yesterday, *Le Devoir* received a phone call from a woman saying that the Brink's company had been attacked and that a communiqué could be found at the newspaper's entrance."

The woman on the phone was me. As soon as he arrived at my apartment after the event, Michel Frankland worked at the rough draft of a communiqué. He returned the next morning and asked me to transcribe the communiqué in square letters. We still did not yet have the official paper, so we drew the *Patriote* of the 1837 rebellion in outline on a sheet of paper and then transferred it to a stencil, before running off several hundred copies at Collège Bois de Boulogne.

The communiqué explained why Brink's had been chosen as a target.

We wanted to make them eat their filth from the last provincial elections. We are not through avenging the honour of the people of Quebec. A word of warning to all those who participate in promoting the unjust system under which we live. . . . The André Ouimet Cell has gone into action. It will intensify its activities until the final liberation. The spirit of a people will not be stifled.

It concluded with a *Vive le Québec libre* and a *Vive le FLQ*, and the obligatory: "*Nous vaincrons!*"

We delivered the communiqué during a snowstorm. Michel Frankland drove his car, accompanied by Rose-Marie Parent and me. Michèle Léger claimed to be too tired to accompany us. Michel dropped us off in Old Montreal and continued alone. He was to meet us an hour later. Rose-Marie and I delivered the communiqués tucked in newspapers, in the way Robert Comeau had shown me. Then we phoned the media with the short message from the FLQ telling where to find the communiqué.

It was cold and the storm was raging. We waited and waited at the spot where Michel was to pick us up. No sign of him. After waiting an hour with our feet in the snow, our fingers curled up inside our gloves, we decided to go to a restaurant to warm up over coffee. What could have happened to Michel?

"From what I know of him, that damned Frankland," said Rose-Marie, "it wouldn't surprise me if he were at home."

She began to denounce her lover. I took a coin and phoned his place. Michel answered.

"What are you doing at home? We have been waiting for you for an hour in the snow. We are frozen through."

"Well, I thought that if I kept on circling in the same area, the police would get suspicious of me. It could have been dangerous. So I returned home, I put on my slippers, and now I'm having a glass of gin."

"Dangerous! Dangerous for you? We were the ones with the communiqués. What did you have to fear?" I was furious.

The Molotov cocktail had done relatively little damage to the Brink's garage. But the action proved to Robert Comeau that Michel Frankland was serious, Michel renewed his pleas for dynamite but Robert continued to hedge.

One day at the university, Robert drew me into a lecture room and told me of a place where we could steal some dynamite. It was at Saint Paul d'Abbotsford, about an hour by car east of Montreal. With a piece of chalk, he drew on the blackboard a plan of the area and the route to be followed from Montreal. I copied the plan onto a sheet of paper and gave it to Michel.

We left after midnight on the night of January 14. There were three of us — Michel, myself, and Souheil Rashed, a young Arab of twenty-three, who worked at the Ho Chi Minh Bookstore. Souheil did not look like an Arab: he had pale skin, wavy hair, and he was a Catholic. He was a militant member of the Front populaire démocratique pour la libération de la Palestine (FPDLP). There were contacts and mutual sympathies between the FLQ and the terrorist movements of the Middle East. It was not unheard of that someone from the FPDLP should take part in an attempt to steal dynamite.

We drove along the south shore of Montreal. The map that Comeau had drawn for me was not terribly precise. We left the highway and explored a maze of secondary roads. By the time we discovered the shed where the dynamite was stored, the sun was already on the horizon.

"We can't steal the dynamite now, that wouldn't make sense," said Souheil. "We are in the country and the farmers get up early."

Michel agreed and suggested we return the following night.

Two days later, we were to go out again and I phoned Michel Frankland to set the time. He couldn't come, he said, because his wife Jeannine had suffered a heart attack. (When I expressed my sympathy to Jeannine some days later, she was surprised to learn that she had been ill.)

I called Souheil to tell him that Michel could not come. He came over immediately with two of his friends, Charles Meunier, a

Quebecker, and a South American by the name of Domingo. The three belonged to the Mouvement de Solidarité Québec-Palestine.

Souheil was beginning to know Michel. They had gone together to buy wire-cutters to break the padlock of the dynamite shed. He told me that Michel had been terribly nervous and had insisted that Souheil should pay for the wire-cutters, and not he. Was it because he feared to be described to the police, or because he did not want to use his own money? Knowing Michel's courage and his thrift, I suspected that both explanations were equally valid.

On the evening of January 16, we discussed the project and the decision was made that three people would go to Saint Paul d'Abbotsford, that the driver of the car would leave the other two, who would carry out the theft while he drove around. Then the driver would pick up his accomplices and the dynamite later at a set time. Charles Meunier offered to replace Michel Frankland. We were to meet him again later in the evening.

Souheil returned at 11:35 that evening in an orange Datsun. We loaded the tools into one of the two canvas bags that would be used to carry the dynamite. We had wire-cutters, a flashlight, pincers, a metal saw, a monkey wrench, a crowbar, and a file. We put all the equipment in the trunk of the Datsun. Then I told Souheil that I had forgotten to make a phone call. And so, a few minutes after our departure, he parked the car by the Laurier Métro station. I ran to a public telephone booth, and notified Julien that we were on our way. We picked up Charles Meunier at Souheil's apartment. With Charles at the wheel,* we crossed the Saint Lawrence on the Jacques Cartier Bridge, took the highway for the Eastern Townships, and arrived at Saint Paul d'Abbotsford at 1:05. On the way, Charles told us that a group of people from Saint Henri were preparing a kidnapping in the name of the FLQ. The hostage would be kept in the slums of Saint Henri.

The village was asleep. I remember passing by a service station and a few houses. Then, all around us, there were fields, woods, and finally a field crossed by a railway track. According to our plan, we were to leave the car where the track met the highway, and follow the tracks till we reached the dynamite shed. We would then have a fence to climb, after which we would break into the shed, gather up the dynamite, and return the way we had come. We would then wait for Charles at the junction of the railway track and the highway.

Souheil and I got out and started walking along the railway tracks.

---

*Contrary to what has been said, I did not drive the car. I have never had a driver's licence and, even today, I don't know how to drive.

It was terribly cold, perhaps twenty-five below Fahrenheit. Our breath came out in a cloud. We could hear the sound of our boots in the dry snow.

At first, we couldn't see the shed, but we could see a light in the distance — the only light for a mile around. We spoke in hushed tones, even though there was little chance that anyone could hear us. On either side of the railway, a row of trees protected us from unwanted eyes. I could feel the cold on my cheeks, between my wool toque and my wool scarf.

Soon, we could clearly make out the light and the shed, the door of which was at right angles to the railway track. Now, the shed was only about forty feet away.

We were about to climb over the fence on our right when we saw a beam of red light dancing on the snow, on the trees, and on the shed. Then we heard the sound of a motor. Without a word, we threw ourselves flat between the two tracks of the railway. Raising our heads, we saw a Sûreté du Québec patrol car approaching with its dome light flashing.

Had someone seen us and alerted the police? We saw the car come towards us and stop a few feet from the shed. The headlights sent their beams over our heads; we were too low to be caught in them. The front of the car almost touched the fence. At first, we hardly dared breathe in case the steam from our breath should be visible in the headlights. We didn't dare whisper.

What would happen? Did they know that we were there, a few feet from them? Would they get out of the car to examine the shed and check its padlock? Nothing happened. There was only the ditch, the embankment, and the fence between us and the car. Souheil and I were so close together that our bodies touched. On each side of us the canvas bags were lying on the snow. He was stretched out between the police and me, and the patrol car was no more than twenty-five feet away.

It was cold, oh, it was so cold! After a while, the headlights went out and only the flashing dome light made the landscape seem to rotate dizzily. Still nothing happened. Now and then, we could hear the chatter of the radio over the hum of the motor. Second by second, I could feel my body freezing.

I raised my head. A light was on inside the car. There were two men. I heard Souheil murmur:

"The swine are drinking coffee!"

Coffee. What I would not have given for a cup of coffee. I was terribly cold, even though I was wearing a toque, scarf, thick corduroy coat with a lining, jeans, two or three pairs of wool socks, and leather boots. Through his duffel coat and his sweater, I could feel Souheil shivering beside me. We were both chilled through, but we didn't dare move.

"What do we do if a train comes?" I whispered to him.

"We roll in the ditch."

I decided that I would roll on his side of the track. We would be less visible in the ditch below the fence than on the other side.

Along with the cold, what tension and misery we felt! I raised my head to look again. They were eating sandwiches. It must be their lunch hour. They were warm and they had coffee that they were pouring from a thermos.

I was certain that we would catch pneumonia or die of exposure if we stayed here much longer. And what would I say if they spotted us and took us to a police station? It would not be easy to say that I worked for the Montreal police. They could hardly arrest Souheil and let me go.

"If they catch us, what will we say?" I hissed to Souheil.

"We'll say we're out for a walk . . ."

"A walk in the middle of the night with a bag of tools and next to a dynamite shed?"

"We'll say we're waiting for a friend."

I didn't know how much longer I could stand it. We had been lying there without moving for about forty-five minutes. Suddenly, the headlights came on and the car began to back up. It went a long way back up the lane leading from the shed to a highway.

"Come quickly," Souheil said. I tried to stand up. "No, they will see you. Crawl."

How hard it was to move after being still for so long! Any idea of stealing dynamite that night had gone. We crawled on our hands and knees and dragged the bags behind us. I couldn't feel my arms or my legs. I had to check that my bag was still following me.

After we arrived at the junction, we decided to hide behind a snow bank beside the road. Now and then a car passed and we crouched down in case it should be the police car. But Charles, our driver, did not know where we were hidden and he drove right by us before we had time to stand up and signal. I despaired at the thought of waiting longer but Charles was back again within ten minutes. This time we were ready. As soon as we recognized the Datsun, we threw a snowball at the windshield and he stopped.

It was 3:15 by the time we reached my apartment. Souheil came in briefly to help me remove my boots, because my fingers were so frozen that I couldn't take them off myself.

Souheil, of course, was bitterly disappointed. He was to have taken part of the stolen dynamite. And I didn't feel like laughing when I next saw Julien. We had been, of course, under surveillance during our whole escapade. A provincial police patrol car had been sent to keep watch on the dynamite shed. Why had Julien thought it necessary to keep me freezing for an hour on the railway track? The life of a police informer is not always a bed of roses.

CHAPTER 22
Attack on a Post Office

※

It was almost midnight when we left my apartment with the bomb. It was in the blue canvas bag and Rose-Marie Parent and I each held a loop. We took the bus and the Métro to go and meet the head of the Wolfred Nelson Cell, whose name was Jacques Primeau. He was waiting for us with Louise Lavergne, the other member of the cell. We joined up with them and the four of us left on foot about half-past midnight. Our objective was the post office on Papineau Street.

The walk took thirty-five minutes and it was cold in the early hours of February 20, 1971. Primeau and Louise Lavergne were in front; Rose-Marie and I followed with the bomb. Rose-Marie wore a fur hat, while I was bare-headed. I had a toque in my pocket in the green, white, and red colours of the rebellion of 1837. It was the fashion for students to wear the defiant colours, but I didn't think this was the time to attract attention, when I was carrying a bomb. However, it was so cold that I finally pulled out my toque and put it on.

Only Rose-Marie seemed nervous. Jacques Primeau and Louise Lavergne were feeling light-hearted. They joked:

"Be careful back there. Don't drop your bag!"

The bag was not very heavy. It contained four sticks of dynamite tied together by black tape. Each stick was sixteen inches long, two inches in diameter, and weighed three pounds. Between the sticks, Primeau had inserted a detonator with a long fuse.

As we walked along Mont Royal Street, a police patrol car pulled up beside us and a constable lowered the window, hailed us, and began to flirt with Rose-Marie and me. Suddenly the radio spluttered and they drove quickly away.

"If only they knew what we are carrying," said Jacques Primeau with a laugh.

We had agreed that I would not go into the lane to plant the bomb. I told the others that I was too well-known to the police because of my previous deeds in the FLQ, and that it would be too dangerous for me to accompany the bomb as far as the wall of the post office where it was to explode. I handed the bomb to Jacques Primeau, who was to place it beside the building and light the fuse, while Rose-Marie stood guard at the entrance to the lane.

Louise Lavergne and I went into a restaurant called La Pizza, two minutes away from the post office. Jacques Primeau and Rose-Marie were to join us there to await the explosion. We drank coffee as we waited for them. I barely knew Louise Lavergne; I had only met her a few days earlier through Jacques Primeau. She was a student at the Université du Québec à Montréal in cultural animation. She was twenty-three years old but looked about thirteen; her body was without curves, and she limped a little. She seemed to know everyone in the FLQ. She had baby-sat with Boris, the child of Jacques and Suzanne Lanctôt. Politically sophisticated, she was more serious in her revolutionary commitment than Jacques Primeau. I had got to know him one night a few weeks earlier when he had turned up at my door, sent by someone from our world. He had the appearance of the perfect terrorist: beard and moustache, jeans, a khaki parka. He had asked me for dynamite. He claimed to have several terrorist exploits to his credit, and even to have taken part in the kidnapping of Cross. But I was sceptical.

In the restaurant, we were seated at a table by the window. Soon we saw Jacques walking towards us, but Rose-Marie was not with him. He came over to our table and told us that he had been unable to light the fuse, because the wind was too strong. Rose-Marie, standing watch, had seen someone coming into the lane. She had let out a cry and run away.

Jacques didn't want to go back into the lane. He wanted to leave the bomb there and get away. Louise Lavergne would not hear of it.

"We can't just leave the bomb like that in the lane. We will go, the two of us. Come on, Carole, we'll go light the fuse."

Jacques left, after lending us his lighter. We went into the lane and found the bomb. I got down on my knees in front of it to try to protect it from the wind. Louise played with the lighter. It was true that the wind was strong in the lane. After a few attempts the flame spurted and ignited the fuse. We went off at a fast pace, but without running, because we didn't want to attract attention. As we walked, we listened for the explosion. A few blocks away, we took a taxi to my place, Louise was nervous. She took off the toque that she had been wearing.

"Will you lend me your toque? You can keep this one or do what you want with it, I don't want to wear it any more. People might have noticed us and described the toque. It could get me arrested. I'll never wear it again."

Stretched out on the bed, we turned on the radio to hear what they would say about the bomb. We turned the dial from one station to the next. Nothing. Not one word.

What had happened? Where had we got our dynamite? How had we come to be planting a bomb? Who were Jacques Primeau and Louise Lavergne? It was a long story going back to the month before, and our unsuccessful trip to steal dynamite at Saint Paul d'Abbotsford. Since then, Michel had been more insistent than ever that Robert give him dynamite, now that he had proven himself by throwing the Molotov cocktail at Brink's.

Robert finally agreed to give it to us and asked me to meet him at his office on Friday, January 29. I went there and waited for a long time, but he never showed up. After an hour I called Julien Giguère.

"Julien, I've been waiting for Comeau for an hour and I'm getting fed up."

"I'm sorry, but you'll have to wait another twenty minutes, because Comeau is driving around the north end of the city with someone else." Comeau, of course, was being followed.

"Where in the north?"

"On Saint Zotique Street, where the other man lives. I just got a call from the boys on the surveillance team and Comeau is driving around in circles while talking to this other man."

Robert Comeau finally arrived. He said that he had just met his contact and that our cell would get the dynamite. He asked me to meet him in the late afternoon at his office with Michel Frankland.

I phoned Michel at once and we agreed to meet in the UQAM cafeteria. We then went together to Robert's office and he told us that the transfer of dynamite would take place on the weekend. He would give me the final arrangements the next afternoon at the Cinéma Verdi, where I was to meet him.

Michel Frankland was overjoyed. Dynamite at last! He decided to call a meeting of the André Ouimet Cell that very evening in my apartment. For the first time, all four of us would meet each other.

I had met both Rose-Marie Parent and Michèle Léger with Michel. But neither of the two *princesses* had yet met the other. I was certain that neither of them suspected a rival for Michel's affections.

When Michel arrived, I could tell that something was wrong. He was talking even more than usual, but Rose-Marie seemed unhappy, and didn't say a word. She must have caught on immediately when he came to pick her up in Michèle Léger's car. Rose-Marie had to get in the back while Michel and Michèle rode side by side in front.

Michel explained his plans for two hours, then got up to leave. Rose-Marie asked if she could spend the night with me. Once the others were gone, Rose-Marie's anger burst out. She wanted to hear no more of Michèle Léger and she had had enough of Michel Frankland. She would continue to see him only as a member of the FLQ.

We spent part of the night talking while downing an almost full bottle of Martini vermouth.

The Verdi theatre where I was to meet Robert Comeau was just a few blocks from my apartment. Rose-Marie and I arrived a few minutes before one o'clock, but the doors were locked. We went into a restaurant nearby, the El Asador, to have a bite to eat. Then we returned to the Verdi. Since I couldn't see Comeau, we sat down and waited. The film started.

What a film it was! It was a South American production, called *Viva la Revolución!* It was the kind of film Robert Comeau never missed. It was in Spanish, with only a few sub-titles in French, so we couldn't quite follow the story. I remember a sequence in which Eva Peron made an interminable speech. The film began at one-thirty and didn't end until six-thirty, five hours of boredom!

Where was Robert Comeau? I finally saw him seated with someone else about five rows behind us. I waited for him to make the first move. Meanwhile, a man had taken the seat next to Rose-Marie and had begun to flirt with her.

At the intermission we went out to the lobby to have a cigarette. While Rose-Marie talked to her suitor, Robert passed by with a man that I recognized. He was of medium height, and wearing a blue and white toque and a suede jacket. He had a thick beard and a paunch.

Robert didn't make any introductions. He just told me in a low voice that the delivery would take place the next day, Monday, at ten-thirty in the morning at Michel Frankland's office at Collège Bois de Boulogne. The bearded man mumbled his agreement, then they went back together into the theatre.

Monday, February 1, I went to meet Michel Frankland at his office, where the delivery of the dynamite was to take place. I took for granted, as did Julien Giguère, that it would be the bearded man from the Verdi theatre who would deliver the dynamite. Since he had left the Verdi, he had been under constant surveillance by the police. That morning, he left his home shortly after eight o'clock, followed by a swarm of unmarked police cars. He bought a newspaper, took a bus, went down into the Métro and arrived at nine o'clock at the home of Gilles Cossette, a member of the Viger Cell. He only stayed there five minutes, went out, took the Métro again, went into one of the buildings of the UQAM, left by a back door and went into another UQAM building where he stayed for three hours.

Suddenly the surveillance team received a call:

"Get to Collège Bois de Boulogne right away! The transfer of dynamite has already taken place."

The police had followed the wrong man.

I woke up late that morning. When I looked at my watch I could see that I would not have time to get to Collège Bois de Boulogne by ten-thirty. To go there, I had to take two buses and the Métro, so I telephoned Julien and he agreed to drop me off near the college. I went to Michel's office and we both waited for the person who was to hand over the dynamite. At one point, we were looking out the window and saw a white car come slowly into the entrance that leads off the street to the various buildings of the college. The car went twice around the driveway and parked. The driver did not seem familiar with the place and we were certain it was our man.

Michel sat down behind his desk and I perched on the edge. Soon there was a knock at the door and Michel called out: "Come in!"

A man came through the door. To our surprise, it was not the man we had met in the theatre.

He was wearing a navy-blue toque. I could make out brown hair, slightly wavy. He had neither glasses nor moustache. I tried to imprint his appearance on my memory. I had never seen him before.

Michel spoke first.

"Hello, my name is François."

Michel was using his code name, and he introduced me as Séverine. There was no expression on the face of the man.

"I am Jean." A fictitious name, of course.*

He put a hand inside his coat and drew out a brown envelope, eleven by fourteen inches. It was unsealed. He opened it and placed on the desk about twenty sheets stapled together. He was wearing leather gloves that he never took off.

"These are plans for making explosives. You can study them."

Michel got up and bent over them. "Jean" and I stood side by side. He took out two other sheets, unstapled, which carried in outline the familiar figure of the 1837 *Patriote*.

On one of the sheets, across the left margin, were the words, going from the bottom to the top of the page: *Opération Libération*. That was the paper used by the cell that kidnapped James Cross!

Jean told us not to use this paper. What we could do is cover over those words with paper or cardboard before photocopying it. On the second sheet, a photocopy of the first, we could make out the traces of the cardboard that had been used to mask the words *Opération Libération*. Jean told us that these were the last two

---

* In 1980, before the Keable Commission, I identified "Jean" in a photo. The name was an alias for Gilles Cossette.

sheets that the FLQ had. Then he pulled out of his pocket a key with a number engraved on it. He set it on the table.

"This is the key that opens a locker in the Voyageur bus terminal. You have until midnight to pick up the contents."

He put the sheets back in the envelope.

He turned on his heels. Michel extended his arm to give him the revolutionary salute but "Jean" had already disappeared.

Michel put on gloves, picked up the envelope and examined its content. I went to the window to see Jean driving off in the white car.

Julien had given me a special number that I was to call as soon as I had the dynamite. I was anxious to phone, but I spent another twenty minutes talking with Michel. I couldn't just leave. We agreed that he would pick me up in his car in the afternoon and that we would go to pick up the dynamite at the bus terminal. We had expected to get twenty-three cases — Robert Comeau had used that figure. But there would certainly not be room for twenty-three cases in a locker.

I took with me the envelope and the key and went off in search of a public telephone to dial the number Julien had given me. I left a message that the meeting had taken place. Then I went to the bus stop.

Julien was there waiting for me. I ran up to him, all excited.

"Did you see him? Who was it?"

Julien looked at me, astonished.

"Who was who?"

"The man who came."

He hadn't seen him. He had put a few surveillance cars on the man from the theatre, and posted a few men in the college parking lot. But they were expecting the delivery of twenty-three cases of dynamite, just as I was, and they paid no attention to someone who drove up in a white car and got out of it empty-handed.

I described for Julien the white car. The surveillance team fanned out and soon spotted a white Cougar. They chased it into the grounds of a Dominican monastery, but the venerable man who stepped out of it was clearly no terrorist.

Michel came by to pick me up towards the end of the afternoon. Darkness was falling. He was nervous and kept looking into his rear view mirror for cars following him. He twisted and turned to baffle his invisible pursuers. Michel was always convinced that he was being followed, and sometimes he was right.

When we reached the bus terminal, Michel stopped his car without parking it. He looked at me and said:

"You go and get the dynamite. I'll keep driving around to see if we're being followed. I will come back for you here."

I was furious. "Michel, you don't mean to say that you want me to go in there alone?"

"Certainly you can go alone. It's important to find out whether we are being followed."

I took with me two canvas bags. I walked into the terminal, which was crowded as it always is at rush hour. I made my way through the crowd and went in search of the locker whose number matched the key that Jean had given me. I found it, at floor level.

I inserted the key in the lock and turned. Startled, I immediately closed the door again. I had seen an open bag and sticks of dynamite that had tumbled out of it. How was I supposed to remove the explosives without passers-by noticing?

I knelt before the door to hide the interior of the locker. I opened my coat and spread it out on either side. Bending forward, on my knees, I tried to stuff the sticks back into the bag and zip it up. It was no use, the zipper was broken.

With each attempt, the sticks tumbled out once more and knocked against the metal of the locker. There was only one solution: I would have to transfer the sticks into the bags I had brought with me. I was about to do so when a fat woman heaved her suitcase into the adjacent locker.

I couldn't pull out the sticks of dynamite while she was there! She might scream down the whole bus terminal if she saw what I was handling. While she searched in her handbag for a coin and studied the instructions for using the locker, I, on all fours tried to conceal my contraband.

At last she left. I began to transfer the sticks, one by one. There were fifteen of them, each weighing about three pounds and about eighteen inches in length. I put them in my bag and closed the zipper. The bag was heavy.

There were some other things in the locker: two transparent plastic bags, one containing electric detonators, and the other containing fuse detonators; there was also a ball of fuse that was about seven inches in diameter. It looked like a ball of clothes-line rope. I put the detonators in the smaller of the two bags and I thrust the ball of fuse into my coat, under my arm. At last everything was in place. I got up and begin to carry off my load.

I was terribly nervous. Never had I handled dynamite before and I was afraid that the dynamite sticks would knock together, blowing up the terminal and me with it.

I trembled at the idea of getting arrested.

Two policemen were making their rounds. They came up to me, wanting to be helpful.

"That looks heavy. Can I help you carry your bags to the door?" I was bending under the weight of the two bags. In addition, I had my purse to carry and I didn't dare move too much in case the ball of fuse under my arm rolled out on the floor.

I smiled sweetly at the policeman, trying to show him it was nothing at all, and I shook my head.

Just at the entrance there were a couple of steps. A man offered to help me with my baggage. I refused again, acting independent.

Outside, the sidewalk was icy on that winter day and I was wearing boots with high heels. I inched forward, praying: "God, don't let me fall."

Michel, of course, was not there. As I waited with my wares on the sidewalk, I had visions of Michel sitting in an armchair at home in his slippers, sipping gin. But no, he arrived and we put the bags in the trunk of the car. I wouldn't allow him to smoke all the way to my apartment.

We laid out the dynamite on the carpet. Michel put on gloves to examine our treasure. He was really happy to have at last got his hands on some dynamite, but he was a bit nervous, too. He preferred that I keep it at my place for the moment. Later, we would transfer it to Rose-Marie's.

As soon as Michel left, I phoned Julien. He asked for a precise description of all the objects I had found in the locker. He hung up, saying he would soon be at my place. He arrived with another detective. They took the sticks of dynamite and replaced them with counterfeit sticks and electric detonators. But since they had neither phony fuse detonators nor fake fuse, they left me with what I had.

After their departure, I opened the bag of fake dynamite. To my consternation, it didn't look at all like my sticks of dynamite. When you shook them you could hear the sand sliding around inside. And they were much lighter than those I had had.

I called Julien. "There is not a terrorist alive who would take these for real dynamite."

He said he would see what he could do. I met him later in the evening and we exchanged the fake sticks for other fake sticks. The transfer took place behind the convent of the Carmelites. It was very dark and for the occasion I was wearing a blonde wig. I was afraid I might be seen by someone from the FLQ.

Back at home, I looked at what the police had brought the second time. It was better, but still far from perfect. I phoned Julien again. He said that he would see what he could do. The next day he made a special request, of the highest priority, to the C.I.L. at Beloeil which manufactured explosives. The Montreal police sent a helicopter to pick up the dynamite, causing alarm in the factory. If the helicopter had crashed, what an explosion it would have caused! They had made perfect fake sticks of dynamite, and I had them within twenty-four hours.

A few days later, Michel and I put the sticks in a trunk and carried them to Rose-Marie Parent's apartment. They would stay there until April, when she was to leave for Algeria. Then I would take them to my mother's, who had agreed to hide them in the attic. Brave mother! She thought she was helping out the FLQ! If my father had known!

It was a few days after I came into possession of the dynamite that Jacques Primeau appeared at my door. Jacques declared that he was in the FLQ and offered his services to reorganize the FLQ, thrown into disarray by the October Crisis. A few days later, he asked me to get him some dynamite. He had heard that I had a supply of it, and asked me to show him a stick of it to prove that this was the case.

One evening shortly afterward, when we were at the home of a mutual friend, I called Rose-Marie, the custodian of our dynamite, and asked her to bring over a "flower." This was the FLQ name for a stick of dynamite. A bomb was called a "bouquet."

When Rose-Marie arrived, Jacques was upstairs. We wrapped the stick in Christmas wrapping paper, with a red ribbon. When Jacques came down, we offered him the present and he quivered with joy at the sight of his beautiful stick of dynamite, on which was printed: "CIL Beloeil Qué. DANGER EXPLOSIVE POWER FRAC 75%."

He soon found a target: the post office on Papineau Street, near Mont-Royal.

One evening, at Jacques' request, I brought to the apartment where he was staying all the material necessary for making a bomb: an alarm clock, dynamite, two kinds of detonators, and official FLQ paper. At first, he tried to build a time bomb, but the idea of linking an electric mechanism to the dynamite made him nervous. He decided that a time bomb was too complicated for a mere post office: one assembled with a fuse and a detonator would do.

I spent the following days in strange diplomatic negotiations. Julien was urging me to calm down Jacques, who planned to climb up to the roof of the post office and plant his bomb there. Julien was shocked. This was out of the question! We presumed that Jacques would use the fake dynamite that I had given him — but we couldn't be absolutely sure. Jacques might get hold of some dynamite from elsewhere. Julien intended to dismantle the bomb before the burning fuse reached the detonator, just in case the dynamite turned out to be real. But it was too great a risk to have to climb up on the roof of the post office after waiting for Jacques to climb down. The bomb might go off in Julien's hands.

I finally convinced Jacques that it was too dangerous for him to plant a bomb on the roof. It might explode while he was climbing down and then he might be caught. He was easily persuaded. I don't think that the thought of climbing up to a roof particularly appealed to him.

He held to his next notion more stubbornly. He wanted to toss his bomb into the mail chute of the post office. Julien was disturbed when I told him about it. He had seen the damage caused by an explosion in a letter chute once before.

"It's awful, the letters went flying in every direction, the cheques were in shreds. If there are coins in the envelopes they shoot off everywhere, and it makes a terrible mess. They go into the ceilings and break the windows."

Besides, even if Jacques had fake dymanite, he had real fuse and real detonators. The detonator, when it exploded, could cause a fire in the chute, burning the letters and possibly burning down the post office.

I had to convince him that it was a bad idea to plant his bomb in the chute. It was several days before I could get him to agree to place his bomb near the outside wall of the post office. In the end, everyone was happy, and particularly Julien.

On the day when we set off to plant the bomb, we were, of course, under police surveillance. As I described at the beginning of this chapter, while we were walking with our parcel, a police patrol car slowed down beside us and the occupants began to flirt with us. Our surveillance team feared that these innocent policemen might search our bag and find the bomb.

Over the police radio, they called the patrol car and ordered it to report instantly a few blocks away, where detectives were waiting. That is why we saw the patrol car drive off so suddenly after hearing a message on its radio.

While we were waiting for a red light at a corner, a man stumbled into me and grazed the bag. I paid no attention to this incident, so apparently ordinary. But Detective-Sergeant Jean-Guy Rousselle of the anti-terrorist section wrote in his report:

"About 1:05 I, Detective-Sergeant Rousselle, encountered on the south side of Mont Royal, west of Chartier Street, in front of the La Pizza Restaurant, three people." He then went on to describe Jacques Primeau, Louise Lavergne, a young woman in the cell, and "a young woman, about twenty years old, wearing glasses, a burgundy-red corduroy jacket, and a *Patriote* toque. She was about five foot two and weighed 115 pounds. It is to be noted that she carried a leather bag of a dark colour, and when I passed them, I bumped against her and I was able to feel that inside that bag there was a heavy object." He was referring to me, carrying the bag of dynamite.

While we were walking, Julien and an explosives expert were checking out the lane behind the post office. They saw a depot with an enclosed stairway that overlooked the lane. They went up the stairway to the top floor and settled themselves there. It was unheated, and the wind whistled in between the cracks in the boards. But from there they had a good view and they kept in touch by walkie-talkie with the surveillance team.

At last Jacques Primeau arrived. He entered into the lane while Rose-Marie stood guard at the entrance. He bent over and opened the bag. At the other end of the lane, the police saw a man who was walking his dog, but Primeau could not see him because of a snow bank that separated them. The police saw Primeau take the bomb out of the bag and unroll several feet of fuse. They were relieved: they would have lots of time to dismantle it!

Jacques took off his gloves, took a lighter out of his pocket, and tried several times to ignite it. Nothing. The man and his dog were getting closer. The dog was sniffing about everywhere and urinating on the walls. Jacques adjusted the flow on his lighter. This time, the flame spurted out. At that moment, Rose-Marie Parent saw the man and his dog and whistled to attract Jacques' attention. They both started running. Rose-Marie took a bus and fled all the way home. Jacques went to the restaurant where Louise Lavergne and I were waiting for him.

Taking advantage of Jacques' flight, the two policemen left their hiding place, removed the detonator from the bomb and replaced the tip of the fuse, without a detonator, among the four sticks of dynamite. The plan had worked. Now there was no danger that the bomb could explode.

A few minutes later, Louise Lavergne and I returned to the lane to ignite the fuse. Of course, nothing could happen without the detonator. In any case, the fuse went out once again almost as soon as Louise and I turned our backs.

As we left the lane and walked along Papineau, I noticed Julien standing at a bus stop, as if he were waiting for a bus. He gave me an angry look. I knew why. He had ordered me not to take part in the planting of the bomb.

It was Julien himself who called the police, without identifying himself, and told them where they could find a bomb.

The next day, the newspapers published a picture of the bomb and reprinted the communiqué of the Wolfred Nelson Cell. The three of us had composed it together. I had typed it. A big headline in the

Journal de Montréal, beside a picture of the bomb, said "This bomb announces an FLQ offensive."

Jacques went underground, convinced that all the police forces on the continent were on his trail. Rose-Marie hid him at her place. Soon all her beer, her gin, and her Martini disappeared. She found the empty bottles thrust into the snow. Jacques maintained that it was none of his doing.

On Rose-Marie's telephone, which was being tapped, Jacques Primeau called his girlfriend, Jacqueline, and told her not to worry about him. The FLQ had hidden him in a safe place where the police would never think of looking.

The police, listening to the conversation, smiled.

CHAPTER 23
Felquiste Friends and Lovers

— �֍ —

Why did I continue as an informer after the October Crisis? The answer is not simple. In part, it was because I expected a new flare-up of terrorism in 1971. If that happened, I wanted to be ready, in position. It had become a challenge to get to know all the people in the FLQ and to become privy to their secret plans. There was a lot of romanticism involved: the romanticism of the Felquistes who played at revolution, at grandiose clandestine acts. But my role was even more complicated: I lived a double secret life, as part of the FLQ, and as a spy.

Now I was paid for giving information. From the beginning of 1971, my controller, Julien Giguère, brought me $30 each time I met him, which was generally twice a week. In addition, in November, 1971, he brought me a lump sum of $15,000. What a fine surprise! I put it in the hands of a relative, with instructions to invest it for me. But, even though I was paid, I never worked for the money. I had other concerns in spying on the FLQ.

How could I betray my friends? This was a question that I would often be asked later, after my role was made public. The fact is that I did not see what I did as a betrayal. Insofar as FLQ actions had serious consequences, I seriously wanted to counter the FLQ. And insofar as they were only playing a game suited to naïve adolescents, I, too, was playing a game.

No one went to jail on my account. The police were worried about another outbreak of terrorism on the scale of the October Crisis. When lesser acts were committed, the police tried mostly to contain them rather than send Felquistes to prison. I was there in case a crisis blew up.

Soon after James Cross was freed, my controller informed me that many Felquistes hung out in a bar called Le Chat Noir. He suggested I start going there and try to make friends, which is what I did.

Le Chat Noir was not far from two of the buildings of the Université du Québec à Montréal, and in the afternoon you could always find a few students there. At night the clientele changed, as I soon learned.

It was dark, dirty, stinking, noisy, and ugly, and it was the place where the apprentice revolutionaries felt most at home.

There was always a crowd. At the entrance, a student acted as a doorman. It was he who supplied the white regulars with marijuana and hashish. Sometimes he handed out precious advice to those who entered.

"Be careful tonight. Leave before eleven o'clock because the police from No. 4 Station are coming. If you have drugs, get rid of them."

You went into the darkness. What little light there was came mainly from the street, through the windows. An illuminated jukebox and, behind the bar, a few lit-up signs also provided light.

There were several groups of regulars who kept their distance from each other. The black anglophones wore jeans and sleeveless vests, had naked shoulders and threw out their chests. They were constantly saying: "Hey, man!" White French-speaking prostitutes, in white slacks and spike heels, sat together at a table while waiting for their clients. Men of fifty, in suits bought on Saint Hubert Street, stared at the women from their tables by the dance floor.

The leader of the black group was a pimp called Charlie the Horse. He was tall and muscular, and everyone treated him with caution. He always sat at the table closest to the entrance. From time to time during the evening, one of his three or four charges came in, walked up to him with her hips swivelling, gave him some bills, then went back to the street. Charlie the Horse also supplied the blacks with drugs.

Charlie the Horse's hookers were white and English-speaking. The women who worked inside Le Chat Noir were French-speaking. They wore beehive hairstyles, garish make-up, and low cut, see-through lace blouses. From time to time, one of the older men would come over and ask one to dance. Then they would go to his table, and he would offer her a drink before they discussed the price of the transaction.

In the women's washroom, where one of the two sinks had often overflowed and the floor was slimy with vomit, you could hear one woman consulting another.

"How much for an old man of sixty, not very healthy, and not very rich? I've had a proposition."

"Does he appeal to you?"

"No."

"Well, if he doesn't appeal to you, $50 for an hour, and nothing extra, just the trick."

They applied their lipstick and their Yardley perfume and adjusted their skin-tight slacks. Then they would go out together, laughing, holding each other by the waist and smoking cigarettes.

I spent many long hours at Le Chat Noir in 1971. The first time I went, it was during the day and I recognized no one. I returned by night and saw the three musketeers who had crept into Robert Comeau's office: François Séguin, Pierre-Louis Bourret, and Jean-Pierre Piquette. They were sitting together, chatting. I didn't dare join them, much as I would like to have. My opportunity came a few weeks later, when I ran into Louise Lavergne, who went to Le Chat Noir almost every evening. She introduced me to François Séguin.

"You can call me Fritz, that's what everyone calls me," he said.

From the very beginning, we got along well. To be heard over the music, which was playing at full volume, we had to bring our heads close together and shout. He had broad shoulders, and was still wearing a toque. A heavy beard covered most of his face. I learned that he was a political science student at the UQAM and that he has a degree in commerce from the École des Hautes études commerciales. He attracted me from our first meeting. And, of course, Poupette was happy to be meeting another one of the members of the Viger Cell.

Soon I met Jean-Pierre Piquette and Pierre-Louis Bourret, both very good friends of Louise Lavergne. She was very close to Pierre-Louis. I also met Pierre Carrier, who had been suspected by the police of involvement in a plot to kidnap the American consul. He took me to visit the farm of Gérard Pelletier on the Richelieu. Pelletier would be arrested a few months later at a hold-up in the course of which a policeman, struck by a bullet, was seriously wounded. Pelletier would be sentenced to seven years in prison.

I had become an informer by accident, in spite of myself. Now I learned to enjoy the game. I led a double life. I came home after my courses at the end of the afternoon and had a quick meal. Michel Frankland sometimes dropped by to bring me up-to-date on his projects and to drink my vodka. Then I would take off my blouse and skirt and get into what I considered my terrorist's costume. I would remove all my make-up, and put on a pair of jeans on which I had embroidered an orange sun, a red moon, a violet star, a blue flower with green petals, and a little brown man with his head in a white cloud. With these I wore boots and a thick sweater, two sizes too big. And then I would go off in the Métro to meet my gang at Le Chat Noir. There we would talk of films we had seen, and rehash the latest episode of Lucky Luke, the cowboy who ran faster than his shadow, or of Arsène Lupin, everybody's favourite. We rarely talked politics. If anyone had read Franz Fanon or Albert Memni, he kept it to himself.

Other evenings I had to meet my controller, and I dressed altogether differently. I wore a dress in one of my favourite colours, burgundy red or black or sometimes green. Or a skirt and blouse. With these outfits, I wore nylon stockings, high heels, make-up, perfume, and jewellery. I felt feminine. If my friends from Le Chat Noir had seen me, they would have written me off as bourgeoise and reactionary, but I met my controller in a restaurant in the east end where the regulars of Le Chat Noir never went. There, I could talk and laugh without restraint, without the constant caution I had to maintain most of the time.

I met Louise Lavergne almost daily. She visited me often in Montreal and came with me to spend a week or two in Sainte Anne de la Pérade. I suffered with her when Pierre-Louis Bourret was killed during a robbery at Mascouche.

One afternoon in September, I got a call from Julien Giguère. He informed me of a raid that the FLQ had carried out in the town of Mascouche, seventeen miles from Montreal. A few members of the assault group had broken into the police station, handcuffing and gagging the two people they found there. Others held up the Caisse Populaire and made off with more than $7,000. When they tried to escape, citizens of Mascouche pursued them, shots were exchanged, and Pierre-Louis was critically wounded in the head. The Felquistes abandoned him in a car with the money. He had been taken to hospital where he was now lying in a coma. Julien wanted me to check on the whereabouts of Louise Lavergne and Lisette Poisson. There had been two women in the raid, and since Pierre-Louis was involved, Julien suspected Louise and Lisette of having taken part.

The media had not yet been informed. Julien told me to pretend I was unaware of what had happened. Later in the day I reached Louise, and I said that I had something important to tell her. I asked her to meet me at the Bouvillon Restaurant. When I saw her, I felt certain she knew absolutely nothing about what had happened at Mascouche. She was relaxed and cheerful, and wondered why I had asked her to meet me.

Despite Julien's warning, I told her that I had heard it broadcast on the radio that Pierre-Louis had been wounded during a hold-up.

"I think they said he is in the hospital."

I wanted to spare her the brutal shock of learning from the television that her lover was critically wounded. I also wanted her to know that Pierre-Louis' condition was serious.

She hurried back home and spoke to Pierre-Louis's mother, who confirmed what I had told her. I went to see her later: she was in a nightgown, her hair plastered against her head, pale and sad. All the curtains were drawn. I encouraged her to eat while she listened to the radio, which was now going on at length about the Mascouche robbery and the condition of Pierre-Louis. I phoned the hospital for a report, but at first they refused to tell us anything. When I said that I was Pierre-Louis' sister, calling from outside Quebec, the nurse replied:

"Since you are his sister, I can tell you that he is in a coma, his brain is affected, and we give him at most two or three days to live, perhaps less. He will certainly not regain consciousness."

I kept from Louise the critical condition of her friend.

Pierre-Louis, shot on September 24, died during the night of the 25th. I cried when I heard the news. He was only twenty years old, a college boy, a great dreamer, and a romantic. He thought he had a mission to transform society. He had innocent eyes, long eyelashes, wavy hair. He used to smile a lot, he was sentimental, he would bring Louise an ice cream cone with three scoops. He had rosy cheeks, freckles, and the affable face of a choir boy. And he was dead! This innocent really had the mind of a terrorist. He believed that Quebec lived in a police state, under fascism, that the *Anglais* controlled us all and left us only a pittance. He respected René Lévesque, but thought that the Parti Quebecois would never achieve anything because the solution was not in independence alone, but in a social revolution. How sad it was, this death of a young man destroyed by his romantic naïveté.

When Pierre-Louis was buried, on September 29, his parents had a religious service at the parish church. But Louise did not go, nor did anyone from the FLQ. They feared that the police would be there — with reason, as it turned out. The police photographed everyone going into the church.

I never harmed Pierre-Louis Bourret nor Louise Lavergne, even though we were playing a complex game in which we were on opposite teams. But there is one person whose life I surely changed, and that was Fritz, François Séguin. Without knowing it at the time, I was instrumental in turning Fritz around.

When I first met him, François Séguin had already proven himself as a revolutionary. He had planted bombs. He and Nigel Hamer had stolen two dozen cases of dynamite in September, 1970, shortly before Cross's kidnapping. Later, he had served in a cell supporting the kidnappers. He was one of eight people in the attack on Mascouche. It was he who had cut the telephone lines, isolating the town.

He was highly respected in our milieu; he had a reputation as a serious revolutionary. To me, he seemed more mature than the others in the group. He spoke easily and pleasantly, laughing, telling stories, never speaking of the FLQ. I found him attractive.

One night, several of us were at the La Fontaine de Johannie

Restaurant. Fritz offered to drive us home. He dropped the others off first, and then stopped in front of my door and asked me if he could come in for a cup of coffee. I agreed, with pleasure. We went in, and Fritz sat down. For the first time, he spoke about the FLQ. He told me that Robert Comeau had spread it around that I was a woman cop, but that he, Fritz, did not believe it. The Front had even considered excluding Robert Comeau because he talked too much (as I was well aware!).

While he was talking, Fritz got undressed: his shoes, his socks, his sweater, everything. I found this an odd way to go about it, but I liked him. It was his first time, at the age of 25.

He took a bath the next morning. I was pleased, because there was a certain "air" about him. After him, I went to take a bath myself but the tub was filthy. I had to take a cloth and abrasive powder to it before it recovered its colour. In that respect, Fritz was not exceptional: many of the revolutionaries despised cleanliness and hygiene as bourgeois vices.

In April, 1971, Fritz and Pierre Raby committed a robbery at the Bank of Montreal. They went in and told the clerk that they wanted to buy American Express travellers' cheques. The clerk came back with a batch of blank travellers' cheques; Fritz and Raby grabbed them and ran. Raby was caught by bank employees but Fritz, losing his toque, managed to escape.

Not long afterwards, I was having a beer at La Fontaine de Johannie with Pierre Raby. I wondered at the absence of Fritz, whom I had not seen for several days. Raby confided that Fritz was now in Cornwall, Ontario, on FLQ business.

"You understand that it's better not to talk about it; it concerns the Front."

Of course, I told Julien that Fritz was in Ontario. He checked it out, and discovered that Fritz had cashed American Express travellers' cheques, under the false name of Paradis, in several Ontario cities, including Cornwall. He was in the company of Robert Comeau, and on that trip they slept in Ottawa at the home of Nigel Hamer.

I was never able to find out exactly what happened after that, but I deduced that the police must have convinced Fritz that he should become an informer, under the threat of going to prison with the *Anglais* in Ontario. No doubt, as a good Quebecois revolutionary, he could not face the prospect of spending a few years in an English prison in Cornwall.

What aroused my suspicion was that Julien no longer insisted that I keep close watch on Fritz. I decided to set a trap to see whether Fritz was an informer.

One evening late in 1972, I was at a bar in Old Montreal, the

Imprévu, and I noticed Fritz seated at a table at the back of the room. He beckoned me over and I sat at his table. In a flash, I had an idea. In confidential tones, I asked him:

"Fritz, can you get me a few guns, because I have some friends who want to break out of Saint Vincent de Paul penitentiary. I need at least two revolvers. What do you think?"

He thought it over.

"You know, for the moment we don't have any in the group, but perhaps later."

After I had finished my next report to Germain Tourigny (who had replaced Julien Giguère as my controller in November, 1972), at the Chez Lanni restaurant, he said:

"That's all? Are you sure you haven't forgotten anything?"

At our next meeting, he asked the following question: "Carole, have you heard anything about an escape from Saint Vincent de Paul in the near future?"

That was it! I knew then that Fritz was likely working for the police, because he was the only one who could have passed on the information that I had made up. I learned, when I finally admitted my ruse, that the police had spent hours at Saint Vincent de Paul penitentiary trying to uncover an escape plot. Germain Tourigny was not amused with me.

I never spoke of my suspicions to Fritz or to anyone else. Later on, someone else would publicly accuse him of working as an informer.

CHAPTER 24
Two New Cells

⚜

The fall of 1971 was a very busy time for me. When I try to recall those days and those nights, I see myself moving in a fog of fatigue. I had just started teaching international relations at two colleges and at the Université du Québec à Montréal. But I still carried on my work as a police informer.

In October 1970, Michel Frankland appeared at my place with a new plan. He told me that, at the beginning of the month, he had become acquainted with a businessman ready to finance the FLQ. This man sympathized with the FLQ, according to Michel, and he was in the habit of sending letters with a revolutionary content to the newspapers. He used to sign his messages with the initials L.W.

According to Michel, these initials stood for the English name Lone Wolf. Since I had never heard of this mysterious Lone Wolf, Michel showed me a newspaper with an article about a message from L.W. This man, according to Michel, had already given $20,000 to the FLQ and was ready to contribute more.

I was anxious to meet this unusual businessman. One day Michel drove me to the north end of Montreal. He parked his car in front of a large house with a flagpole on the roof, flying a big *Patriote* flag.

We rang the doorbell and a middle-aged woman opened the door and led us down to the basement rec room. She served us gin and tonic and we waited.

Lone Wolf soon appeared in person, about forty-five years old, thin, and fair-haired. He introduced himself. Michel told me that he was the man who was ready to finance the FLQ. Lone Wolf agreed, but made it clear that before he gave us anything, he required proof that we really were from the FLQ. To this end he suggested that we issue an FLQ communiqué that contained the words: "Thanks to L.W." The man added that he was ready to give us up to $10,000 if we would carry out some ambitious and attention-getting operation. Then he signified his desire to speak alone with Michel, and they went off together briefly. Michel returned with a big smile and announced that Lone Wolf would like to drive me back home, alone. I answered that I was not interested.

On October 28, Michel Frankland took a sheet of FLQ paper and drew up the communiqué required by our businessman. He then tossed the message in a trash can at the corner of Esplanade and Bernard and I called the *Journal de Montréal*. I can't remember whether the newspapers printed the text of our communiqué and its sentence, "Thanks to L.W."

A few days later, Lone Wolf himself appeared at my door. Michel Frankland had given him my address. There he was, all smiles, wearing a short black leather jacket. I let him into the hall, but I soon discovered that the purpose of his visit was more amorous than revolutionary. I showed him the door, and never saw Lone Wolf again.

One or two days later, Michel arranged to meet me and Louise Lavergne at the Cherrier Restaurant, on Saint Denis Street. Waving a hamburger with all the fixings, and greatly pleased with himself, he told us of his plan to hijack a plane. He hoped that Lone Wolf might be impressed enough with this idea to give us $10,000. While eating, he developed his idea. It was a good one, but it had a serious flaw: we didn't know anyone ready to hijack a plane. Michel was the last person to volunteer for a mission that involved the slightest risk. Louise Lavergne wouldn't hear of it. So we would not hijack a plane. Instead, we would simply place a bomb aboard a plane.

Good idea! We would let it be known in what plane the bomb was hidden and how to dismantle it, but only on condition that the federal government deposit $100,000 in the account of Jacques Lanctôt in Cuba. Later, the $100,000 was upped to $200,000. Frankland, close with his own money, allowed himself to be generous with the public purse. Once Jacques Lanctôt or another member of the Liberation Cell had confirmed by radio that they had received the money, we would let the authorities know where to find the bomb.

But who would agree to carry the bomb aboard the plane? How would we get it there? These were daunting difficulties, and when we went our separate ways that night, it was clear that the plan was not entirely worked out.

It was November 7. The next day would be my birthday and I met Julien at the Chez Lanni Restaurant, our usual meeting place. Julien was in great good humour and, to celebrate, he did not want to hear a word about Michel Frankland before dessert. We chatted like two friends over a bottle of Secco-Bertani.

The meal over, Julien took out his black notebook and wrote down Michel's latest scheme.

I still had eight sticks of fake dynamite, and Julien feared that

Frankland would want to use them for his bomb. Michel's plan could have serious consequences, even with fake dynamite. So Julien asks me to give him back the remaining sticks. The next day, I put the dynamite in a suitcase and carried it to No. 17 Police Station.

As we had anticipated, Michel asked me for dynamite. I answered that I had no more left. Michel was disappointed, but he didn't give up his idea. He turned to one of his acquaintances of the moment who had contacts in the underworld.

This contact was a big man, heavyset, with a prominent paunch. He was thirty-seven, but looked older. He wore jeans and a T-shirt and did odd jobs as a painter or a carpenter to earn a living. He also was a pornography salesman, and he supplied Frankland with marijuana.

Michel hoped to get dynamite through him. It was also this man, according to the plan, who was to go to Dorval airport with a dismantled bomb.

The original plan had evolved. Faced with the difficulty of planting a bomb on a plane, Michel had decided that we would plant a dismantled bomb in the airport, along with a communiqué. The communiqué would claim that a bomb was hidden on board a plane, but it would be just a bluff. Michel was convinced that the authorities would not want to take a chance and that they would comply with our conditions.

Michel's acquaintance was supposed to bring us explosives, but he never did. Meanwhile, the police had put both Michel and his contact under surveillance. The team following them was watching for any indication that dynamite had been turned over to Frankland.

One night, Michel confided that we would have to replace his contact because he was unwilling to go to the airport. No problem. He drove me to the home of another candidate for the FLQ who was willing to serve as a replacement. He parked his car on la Terrasse Fleury, in Ahuntsic. Michel then told me that his recruit was a cook at Collège Bois de Boulogne, where Michel taught. Michel went to the door and rang, but there was no answer. We waited in the car and the man finally appeared. He was forty or forty-five, with a moustache and a Vandyke beard. He was of French nationality. I met him under his nom de guerre, Dagobert.

Dagobert climbed into the back of the car. While they talked, Michel drove around the block about thirty times. Dagobert and Michel preferred to speak in the car because they feared the police might have planted a listening device in the cook's apartment. Dagobert wondered how to dress without drawing attention on his trip to the airport. He did not know what kind of a bag he should use to carry the dismantled bomb, nor in which locker he should hide it. This was the cook's first terrorist operation, and he was rather fearful. But Michel, the veteran, had all the answers.

At about eleven o'clock, a police car, its lights flashing, cut in sharply in front of us and stopped. Frankland braked. The police came running out of their car and ordered us to get out of ours. Michel showed them his identification while they searched the car thoroughly. Finding nothing, they drove off, after telling us that a theft has been committed in the neighbourhood. A routine check.

Dagobert and Michel were shaken. They did not believe for a minute the story of the theft. They were convinced that the police had been following them. Dagobert asked to go home immediately, and then Michel drove me home. The next day, I related the incident to Julien and he promised to check on it. There really had been a theft in the neighbourhood, and the police had searched Michel's car simply because he had aroused suspicion by driving around in circles.

The next afternoon, I received a phone call from Michel, telling me that today was the day. I was to go to his office at Collège Bois de Boulogne and take with me all the parts that go into making a bomb (except the dynamite itself) and some FLQ paper. So I put an alarm clock, batteries, wire, an electric detonator, and black tape into a bag. Then I telephoned Julien Giguère.

I explained to Julien that the extortion attempt would take place in the late afternoon. It was understood that I would phone the anti-terrorist section if I saw that Michel had got hold of real explosives.

I dressed and took the Métro. Michel was waiting in his office. He told me that he would simply send a detonator in an envelope with a communiqué, and that Dagobert would carry this to the airport. There was to be no dynamite. While waiting for Dagobert, he put on his gloves and began to write out a communiqué in the usual square letters.

Jalbert Financing Cell
Communiqué Number 1 November 19 1971
In a plane presently in flight, there is a time bomb made up of eight sticks of dynamite (power frac 75%). If the federal government does not transfer $200,000 (two hundred thousand dollars) immediately to the account of Jacques Lanctôt in Cuba it will be responsible for the death of the passengers. If on the other hand, it deposits this amount as indicated we will let you know immediately how to dismantle the bomb. If you act quickly you will save lives, otherwise . . .

As he wrote, Michel's hand tired and he asked me to take over the writing while he dictated the text. So I put on my gloves and continued:

To prove that the $200,000 has been transferred to Cuba, Jacques Lanctôt (or Marc Carbonneau — Yves Langlois — Jacques Cossette-Trudel — Louise Cossette-Trudel) will announce it directly (by telephone) on the air on CKLM. Only then will we tell you how to proceed.

The FLQ is not a "money-maker." We are only taking back the money extorted from Quebecois workers by the political-financial establishment. The FLQ will use this money to advance the cause of the liberation of the Quebec people. The people of Quebec will not be truly free until power is in the hands of the workers.

Vive le FLQ!

Nous vaincrons!

P.S. To be divulged only to the proper authorities. The code of this operation is Z 35. Every telephone message that we will send you will begin by "FLQ Z 35." Otherwise you are dealing with imposters.

Front de Libération du Québec
The Communiqué must be broadcast on the air by CKLM. Otherwise...

Michel was ecstatic. He was particularly proud of that little touch, Z 35.

We put the electronic detonator and the communiqué in an envelope. Then we waited for the arrival of Dagobert.

When he arrived, Frankland gave him the envelope, explained what it contained, and repeated his instructions: once the envelope had been delivered, he was to call certain radio stations, some newspapers, and a few airline companies to tell them that the FLQ had planted a bomb on a plane in flight.

Dagobert went off. We waited in Michel's office. About half an hour later, he turned on the radio and tuned in the stations that Dagobert was to call. Time passed. Michel changed stations constantly, but none interrupted its broadcast to announce the dramatic message of peril in the sky. Michel began to think that Dagobert had not followed his instructions. Finally, he drove me home.

What had happened? According to the police investigation, calls were made that night to radio stations CKLM and CJMS, to the *Journal de Montréal*, to Air Canada and KLM. CKLM received three phone calls altogether, the first at about eight-thirty.

During the evening, airport employees had found the communiqué and notified the airport management. But the police, filled in by Julien Giguère, told the officials that they had every reason to believe that there was no bomb on a plane. The Dorval authorities, however, were reluctant to expose passengers to even the slightest risk, so Staff Sergeant Donald McCleery of the RCMP phoned the force's superintendent in Ottawa. He, in turn, spoke to the senior management at the airport to tell them that the communiqué was not to be taken seriously.

Another plot had come to nothing. There was no suspense, no panic, and no money. Worst of all, there was no publicity! Did Michel Frankland lose heart at the thought that his plan had come to nothing? Not at all! He was soon on to another plot.

Jacques Primeau, the patriot whose bomb had fizzled in the snows of February, told me at the beginning of October that he was creating a new cell and he asked me for dynamite. I refused. I said that I couldn't give dynamite without knowing the others involved and how trustworthy they were. In fact, my reason for refusing was that I wanted to know more about the cell, its members, and their plans. Jacques agreed to put me in touch with a member of his new cell.

One evening shortly after, he asked me to meet him at the Cartier tavern in Old Montreal, where he worked as a bartender and doorman. I went there and knocked at the window at the back, as I had been instructed. Jacques brought me inside the tavern and hid me behind the counter. At that time, women were not admitted into taverns. He handed me some draft beer and told me that one of his recruits was in the room. Jacques went over to speak to him, but the young man answered that he could not meet me that night as he had an appointment. Instead, he gave Jacques a telephone number where I could reach him by asking for Michel.

The next day, I called Michel and he suggested that we meet at the Select Restaurant, at the corner of Saint Denis and Sainte Catherine. He gave me a quick description of himself: he would be wearing a blue and black checkered shirt and glasses.

At the restaurant, he told me his full name: Michel Guay. He confirmed that he wanted to join the FLQ, that he would do anything for the liberation of the Quebec people, and that he was ready to fight to the death. He was a young student of twenty, a bit naïve, full of enthusiasm. At the end of our conversation, he asked me for dynamite. I answered that I couldn't make the decision to give him dynamite without an okay from the other members of our group. I told Michel that he would have to meet them.

The next meeting took place at the Cherrier Restaurant. In addition to Michel Guay and me, Louise Lavergne, Michel Frankland, and Michel's underworld contact were there.

Michel Guay explained once again why he wanted to be in the FLQ: the Quebecois were exploited by the *Anglais*, we had to get rid of the *Anglais*, become independent, and create a socialist state. He added that he knew other young people who shared his ideas and were ready to take action, but he named no names.

He made a good impression on the group. We decided to give FLQ paper to this new cell so that it could announce its formation to the world.

On November 14, Michel Guay came to my apartment. I took out my paper and begin to type what he dictated to me. He named his cell after Michèle Gauthier, a young woman who had died of an asthma attack during a recent demonstration in support of strikers at the newspaper *La Presse*; in the popular mythology, she quickly became a martyr of the working class.

Michel Guay dictated with a seriousness that approached religious solemnity. It was an important moment for him. For the first time, he saw the official paper of the FLQ, which previously he had only seen reproduced in newspapers and on television. He had the sense that he was making his entry into the History of Quebec, into a great movement that would culminate in Humanity's Liberation, as he dictated the communiqué. Here is an extract:

This present communiqué announces the coming activation of our cell. We have decided to act within the Front de Libération du Québec because no other political formation (or grouping) works for the true liberation of the workers . . . the true liberation of Quebec and of Quebeckers will not happen at the level of political independence, as René Lévesque seems to think, but solely when the workers have at last taken power. And that is why we struggle. It is also the reason we are in the FLQ.

Guay then left me to deliver his historic document, and the newspapers faithfully published his birth announcement for the Michèle Gauthier Cell.

At about eight o'clock the next evening, Michel Guay met us again at the Cherrier. We were all seated at a table by the window and, heads together, we talked in hushed voices. What a conspiratorial appearance we must have presented to the other patrons of the restaurant! Now and then a great burst of laughter shook the group. With two clowns like Michel Frankland and Jacques Primeau among us, there was a lot to laugh about.

Guay confided that his group was made up of a few young people as inexperienced as he, and he asked us for help. Alone, they didn't know what to do next. So we decided to provide someone to help them and perhaps, to advise them.

Michel Frankland had asked a friend of his to set up an FLQ network in the junior colleges. She had recruited a tall, loose-jointed young man of nineteen, a student at Collège Ahuntsic, whose name was André Lavallée.

Michel Frankland had the idea of introducing André Lavallée to the Michèle Gauthier Cell. For additional maturity and experience, he recommended Dagobert, the cook who had gone through his revolutionary baptism of fire by carrying the communiqué to Dorval airport.

I was assigned to introduce André Lavallée and Dagobert to Michel Guay. I did not have the phone numbers of the first two, but I made arrangements through Michel Frankland. I brought Michel, André and Dagobert together at Chez Harry's Restaurant on the night of December 2 at about ten o'clock. This restaurant was a meeting place for Felquistes and their sympathizers, for bohemians, drug traffickers, poets, and students.

Michel Guay and André Lavallée fitted right in: they were wearing jeans, windbreakers, checkered shirts, and long hair. But Dagobert was another matter. The cook dressed with care. His moustache and his little beard were trimmed. His trousers might have just come back hot from being pressed. He wore an almond-coloured turtleneck sweater and a fedora decorated with a plucky red feather. His hands were encased in leather gloves.

The two students hit it off immediately and discussed the student life and the revolutionary films they had seen. Dagobert listened, occasionally interrupting their conversation with brief, anxious comments.

"I am ready to help you, but things will have to be well run. I don't like amateurish work."

Over the next couple of days, the Michèle Gauthier Cell shaped up. Michel Guay talked of robbing a Caisse Populaire at one college; at one of our meetings at the Cherrier, he asked us to get him guns and a getaway car. Michel Frankland said he would see what he could do. The next day, Michel turned up at my place with a bottle of chloroform, a pair of handcuffs, and a revolver. He didn't want to keep these things at home in case his wife should find them. He had gotten the handcuffs in a pawn shop, and the chloroform and the revolver had come from Michel's underworld contact. I asked him why he wanted to give the Michèle Gauthier Cell chloroform and handcuffs when they only had in mind a robbery.

"It's for our kidnapping. We might as well get everything at the same time. The handcuffs will be to restrain the hostage until the chloroform has put him to sleep."

Michel left, and I phoned Julien Giguère. He picked me up in his car and I showed him the objects Michel had put in my care. While we were waiting at a red light he examined the revolver.

"It's only a toy, an imitation of a Cobra revolver," he told me. Then he opened the bottle and sniffed.

"The revolver may be fake, but the chloroform is real. I wouldn't advise you to put your nose in it, Poupette, unless you want to fall asleep."

He then looked at the handcuffs. They were in perfect working order.

"What does your crazy Frankland want with all that?" I explained that Michel Frankland was again dreaming of carrying out a kidnapping.

At our meeting that evening at the Cherrier Restaurant, I gave the handcuffs, the chloroform, and the toy gun to Michel Guay, letting him know at the same time that the revolver was not real. Michel Frankland reassured him, saying that it would have exactly the same effect as a real gun.

"True, it's not real. But when you stick a revolver under someone's nose, he does not ask you before he gives you the money whether it's real or fake. In any case, when you rob a bank with a toy gun, the sentence is the same as when you rob with a real revolver. So it makes no difference at all."

Michel Guay was pleased with his acquisitions. But he had an idea. The toy revolver would look more authentic if it contained real .38 calibre bullets. Everyone agreed that that was a good idea and, the next afternoon, Michel Guay and I went to the International Fire Arms store on Bleury Street. He went in, while I kept watch on the sidewalk in case we had been followed by the police.

Michel had a setback. The clerk would not sell him .38 calibre bullets because he did not have a gun permit. Michel came stalking back out, furious.

Now that Michel actually had his equipment, he began to dither. He told us one evening that he had actually gone out to rob a Caisse Populaire, but he had been dissauded from carrying out the robbery by a snowstorm that would have made flight difficult. He finally admitted that his cell was nervous at the thought of holding up a Caisse Populaire as their first robbery attempt. They would prefer to start with something less dangerous.

Suddenly Michel Frankland had an idea. Bingo! Dozens and dozens of parish churches in Montreal organize evenings of bingo to raise money.

"There is money to be made in bingos, and it's not dangerous!" Everyone burst out laughing at the idea of committing a robbery at a bingo. But Frankland persisted, and soon everyone agreed with him. I said that it wouldn't make much of a revolutionary impression to rob poor women who were playing bingo in the basement of their parish church. But the idea had gained adherents. The next day, Michel Frankland and I went off to reconnoitre bingos.

Michel drove his car from church to church while I took notes. We had to check on the evenings when the bingos were held, because the student members of the Michèle Gauthier Cell had lectures to attend on certain nights. We couldn't plan a hold-up for just any time.

We made a second round of the churches to choose our winner. "Carole, take that church off our list, look, it's so shabby. The steeple is not very tall. We're not going to rob that church, it would be a sacrilege!"

Finally we came upon a big stone church adorned with a tall steeple. "What's the name of that church? It looks not bad at all," said Frankland.

It was the Church of Sainte Catherine, at the corner of Amherst and Robin. Frankland was enchanted.

"There's no doubt about it, Carole, this is where the robbery will be. Robin Street! It's a predestined name. Think a moment. Robin Hood, who robs from the rich to give to the poor. That's exactly what the FLQ does!"

Again we all met at the Cherrier. Michel Guay liked our choice.

I notified Julien Giguère of the place where the robbery would take place, though I didn't yet know the date. Julien, through one of his men, warned the parish priest that a robbery might be committed in his church. The good priest was advised to keep as little money as possible in his cash box.

The robbery was finally scheduled for December 7. Michel Guay was under surveillance and the police saw him meet several other people. They were eight altogether, including a young woman.

Under the eye of the police, they went by bus to the Church of Sainte Catherine. For about thirty minutes, they went into the basement of the church and played bingo, then they came out, walked around, went into a restaurant, and returned to the church. But after a short while they came out again. In addition to two policemen in the basement, playing bingo, six detective-sergeants and a surveillance team of twenty were patrolling the area.

Michel Guay, the police noted in their report, "seems nervous."

At last Michel went into the hall where the bingo game was in full swing. He went up to the woman in charge of the cash box, talked to her for a minute, then grabbed the cash box and ran. There was a chase. Guay and the others scattered in different directions. Guay ran to the sidewalk and turned right, sped to a lane, and came out the other end with a policeman at his heels. He ran three blocks north, dropped the box, and continued running. Two of his accomplices were now running with him. They reached the next corner. Guay and one companion ran down the street, looking for a taxi, while the third, André Lavallée, ran across the street, jumped into a taxi, and headed west. A block later he was intercepted by a patrol car and arrested.

Guay and his running mate also found a taxi and headed east. At that moment a policeman fired his revolver in the direction of the taxi, but it kept going. It turned left at the next corner, climbed a hill to Sherbrooke Street and there turned right. A patrol car cut off the taxi, and Michel Guay and his companion were arrested.

They were then taken to the police station and Julien Giguère phoned me at home to say that the robbery was over. In addition to Guay and Lavallée, he told me that two other young men were arrested. Their names meant nothing to me.

In a sense, I felt sorry for these young men. They had been carried away by their dreams of becoming heroes in of what they took to be an historic movement. But I also knew that I had done them a favour. They had been arrested for simple theft. They had not even used the toy revolver that Michel Frankland had got for them, and, because the parish priest had been notified, they had made off with only $31.90. If the police had not warned the priest, they might have stolen several thousand dollars, and the charges against them would have been much more serious. As it was, they were fined $25 each. Their little adventure had cured them for good, and they never again dabbled in terrorism.

As I learned later, they thought that Dagobert had betrayed them to the police. He had not taken part in the theft, for what reason, I do not know. No one suspected me for a moment.

The Michèle Gauthier Cell had come to nothing. Michel Frankland cheered himself up by dreaming up another scheme.

CHAPTER 25
A Robber in a New Light

I saw my robber again, the one who had robbed me on November 12, 1970 to fill the coffers of the FLQ. It happened more than a year later, at Le Bouvillon, a café not far from the University of Montreal, patronized mostly by students. In the middle of the dance floor, a man by himself, stripped to the waist, was dancing. Everyone had gathered around him to watch. He danced very well, and had a fine body, both elegant and athletic. But the more I looked at him, the more familiar he seemed. Intrigued, I looked more closely at his face. Suddenly I recognized him: my robber! Luc Gosselin!

He soon stopped dancing, put his T-shirt back on and returned to his table. I watched him from the corner of my eye. He looked at me as though he, too, recognized me. He got up, came over to my table, and asked me to dance.

"We know each other," he said as we danced.

"Yes, I know we know each other, but I can't remember where we met." I didn't want him to know that I recognized him as my robber.

"Does 1970 mean anything to you?"

"1970? You were a student at the UQAM?"

"Yes, that too. But, more precisely, the fall of 1970? The October Crisis?"

"Oh! Now I remember. My robber!"

He smiled with pleasure. "And you are Carole de Vault, aren't you?"

We were like two friends who met after losing touch.

I had not seen Luc Gosselin since November 16, 1970, the day I testified at his preliminary hearing. He had appeared at the court accompanied by his father. He had worn, that day, a shirt and a tie. There had been nothing threatening about him, nothing about him of the man who had frightened me so much. At the courthouse, he had the look of a young intellectual.

Called as a witness, I acted as though I had never seen the accused before the moment of the theft. I claimed that I was not even absolutely certain that this man was the same one who had robbed me. There was no mention of the FLQ. The Crown prosecutor tried to prove that Gosselin robbed me and that he intended to make off with the bag containing the money of the company rather than a bag containing my personal things. Why would a man armed with a revolver grab a bag with only $12 in it?

The judge was sceptical. If my memory serves, he spoke in these terms to the prosecutor:

"If I understand you properly, you are suggesting that this pretty young woman is the accomplice of the accused. If so, I don't understand, because if they were accomplices, she would have told him to take the company's bag and she would not have let him flee with her personal effects."

Gosselin was sent to trial. As soon as the hearing was over, I went to see Noel Vallerand, as I had agreed to do.

"It's over. They found him guilty," I said to Noel.

"Did they talk about the FLQ?"

"No. The policemen who are conducting the investigation are members of the armed robbery squad."

"Ah! So they think it's an ordinary robbery. That's fine. I'll tell Robert Comeau; he will be pleased."

I was not called on to testify at the trial itself. Robert Comeau was anxious to know what was happening, but he did not want to go to court in case the police made a link between Gosselin and him. Michel Frankland, cautious as always, also refused to attend. Instead, he recruited a young woman to attend the trial and inform him of the results. Unfamiliar with court procedures, she reported back that Gosselin had been found guilty, but she did not hear what sentence he received. In fact, he was fined $50, which his father paid, and sentenced to one day in jail. But he did not even spend the night in jail.

That evening, Michel Frankland arrived at my place with the news. He wanted to let Robert Comeau know about it as quickly as possible, but he did not want to talk openly on the phone, in case his line was tapped. He decided to put the message into a code that Robert Comeau would understand, but not the police. He decided to appeal to Robert's erudition, feeling certain that ignorant cops would not catch his meaning.

Michel came up with a sibylline message. According to him, a reference to the writer Kafka would remind Robert of the novel *The Trial*, and would tell Robert plainly that Michel Frankland was referring to Gosselin's trial. So he wrote on a sheet of paper: "I read Kafka."

He also wanted to let Robert know that Luc had been found guilty. So he wrote "Cicero" to suggest a lawyer. As he was casting about for the name of a trial in which Cicero had been involved, I suggested the Catalinarians, but Michel said they would not do.

"No, no, that's too well known. The police might catch on. Find something else." I suggested the speech against Verres.

"Ah, that's much better. The police will never get it."

A reference to Cicero and his prosecution of Verres surely ought to put Robert on the right track. So he wrote: "Cicero did not succeed as well as against Verres." Now Robert would understand that Luc Gosselin had been found guilty.

The third sentence must tell Robert that the police had made no link between the robbery and the FLQ. He decided to allude to the Jacques, those French peasants of the Middle Ages who revolted against the nobility for more bread. Robert Comeau would surely make the connection between the Jacques and the Felquistes. Then he chose Zeus as a code name for the authorities. He wrote his third sentence: "The Jacques can continue to till their fields, for Zeus has not seen them." Michel was about to use my phone, but I insisted that he call from a public booth in case the police had taps on my line. His message, in my opinion, was ridiculous. What could Robert possibly make of such gibberish? But Michel was confident. "Robert Comeau is cultured, he is a man of letters. He will understand."

Off he went to phone, while I burst out laughing. As soon as he reached Robert on the line, he read off his message without a pause: "I read Kafka. Cicero did not succeed as well as against Verres. The Jacques can continue to till their fields, for Zeus has not seen them." Then he hung up. And he came back, a smile of satisfaction on his face, convinced that the learned Robert had understood the coded message.

When I next saw Robert Comeau, he was highly indignant. He had decided that Michel Frankland must be a police informer. Michel, he said, had phoned him and rattled off a coded message that he could make neither head nor tail of, something about Kafka.

"If the police are listening in on my line, they will certainly be convinced that I have something to hide, since I receive messages in code."

Now, a year later, I was meeting my robber, Luc Gosselin, in circumstances altogether different. He was handsome and I immediately felt strongly attracted to him.

After we danced, I left Le Bouvillon. About a week later, I met him again, in the Métro. This time he suggested a date and I accepted. As a woman, I found him very sexy, and as Poupette the police informer, I was curious to know what he was up to.

We met more frequently. Luc adored the cinema. He could see a film every day and never tire of movies. He took me to a Charlie Chaplin festival, and to a Luis Buñuel film. We went dancing. He was a physical fitness nut and went to a centre where he ran and lifted weights.

Sometimes I went with him at lunch time for an hour of jogging at the Centre culturel et sportif, but I couldn't keep up with him. While he exercised with weights, I would have a swim.

He didn't drink alcohol, coffee, tea, or soft drinks. He did not smoke and he would not eat pork. He did not have a single hair on his chest, his arms, or his legs. He explained one day that it was a matter of cleanliness and that he was imitating the Japanese, who remove hair from their body. His face and skin were so perfectly smooth that at first I had thought it was a matter of glands. But no! It was a triumph of science over nature. He must have applied a bottle or two of NEET a week, to judge by the smoothness of his skin. He took a shower twice a day.

Luc, like many in the FLQ, worked only now and then. For the moment, he was the superintendent in an apartment building in Rosemont, which left him a lot of free time to pursue his interests. Sometimes he registered for a course but he always gave it up at the end of a month or two.

He did not seem obsessed with politics as Robert Comeau was. One day he told me that for him, the ideal society was that of the Scandinavian countries — a strange choice for a revolutionary. But he loved firearms and physical exercise. When the police had searched his apartment after his arrest in November 1970, they had found a .38 calibre I.N.A. revolver loaded with five bullets, and a 7.65 calibre Beretta pistol loaded with eight bullets. In a bag, they had found more bullets and permits to carry two different Lugers and a Smith and Wesson. He told me that he enjoyed target shooting.

Luc was an agreeable companion and a charming man. We were lovers, briefly, but soon we became just good friends. He often came to my apartment, where Louise Boucher, who had helped Michel Frankland and me prepare to challenge the election results in Ahuntsic, often stayed with me. She quickly fell madly in love with him. Then we often went out as a foursome, Luc, Louise, his friend Jacques, and I.

One evening in 1974, I was alone at the restaurant called Da Giovanni, which was near a club for transvestites, Sous les Ponts de Paris. Sometimes the clientele from the club came to eat at Da Giovanni.

At a table in front of me I saw a woman whose face was familiar. She had brown hair in an Afro hair style, and wore jeans and a white and blue blouse. She noticed me and quickly looked away.

I was reading as I ate, but my eyes kept going back to the woman: who was she? I had certainly met her, but where? She got up, took her handbag, and walked away. Instantly I recognized her: Luc Gosselin! I was thunderstruck. What did it mean? Was I seeing things?

Not long afterwards, Luc called. He invited me to a movie with his friend Jacques. Not a word about Da Giovanni. The three of us watched the film, and then Luc found some reason for going off. I was alone with Jacques, who invited me to a restaurant where he said, with some embarrassment, that there was something he had to tell me about Luc. With many pauses and false starts, he finally came to the point. Luc was a transvestite and he had asked Jacques to tell me, and he wanted me to tell Louise!

At first I was unable to. She loved him; I didn't have the courage to hurt her. I kept silent for a week, ten days. How could I tell her in the morning when she was rushing off to work? And at night, she seemed so tired.

One Saturday morning I prepared a lavish breakfast that I carried to her on a tray. I woke her up. She smiled at the sight of the tray. When breakfast was over I brought up the subject in a roundabout way.

I spoke first of the Japanese and their cleanliness. Then I moved on to Luc. Two showers a day. Not a hair on his body. Then I discoursed on the properties of NEET. Her mouth dropped. She hadn't realized.

At last I mentioned the women I had met at Da Giovanni, who had an Afro hair style. She would never guess who it was.

"No, no. Who was it?"

"Luc."

She asked me to bring over the bottle of gin that was on the table at the foot of her bed. At first she put some in her coffee, then she drank it straight.

Was her heart broken? Perhaps for a few hours. But I thought that the shock would save her from greater pain later on. It all seemed so absurd, as funny as it was painful.

Luc might be an unusual case, but he was far from the only FLQ member with out of the ordinary sexual tendencies. An impressive number of Felquistes were homosexual or bisexual. Many were impotent.

I was inclined to believe that, for many of them, guns and dynamite were a form of sexual expression, a sign of virility.

CHAPTER 26
The Second Front
———————————— ✤ ————————————

In all the annals of Quebec there has never been mention of the terrorist movement known as the Front National — the FN. I hereby reveal its existence for the first time. For the originality of its conception, the daring of its recruitment, the scale of the human resources it attempted to mobilize, the Front National surely deserves to be remembered for as long as people talk about Michel Frankland. For he was its father.

Towards the end of December 1971, Michel Frankland rang my doorbell. He was smiling and proud of himself, for he had in mind a great project.

"Come on, we'll talk about it in the car. Are you free for the whole evening?"

As we were driving along, Michel explained that he had founded, with one of his friends, a new movement which would replace the FLQ.

"You know, the FLQ is finished; the police know all its members. It is time to think of something else."

He parked his car on Jeanne Mance Street, rang a doorbell and soon came back with his friend. The friend was quite young, tall, and had short brown hair parted on the right side. He mumbled. He introduced himself as Pierre. I later learned that he was a former soldier in the Canadian army.

We went to Michel's house, said hello in passing to his wife, who was watching television, and went down into the basement where Michel had an office. Before going into his office Michel put a record on the turntable: it was a fiddler playing Quebec folk songs. He explained to us that this record would scramble listening devices if the police were bugging us. All the time we were there, Michel played the same side of the same record over and over again. I don't know why, but he attributed to it remarkable powers for disturbing the air waves. How many times I was to hear that same record in the months to come!

Michel then unscrewed a panel at the back of his stereo cabinet and pulled out a sheaf of paper.

"You will soon understand!"

He beamed as he screwed the panel back into place. He locked the door of his office and turned to me.

"Carole, Quebec needs us. Pierre and I are planning to create a new movement. The FLQ is too well known, its members all know each other, and that is why the police have always been able to arrest them. I have thought for nights on end about this new revolutionary movement. I'm so proud of it. Then I talked about it to Pierre and he immediately agreed to be part of it. *Voilà*, Carole, we three will be responsible for the new movement, which will be called the Front National — the FN."

He began to unfold his plan. The FN would be structured in such a way that only the three of us would know the identity of its members. They would work in small, decentralized cells. The members would only know each other by their code names. The cells would not be in contact with each other.

Oh, marvel of imagination and of security! Michel had prepared a letter that we would mail to a large number of people likely to be interested in a clandestine and revolutionary movement. The letter would explain the nature of the movement, and would invite the recipient to join it. Enclosed with the letter would be a questionnaire. The fortunate one selected must choose one of nine possible answers. If he chose one, it meant he utterly refused to be part of the FN. If he chose nine, he agreed to join without qualification, and was willing to take part in terrorist activities such as bombings and armed robberies. Between two and eight, the nominee accepted, but with restrictions.

The FN began with a vast recruiting campaign. Its members would be much more numerous than those of the defunct FLQ. And there would be room for different levels of commitment.

But how could we arrange to receive the answers to all these invitations without revealing our own identities? Frankland had found a way. Each recruit would be assigned a code name, which would appear on the letter he was to receive.

We would keep a list of the names, addresses, and telephone numbers of each, as well as the code names. In the letter, we would advise the prospective recruit that we would phone for his answer, and that he was to answer by a number from one to nine. The recruit would recognize our call because we would identify ourselves on the phone by his or her code name.

It was brilliant! Michel tapped his head without undue modesty. Who else could have thought of it?

Michel continued to elaborate his plan. We would recruit our members from all regions of Quebec. In each region, someone would be named regional commander, with lieutenants who were specialists in dynamite, in guns, in robberies, in transportation, who were lawyers, doctors, journalists, and engineers. All of this would be shored up, of course, by a vast support network. Why, a whole clandestine army was rising up at our instigation.

A tactical problem: where would we find code names for each of the hundreds of invitations that we intended to send out? At first, we chose our names from the history of Quebec and its literature. One recruit was named Jacques Cartier, another Alexis Labranche, and so on. But soon we were running short of names and we were afraid of inadvertently using the same name twice.

Michel, the former Jesuit, had a stroke of genius. We would give our candidates the names of the characters and chapters of the Bible. And God knows, they are many!

We sent a letter to the lawyer Robert Lemieux, assigning to him the code name Baruch. As for Michel Leclaire, lawyer for several Felquistes including Jacques Primeau, he would be called Lamentations. The left-wing journalist Nick auf der Maur would be known as Jeremiah and my robber and friend, Luc Gosselin, as Job!

The Front National, on paper at least, began to take shape. And it was no small undertaking: almost every evening we met in Michel's basement. Each time, the same fiddle music foiled the police. Behind the panel of his FM cabinet, Michel hid the impressive lists of the FN and our war manual: the Bible. Each time that we assigned a figure from the Old Testament to the potential revolutionary, Michel ticked off the name in the index of his Bible.

We needed recruits, recruits, and more recruits! Michel studied the calendar of Collège Bois de Boulogne, and picked out the names of the students and professors who seemed to him ripe for the FN. A professor of mathematics became Proverbs, but unfortunately he answered one, a refusal. Another professor was baptised Psalms. Despite his beautiful name he vacillated, and finally said no.

It was my turn to submit names for the FN. I ran through everyone I knew in the FLQ and their sympathizers, with the exception of my suspicious ex-friend Robert Comeau.

Michel Guay, the veteran of the great bingo raid, received the name of Genesis. Jogues Sauriol, investigated in the armed robbery of the Caisse Populaire at Mascouche, was conscripted under the name of Nahum. Before giving us his answer, he asked to meet one of us.

It was against FN regulations, but because Nahum seemed like a promising recruit for the FN, we delegated Pierre, the ex-soldier, to meet him in a bar. Bastien emerged after a few minutes, pale and trembling. Nahum had threatened him, filling him with fear.

"Oh, he's a real tough customer! That guy is dangerous. He said that if we ever move in on the FLQ's territory, they will fix us good," he reported.

Out of caution, the eighth level of the FN — that is, the three of us — excluded Jogues Sauriol from our list of recruits. That would teach him to threaten the FN! Each evening we had to prepare about thirty letters of invitation. Then we had to mail them. This was no simple matter, because Michel thought it dangerous to put several letters from the FN in the same postal box. It could alert the police. So we had to drive around Montreal from letter box to letter box, dropping two or three in each.

After a few weeks, the time came to telephone for the answers of our prospects. This was Phase II in the building of the FN. As a security measure, we telephoned from public booths, but in case the police should be on the watch, we could make no more than one call from each booth. Michel sent us on a tour of the city.

Here is an example of one of our calls. Michel or Pierre, I forget which, dialed the number of Luc Gosselin and asked to speak to Luc. When he came to the phone, the FN representative said:

"Hello, is this Job speaking?"

"Yes, this is Job."

"Your answer?"

"Nine."

"Fine. We will soon be calling you again."

Once back in Michel's car, we wrote down the answer in our records. Luc Gosselin had accepted without reservation. We decided that he should be named commander of a district of Montreal, Section 8G, which included everything south of Metropolitan Boulevard, between Pie IX and Saint Laurent. We had the whole province of Quebec divided into regions and sub-divided into districts.

We soon had an unmanageable number of calls to make for the answers to our hundreds of invitations. Our lists lengthened. Someone, I have forgotten who, gave us a list of garage operators in the Eastern Townships, and each garage man received an invitation. After all, the revolution would need wheels. Michel got from a Jesuit friend a list of the parish priests in the Gaspé and, convinced that the Gaspé *curés* were ripe for revolution, sent each of them an invitation.

But how would we phone so many people? We needed reinforcements. Michel decided to create the additional rank of telephone caller. He chose them from among the *princesses* he knew who had accepted an invitation to join the FN. I called one and asked her to meet me at the Real Steak House, at the corner of Millen and Henri Bourassa. Since we did not know each other, I described my wool beret: I had crocheted it myself in yellow, orange, red, blue, violet, pink, and lilac. I am sure there was not another beret like it in all of Montreal. We met, and I explained the procedure for calling the recruits. She accepted the job. We soon had four or five telephone callers at work. I would meet them, give them a list of names to call, and meet them again a week later to collect their names and answers.

At last I told Michel that these meetings were taking up too much time and causing unnecessary risks. The police might follow me, see me meeting these women, and become suspicious. I suggested that we phone them from one phone booth to another; they would give us the number of a booth where we could catch them at a stated time. And that is what we did.

The structure of the FN was becoming more and more complex. Michel had established eight levels, according to the degree of responsibility. The three of us made up the eighth level; the seventh was made up of professionals such as lawyers, doctors, journalists, or engineers. But one night, Michel had a new idea: we should create a ninth level, a Council of Sages. Those called to the ninth level would be people of intelligence and experience. They would advise us. They would be the FN's brain.

Frankland suggested a few candidates for the Council of Sages. He proposed Noel Vallerand, Gérald Godin and the Jesuit friend who had given Michel the list of Gaspé parish priests. Godin, I remember, refused. I don't recall the answer of the other two.

Michel also designed an emblem for the Front National: two flags crossed, the fleur-de-lys of Quebec and the flag of the *Patriotes*. He had an FN stamp made, which he gave to his Jesuit friend for safekeeping.

Michel looked to the future. He started digging a tunnel in his basement, under the bar. He removed a board of the bar, broke open the floor and dug. After the day's digging, he would put the board back into place so that nothing would show. Above all he didn't want his wife, Jeannine, to know that he was digging a tunnel; she might not like to have a hole in her fine finished basement.

The tunnel was to run under his house and emerge in a wooded vacant lot next to his property. Frankland even proposed to buy the vacant lot so that no one would come along and build a house on top of his tunnel. But, in fact, the tunnel never advanced very far. Michel preferred to conceive rather than to execute great works.

Meanwhile, in November 1972, I had changed controller. Julien Giguère left the anti-terrorist section for homocide. I regretted his departure. We had worked so long and so well together, and we shared so many memories! My new controller was Detective-Sergeant

Germain Tourigny. At first I was ill-at-ease with him and even considered putting an end to my work as an informer. But Germain slowly succeeded in winning my confidence.

He kept the RCMP informed of developments in the FN, and the federal force became alarmed at this new terrorist movement springing up with hundreds of members. One of the officers of the RCMP even suggested asking once again for the War Measures Act to put an end to the FN.

Germain then decided that the FN movement which had had its beginning more than a year before, had gone far enough. His plan was to conduct raids in strategic quarters to frighten off the organizers of the FN.

One day, he told me that a raid would be conducted at my place the following morning. So I invited my friend and sometime roommate, Louise, to spend the night with me. I wanted witnesses. I was at this time living in an apartment with France Lafond, a woman I had met in the Parti Quebecois, and her brother Réjean. France was away, but the three of us, Louise, Réjean and I, played cards until four o'clock in the morning. Then we went to bed. I was the only one who knew the awakening would be brutal.

The doorbell rang, and rang again. Louise, half asleep, stretched out her hand towards my alarm clock and pressed the button to stop the ringing.

"Carole, your alarm clock is broken. I pressed on the button and it's still ringing."

Now we heard knocking on the door. It became more insistent. Réjean thought it was France coming home. From his bed, he called out:

"France, take out your keys, I am in bed!"

The knocking continued. Réjean, draped in a blanket, went to the door. From my bed I heard a loud voice:

"Police! This is a search! You'll have to excuse us, Miss!"

They had taken Réjean for a girl, because he had shoulder-length fair hair. Réjean dropped his blanket and the police realized their mistake.

"Oh! Pardon me, sir!"

I jostled Louise to wake her up.

"Louise, get up, it's not the alarm clock, it's the police. There is a search."

She opened her eyes wide: "The police?"

I saw a tall man in civilian clothes in the doorway. "Good morning, girls. Get up, please. This is a search."

It was Germain Tourigny. I had to pinch myself to keep from laughing. Louise spoke to him.

"Sir, could you go away so I can put on my dressing gown?"

"No, Miss, I am not allowed to leave you. But I will turn my back, so be quick."

Another policeman came into the room. Louise asked him what he was looking for, and whether he had a search warrant.

He went to get the warrant from another policeman who was in the kitchen. There were seven of them altogether, including one from the RCMP and one or two from the provincial police. One of them came back with the search warrant, and Louise and I looked at it. They were looking for explosives, guns, munitions, and literature inciting people to violence. We assured them that there was nothing like that in the apartment.

Louise, polite or half-asleep, asked them:

"Do you want some coffee? Since we have to have you with us, we might just as well have coffee together."

She went to the kitchen, leaving me alone with Germain. From behind the door he gave me a big smile, bringing his finger up to his lips.

Soon Louise came back with the coffee. Germain, in a very serious tone of voice, asked us for our identification papers, our occupation, the names of our parents and their addresses and telephone numbers.

He asked me my name.

"Carole de Vault."

"So you are Carole de Vault. We know a lot about you!"

He tried to open my filing cabinet, but it was locked. "Open the filing cabinet, please!" he told me in a commanding voice. He searched the cabinet. He pulled out a list of names.

"What is this?" he asked me.

"That's the list of my students."

He really did have the list of my students. I had told him ahead of time where he would find the list of the FN members, but he had pulled out the wrong list.

"Your students! You mean to tell me that François Séguin is one of your students?" He pretended to have found the list for the FN.

"No, he is one of my friends."

"Yeah, a friend that we have also heard about."

And he took with him the list of my students. He stared at us intently.

"Do you know anything about the FN?"

Louise stared back at him. "The what?"

"The FN. The Front National. A group like the FLQ that recruits by letter. You are certain that you know nothing about the FN?"

I entered into the game. "No, I don't know anything about the

FN, your Front National, as you call it. If that is what you are looking for, I wonder why you came here? There is no one from your Front National here."

"I'm not so sure. We have information to the contrary."

We heard an outbreak of laughing from France's room. A policeman called out: "Hey, you guys! Come and see this!"

They all went to France's room. A policeman was laughing and reading out loud from France's diary. She had a habit of confiding her sexual escapades to her diary in explicit detail and of exercising her artistic talents by drawing what she most liked about her lovers. The policemen passed the diary from hand to hand. Réjean came forward, saying indignantly, "That's my sister's diary. You don't have the right to read that!"

They stayed on for an hour or two, searching everywhere; in the clothes closets, in the refrigerator, under the beds, under the mattresses. They questioned us, returning often to the Front National, about which, of course, the other two knew absolutely nothing. Finally, they left, taking with them the list of my students and some notebooks belonging to Réjean. We would have to go and get them at the police station a few days later.

France was back by suppertime and Louise came over after work. Louise told France everything that had happened.

"Yes, they were looking for the FN, the Front National. Isn't that right, Réjean?"

I phoned Michel Frankland and invited him to come by. He listened to our detailed accounts of the police search. Michel then drove me over to the home of our co-conspirator, Pierre, and we held a council of war. I explained that the police had made off with a list of the members of the FN, but that there was nothing on the sheets of paper to link the names to the movement.

After discussion, we agreed that it would be better not to do anything related to the FN for some time. It was, in fact, the end of the FN. There would be no more meetings, no more letters or coded telephone calls. The fiddle record went into retirement. The garage operators and the parish priests would never be mobilized. No War Measures Act. The Front National passed into history.

CHAPTER 27
Jacques Primeau

⚜

On the first of February 1972, I received a call from Jacques Primeau.
"Rachel, this is it, they've got me!" Rachel was one of my code
names.
"Who?"
"The police."
"Where are you?"
"At Parthenais."
He was calling me from the headquarters of the provincial police.
If I had been a real Felquiste, he could have finished me. He asked
me to get him a lawyer. I went to the office of Michel Leclaire, a
lawyer who often acted for Felquistes and told him about Jacques
Primeau's call. He telephoned the Crown prosecutor to find out
what charges had been laid against Jacques. They were serious:
making a bomb, conspiracy to plant a bomb, planting a bomb,
inciting to commit a criminal act, and others.

Jacques Primeau pleaded guilty. On March 10, he was sentenced
to two years imprisonment for planting a bomb, to one year for
making a bomb, and to six months for falsifying drivers' licences.
During the next two years, I went every two weeks to visit him at
the federal Saint Vincent de Paul penitentiary on the Island of Laval.
He was now one of the authentic martyrs of the FLQ.

What kind of a person was Jacques Primeau? He was rather an
unusual character. He gave an impression of quickness and intelligence. He had charm and affability. He had no job, and no fixed
address, preferring to crash a few days with one person, a few days
with another. He carried in a brown briefcase all his wealth: two
pairs of woolen socks, two or three creased shirts, gloves, a pair of
shoelaces, and scripts for a theatre course.

For he was an incurable ham. At our first meeting, when he had
asked me to get him some dynamite, he told me that it was he who
had planted the bomb at the Ministry of National Defence that had
killed a woman. He said that he had taken part in the kidnapping
of Cross. He had held up a tavern with a member of the Viger Cell.

"He is the arms, I am the brain."

I didn't believe one word of it.

One day he arrived at my door and took off his khaki jacket rolled up the sleeve of his shirt, and showed me his arm with a theatrical gesture:

"Look, look at what a man can do when he is abandoned by the woman he loves!"

I looked at his arm, which was bleeding from the wrist to the shoulder. "What happened to you?"

"Jacqueline left me! I tried to kill myself!"

He had nicked his arm all over. There were no cuts on veins or arteries, but fifteen or twenty jabs with a penknife into the flesh of his arm. I sat him on a chair and told him to take off his shirt.

"Come, Jacques, you can't just leave your arm like that, it will get infected."

I had neither peroxide nor iodine. I found a bottle of rubbing alcohol, which was better than nothing. I took out some absorbent cotton and soaked it with alcohol. I asked him not to scream so that he wouldn't disturb the neighbours.

"No, no, I won't scream. In any case, I just don't have the strength. After what Jacqueline did, I want to die."

But his strength returned with the first application of alcohol. What roars of anguish! I finished the first aid, then I went to take a bath. Jacques, perhaps revived by the alcohol treatment, asked me if I had anything to eat. Yes, in my fridge there were eleven eggs, bread, and beer. By the time I had taken my bath, he had cooked and eaten all my eggs, finished off my bread, and drunk all the beer.

Soon he had a relapse while staying with an acquaintance, Serge Gagnon. From the bathroom, he called out:

"Serge, do you have razor blades?"

Gagnon told him where he could find some in the medicine cabinet. When he went into his bathroom, he found Jacques inert, and there were a few drops of blood in the tub.

"Primeau, are you dead?"

He administered a few slaps that brought around the unhappy lover.

There was a third attempt. One afternoon I met him at the corner of Saint Denis and Sherbrooke, and he told me that he was going to see a doctor. I accompanied him. He came out with some prescriptions. At the drugstore, he bought a vial containing twenty-four Valiums and another containing twenty-four big red pills. Then and there he swallowed three or four Valiums and as many red pills. About suppertime, we met Louise Lavergne and Serge Gagnon. Primeau continued to take his pills. No one wanted to take him in any more. We dropped by the apartment of one of my friends, Myroslav. We asked Myroslav to keep Jacques while we went to Le Chat Noir.

"You know, Myro, he has taken pills; we want to go out, but we don't want to drag him with us."

"I don't mind keeping him, as long as he doesn't bother me, because tonight I have to fill in an application for a scholarship."

At Le Chat Noir, we met some friends and began to talk about Jacques Primeau. Each could relate a tall tale that he had told.

He claimed, for example, that he had brought back from a trip to Paraguay poison darts dipped in curare. During the October Crisis, with a blow-pipe, he had blown his darts into soldiers' behinds. They had died instantly.

What's more, he had fired on the traffic lights with a rifle to confuse the army in its movements. He had also found a way to poison the water supply leading to the army barracks and the police stations.

He had fought in the Congo. He had gone on to Brazil, where he had met the great German mercenary, Schultz. Schultz, in turn, had taken Primeau to Uruguay where he introduced him to the Tupamaros. Jacques Primeau had learned a lot from those guerillas.

But Serge Gagnon topped everyone else's story. Jacques, sitting at a table in Le Chat Noir with him, had begun to discuss his sexual prowess.

"You know, Serge, I am good with a woman, I can keep her going five hours, six hours. I can do that, but you know, I only have one?"

"One what?"

"Well, a ball, I only have one."

"From birth?"

"No, not from birth. I was the star dancer for the folk dance troupe, Les Feux Follets, and one day we went on tour in northern Yugoslavia. The Feux Follets were learning a native dance that they were going to include in their performance. That day, we were learning a Serbo-Croatian dance. I speak Serbo-Croate, you know. We were practising in national costumes, with boots on. Some Yugoslav dancers were teaching us the dance and they were with us dancing on the stage. I was dancing, and at one point a Serbo-Croatian dancer held a scimitar in his hand and, while dancing, he swung his scimitar with his hand, and then, well, he cut it off!"

"He cut what off?"

"He cut it off!"

Serge Gagnon continued his story. The very night that he had told Serge this story, Jacques Primeau was lying down in his room, covered only by a sheet. Gagnon came over and yanked off the sheet.

"It's not true, Primeau, you have two!"

I was worried about how Primeau was faring at Myroslav's. I decided to telephone Myro.

"How is Primeau?"

"I don't know. I laid him out on the sofa in the next room. The two bottles are empty. He isn't talking, he isn't moving. I am filling in my scholarship application and he is not disturbing me."

Alarmed, we telephoned the Pharmacie Montréal, and we told the druggist what Primeau had swallowed. He told us it could be serious, because the big red pills caused the blood to coagulate.

"You should take him to the hospital. Twenty-four pills, in such a short time, could kill him."

We called Myroslav to tell him of the seriousness of the situation. "Myro, he could die!"

"Let him die, if he wants to. I'm filling in my application. You brought him here. I'm not bothering with him."

I proposed that we go in a taxi for Jacques. We found him motionless. We lifted him up to take him to the hospital. His arms were stiff, and when we tried to raise one, it shot up as though on a spring. Soon both arms were stiff, stretched out in the form of a cross. It was not easy to work him into the taxi.

At the hospital, they put tubes in him to pump out his stomach. A psychiatrist came up to us and asked, "Could you tell me about him?" Oh, yes. We had a lot to tell!

To get over his heartbreak with Jacqueline, Jacques began to go out with a school principal from the Laurentians, a very serious woman who was powerfully impressed by the star dancer of Les Feux Follets. She hired him to instruct her students in dance and theatre. She helped him to buy a car by endorsing a loan of $4,800. But soon, according to the woman, Jacques told the students that he and the principal made love.

On January 26, 1972, Jacques had an accident on the Laurentian Autoroute. The car was totalled. Here is what Julien Giguère told me about what happened next.

"The crazy fool, the damned mental case, had an accident on the Laurentian Autoroute. He lost control of his car and rolled into the field. The provincial police arrived and they found counterfeit drivers' licences in the car. I sent my men. While they were bringing him back to Montreal, they asked him: 'Now, sir, would you explain the meaning of those fraudulent papers?' Primeau looked at them and announced: 'I will tell you everything. It's true, I am the head of the FLQ.'"

So, it was Jacques Primeau himself who confessed to planting the bomb at the post office on February 20, 1971. The police just couldn't shut him up.

CHAPTER 28
Daniel Waterlot

——————————— �֍ ———————————

What an intriguing character Daniel Waterlot was! I was never able to discover the secret of this former policeman who became a Communist leader. Did he work for the KGB? For the CIA? Even today I can't answer these questions. He disappeared after offering me money to spy on the Parti Quebecois.

It was during the summer of 1971 that I saw him for the first time. I was seated on the terrace of Le Chat Noir with a friend, when a stranger came by. My friend introduced him to me as Daniel Waterlot. The name was familiar. Waterlot had been one of the organizers of the demonstration to make a French-language university out of McGill.

I studied his features, in case I should meet him again. He was rather handsome, with short brown hair, blue eyes, and an athletic build. He must have been about thirty, clean-shaven, no glasses. He wore jeans, a sweater, and Adidas.

The conversation turned to Quebec's language conflicts. My friend, who was to be seen in the front lines of every demonstration carrying a flag or a banner, reproached Waterlot for not having demonstrated during the confrontations in Saint Léonard. Daniel replied that those conflicts were bourgeois quarrels, reactionary because they divided the working class rather than uniting it as Marxism proposed.

"You are traitors to the people with your demands for French in Quebec, you act like counter-revolutionaries. I will never support those demonstrations and conflicts over language. You are patsies for the capitalists."

It was almost a year until I saw Waterlot again. In the spring of 1972, the Parti Quebecois held the closing event of that year's fundraising campaign at the Montreal Forum. It was a large gathering. Péquistes came from all parts of the island. As I got on the Métro at Sherbrooke, on my way to this event, I saw Daniel Waterlot, alone. He looked at me intently. Did he recognize me? At Berri-Demontigny station I changed trains, followed by Waterlot. At Atwater I got off and went into the Forum, with Waterlot behind me.

The meeting hadn't started yet, and people were walking around, greeting their acquaintances and buying a beer. Waterlot came over and offered me a beer, which I accepted. He said that he had noticed me on the Métro. I didn't reveal that I had noticed him, too, nor that I had met him the year before: he might think that my memory was too good and that I might have my reasons.

As we were talking, standing side by side, Jacques Parizeau passed in front of us. I greeted him, and he greeted me, but so coldly! I followed his glance down at my pants, my almost military-green uniform with a military belt. This outfit had been given to me by a friend who assured me it was the garb of the Fedayin. The uniform must have put off Parizeau. His lips curled as he looked at Daniel's jeans and T-shirt.

I explained to Daniel that I had worked for the PQ in Ahuntsic riding and that I had met Parizeau there. He asked me if I was really convinced by the PQ's arguments. I answered that I had once been an unconditional Péquiste, but was now less and less in agreement with some of their positions. I knew that Waterlot was active in the Parti Communiste du Québec (Marxiste-Léniniste) (PCQML). The fact was that Poupette wanted to get closer to him.

When the evening's program was over, Daniel asked me in what part of the city I lived. I told him at the corner of Saint Urbain and Pine Avenue.

"Perfect, I live at Pine and Laval. If you wish, we can finish off the evening with some friends who live across from me. They are people from Le Jazz Libre du Québec."

We visited his friends, musicians, who lived in a kind of commune. It was obvious that they, too, were in sympathy with the PCQML. Daniel summarized the PQ's meeting for them:

"What bourgeois! The PQ's coming to power will change nothing for the working class; it will be exploited by the French-Canadian bourgeoisie instead of by the English bourgeoisie."

When the evening was over, Daniel walked me to my door and went home. He came over the next day and invited me for a cup of coffee in a restaurant. I remember that I had a cup in one hand and the other rested on the table. Daniel took my hand and asked me if I had a man in my life. I said no. He told me that he was divorced, had a son, and that there was no woman in his life.

"I find you very beautiful, we could go out together and it might work out between us, you never know . . ."

I found him very pleasant company. As had happened before, I was attracted by a man who interested me both as a woman and as an informer. So we started going out together.

He took me to meetings of the PCQML, which were held in schools or in halls that the Confederation of National Trade Unions put at their disposal. They reminded me a little of my experiences at the convent.

The evening always began with the Internationale, the right arm raised to eye level as if for the Nazi salute, but with the fist clenched. There were usually about fifty members present, most of them English-speaking, many of whom came from Ontario. We always sang the Internationale:

Arise ye wretched of the earth . . .
This is the final battle
Let us unite and tomorrow
The International
Will be all mankind.

The song ended with all fists raised, every throat shouting: "Long live the great leader of us all, Comrade Mao Tse-tung!"

At the time, we were living through the Vietnam war, and the speakers on the platform praised the magnificent popular struggle against South Vietnamese capitalism and American imperialism. We heard of the heroic victories of the Viet Cong; with our fists in the air, we cried out in chorus, "Long live our great comrade, Ho Chi Minh!"

Then the speakers turned to Quebec. We had to carry out the education of the people, not just in our workplaces but also on the street. The decision was made that teams of two would go from door to door every weekday in the Hochelaga-Maisonneuve working-class district.

I entered into the spirit of the thing. Not only had I got close to Daniel Waterlot, but he had moved in almost permanently with me. He still kept his little room on Laval Street, but he was almost never there, except during the day when I gave my lectures at the Université du Québec à Montréal.

Julien Giguère encouraged me. He was curious about the PCQML and about Daniel Waterlot.

"Where do they pick up all the money they spend? They are financed to the tune of thousands of dollars, but by whom? By what power? China? The USSR? One thing is certain, they are financed from abroad. No one in Canada would give them such large amounts of money."

He wanted to know who, exactly, Daniel Waterlot was. I asked him why, and he told me that the RCMP and other police forces suspected him of working for a foreign espionage service, the CIA or the KGB.

I once went to Daniel's tiny room. It contained a narrow cot, a table, a clothes closet, an electric hotplate, and a few books: *The*

Thoughts of Mao, The Revolutionary War, Imperialism, the Final Stage of Capitalism, a book by Mario Bachand that included a few lines about Waterlot, a few books by Camus, by Sartre, and poems by Aragon. There were a few clippings from newspapers about him.

I began to discover certain contradictions in Daniel. After a meeting of the PCQML, it happened that friends invited him out for a drink. He refused, giving as his reason that he couldn't afford a cup of coffee or a bus ticket. I left with him and, on the way, he invited me into a bar where we both had double scotches. Daniel paid for it all. Where did he get the money, since he didn't have a job?

I attended a demonstration of the Communist Party of Canada (Marxist-Leninist), in Ottawa. We were taken there in chartered buses, and we sang revolutionary songs all the way, in many languages. They handed out words in English, Italian, Gaelic, Spanish, and German. In Ottawa, we met in a school hall, and the national leader Hardial Bains made a long speech about the war in Vietnam. Then, all 400 of us ate shrimp on rice and curried chicken. Afterwards, we paraded before the Parliament Buildings, preceded and followed by a great red flag. We chanted as we marched: "Long live the Communist Party of Canada (Marxist-Leninist)! Long live Mao Tse-tung, our great leader! Long live the workers' revolution!" And naturally, we sang the Internationale.

When the demonstration was over, we returned by bus to Montreal, carrying out a critique of the day. Everyone had to express his criticisms. I said that we hadn't spent enough time discussing issues with the people of Ottawa; we should have taken an hour or two to go and sit with them in the parks or on public benches, and carry out popular education. I received congratulations for my critique, and Daniel was proud of me.

These people spent a good deal of time in criticisms and self-criticisms. They went as far as public confessions. For instance, a man had met a pretty bourgeois girl. He offered her a drink, and did nothing but flirt with her, without trying to educate her. He had acted as a male and not as a revolutionary. He made his confession publicly, and everyone approved of his self-criticism.

If someone had a dilemma, he had to put it before the group, which would enlighten him. Once I put before the assembly a question that was bothering me. It was known that the Red Cross of Haiti collected the blood of Haitians and paid them for it. Some Haitians went almost every three days to give blood, in return for money. To lose blood at that rate was undermining the health of those poor wretches. The traffic in blood was lucrative: Haiti was selling it to foreign countries where the demand for blood was great. As revolutionaries, should we not boycott the Canadian Red Cross to make it apply pressure on the International Red Cross to put an end to this traffic in blood?

The answer was no. It would be counter-revolutionary. If the International Red Cross put an end to this despicable traffic, the Haitian people would be deprived of a weapon to throw up against those who exploited them. They must be allowed to fall into the depths of misery, as victims of capitalist exploitation. When they had reached their lowest point, they would revolt.

So I had counter-revolutionary attitudes! Daniel offered, in front of the whole gathering, to educate me. When we were alone he invited me to eat in a restaurant. He took me to Chez Pauzé, on Sainte Catherine Street, and he began my education with a dozen oysters, crab bisque, and trout amandine, washed down with a bottle of Riesling. Then we returned to my place. Revolutionary education? None. But where did Daniel get the money to pay for all that? Certainly not from unemployment insurance.

One day I was told that I was to conduct door-to-door popular education with a man by the name of Bureau. He was not exactly a bright light. He was small, paunchy, about twenty-six years old. What relentless sincerity! He never tired when he had begun to give out the party line on a subject.

We met every afternoon at the Hochelaga Métro station. Bureau would be there waiting for me, his arms loaded with a pile of newspapers, the Peking Information magazine, the Little Red Book of Mao, and other propaganda books and booklets. We began our canvassing in jeans and Adidas, because Daniel had insisted that I buy a pair of that revolutionary footwear.

We knocked at a door, and the door opened. We looked like idiots, and people couldn't understand a word of our spiel. We talked about Vladimir as we called Comrade Lenin, we discoursed on the class struggle, and on imperialism as the ultimate stage of capitalism. People looked at us, open-mouthed.

I must admit that I was embarrassed at disturbing people at home to treat them to such nonsense. I didn't believe a word of it. I let my indefatigable Bureau talk on.

We also peddled newspapers at the Métro entrances every morning at six o'clock. I dragged myself painfully from my bed at five, got into my jeans and a blouse that was far too large for me, and put on smoked glasses so I would not be recognized by people I knew. Then I walked to the Métro.

I was supposed to cry out: "Newspaper of the Communist Party of Quebec (Marxist-Leninist)! Newspaper of the Communist Party of Quebec (Marxist-Leninist)!"

I didn't shout very loudly. Actually, I muttered, holding out to each person my pitiful literature. They were blue-collar workers, at that hour, on their way to work with lunchboxes. Perhaps one person in twenty bought the paper, which I sold for ten cents. At last, at seven o'clock or seven-thirty, I could return home with my remaining newspapers, and went back to bed until nine o'clock.

I finally decided that I had had enough of selling newspapers and going from door to door. To get the others to accept my decision, I spoke about it first to Daniel, who was understanding. He explained to the others that the party had expected too much of me, that I was not yet a party member, and that I was exhausted. Daniel convinced them, and I was excused from my most hated duties.

But I still had to attend the neighbourhood demonstrations organized by the PCQML. Every weekend, rain or shine, we paraded through a block with our red banners, chanting: "Long live the Communist Party of Quebec (Marxist-Leninist)! Long live our great president Comrade Mao Tse-tung! Power to the workers!"

Then we sang the Internationale.

The peaceful wretched of the earth in Hochelaga district looked at us bemused. They must have wondered where such strange enthusiasts came from. To confirm their worst fears, we knocked on every door, we sat down with them on their balconies, we talked to them about the terrible capitalists who took all their money.

Daniel rarely took part in these demonstrations. One evening, after a meeting of self-criticism, the comrades asked him to go to a restaurant with them for a cup of coffee. As usual, he refused on the grounds that he had no money. We returned to my place on foot, and we stopped on the way. Daniel bought two tournedos and a couple of bottles of Bordeaux. He then prepared the tournedos, while giving me a cooking lesson.

He had been born in France. Even though he had arrived in Quebec rather young, he had never lost his French accent. He told me that his father, a miner in the north of France, had always been a Communist; he was beaten up under the Nazi occupation, then died at the hands of the French government.

"He died a true Communist!" he said. "That is why I am and will remain a Communist."

Daniel had worked for six or seven years on the Montreal police force, but was dismissed after a racial incident. Daniel told me that it was his sergeant who had showed himself to be a racist in a nasty scene with a Haitian, but my police contacts told me that it had been Waterlot himself who was the racist, and that was why he had been dismissed from the force.

My controller told me:

"Think about it, a long-time Communist does not hire on with the Montreal police. It doesn't make sense. And look: after a few years, he caused a ruckus and arranged to be removed from the force. And immediately afterward, this martyr to the police became one of the leaders of the PCQML. Don't you find that strange?"

Julien Giguère even predicted that Waterlot would one day ask me to spy on the Parti Quebecois.

Sometimes we walked in Outremont. Daniel looked at the stone mansions and declared: "Soon, all that will belong to us, the damned *Anglais* will leave for Ontario and it will be ours, Carole, it will belong to us!" These were strange words from a man who had claimed that ethnic conflicts are the work of reactionary petty bourgeois.

During the month of September 1973, Daniel announced to me that he had found work at Place Bonaventure with a film company. One morning he phoned me and proposed that we meet for lunch. Over our food at Le Caveau, we talked about Daniel's new job.

When we were through eating, he took me to his office and showed me what he was doing. Seated at a big table like those used by draftsmen and architects, he coloured sheets of paper on which were drawn the outlines of animals, fairies, devils, trees, flowers, and fish of all kinds. When finished, the drawings were assembled into animated films for children.

I let him get back to his work, but he told me that, if I remained in the centre of town, we could go for a drink at three o'clock, when he had a thirty-minute break.

We met at three o'clock. On Lagauchetière Street, he hailed a cab to take us to the Troika on Crescent Street. We could have had a drink elsewhere, even in Place Bonaventure itself. Why waste money on a taxi when we had only thirty minutes together?

Daniel ordered a double scotch for himself and a Campari for me. Then he asked me if I was still in the Parti Quebecois. I answered that I still had my membership card, but that I no longer went to meetings. He brought his head closer to mine, and said: "Would you agree to go back to the PQ as an active member if we asked you to?"

I acted as if I didn't quite understand what he was getting at. "What do you mean?"

"You don't believe in the PQ now that you know the PCQML. We would like you to go back to the PQ and to act as a spy for us within the PQ. Do you think you could do that?"

Oh, I could, but I had no intention of betraying the PQ. I had even warned the Montreal police never to ask me to spy on the PQ. The answer would have been no. "Probably. I don't know anything about spying — what exactly do you want me to do?"

"You would have to become active, first of all in your riding, and show that you were willing to work seriously at the grassroots level. Then you could tell us about what is going on there, the decisions that are made. Then, later on, we could work out a strategy. Would that be all right?"

"I'll think it over and give you an answer when I have made a decision. That's not a small thing you are asking me."

When Daniel returned to his office, I telephoned Julien from a public booth. "Julien, you have the gift of prophecy. Do you remember, a week or two ago, you told me that you wouldn't be surprised if Waterlot asked me to spy on the PQ? Well, you were right, he just asked me."

"Meet me in an hour at Chez Lanni."

An hour later, Julien was waiting for me.

"Tell me in detail about your conversation with Waterlot. This is very interesting." I related the events of the day.

"How much did he offer you for doing it?"

"Two hundred dollars a week. They certainly pay better than you do. If I agree, I will be making almost three hundred a week. It's tempting. But seriously, what should I do?"

"Make the thing drag on. We'll have to consult the other two police forces. We'll have to find out who you would be working for, because you can be sure of one thing, it would not be for the PCQML. Your employers would be the same ones who use Waterlot's services, and that's the intriguing part. Keep Waterlot waiting until we have worked out a plan."

I put off giving Daniel an answer. He understood: it was not an easy decision.

A short time later, in October or November 1973, Germain Tourigny asked me to write a paper on Daniel Waterlot, his life, his tastes, his friends, the places he went to, his loves, everything, without omitting the smallest detail. This request came from the RCMP.

So I complied. I wrote of the double life that Daniel seemed to lead, poor with the party, rich with me. Revolutionary with the party, bourgeois with me. A lover of hamburgers with the party, a lover of snails and *civet de lapin* with me. Going on foot for the party, taking a taxi with me. Criticizing a book violently before the party, reading it in bed at night and praising it to me. There were two people in Daniel Waterlot. And I mentioned his request that I infiltrate the PQ for $200 a week.

I next saw Daniel a week after finishing the paper. He seemed in good humour. We bought tournedos and burgundy and Daniel cooked the meat with shallots and made a sauce with the burgundy. It was a delicious meal!

Then he joined me in my room, leaving the next day after break-fast. He did not come back that day nor that week. I began to worry. It had never happened before that he had been gone for a week without getting in touch with me. I telephoned Yves Charbonneau of Le Jazz Libre du Québec. He hadn't heard from Daniel either. Then I called his mother, but she hadn't been in touch with him.

About two or three weeks later, someone knocked at the door of my apartment. He said, in English:

"Is Daniel Waterlot here?"

"No, he is not here."

"Oh, sorry, you speak French. I have a suitcase for him."

He handed me a suitcase and an envelope.

"Tell him it's Mr. . . . ."

He gave me a name that I have since forgotten. Then he left. He was about fifty, walked slowly, and must have smoked a lot judging by the smell of his breath and the look of his teeth.

Once the door was closed, I took the suitcase into my room and opened it to see whether it had a false bottom. I turned it in all directions, poked and probed at it, but could find nothing.

When I next met Germain I recounted the incident.

"You're sure it doesn't have a false bottom?"

"Certain. I examined it carefully. It is a suitcase of brown leather, very ordinary in appearance, and entirely empty. I left it by the door in case someone comes for it."

"And the envelope?"

It was a sealed brown envelope, nine by eleven inches. There was nothing written on it.

"What will I do with the envelope?"

"Open it up and see what's inside. You never know, it might be important. If Daniel asks you why you opened the envelope, tell him that you wanted to make sure that there was nothing urgent for him in it."

At home, I opened the envelope. It contained $300 in $20 and $10 notes, with no note of explanation. Nothing except the money. I informed Germain.

"Keep the money, deposit it in your account at the bank, and if you see Daniel, tell him you preferred to keep the money in a safe place."

A few days later, Germain told me that he had spoken to some-one from the RCMP who had jumped at the name of the man who brought the suitcase and the money.

So the RCMP was interested.

I never again saw Daniel Waterlot. When I had had no news from him by December 1973, I made up my mind to call his mother. She said that Daniel had left for Europe. The following year, his mother told me that he had gone to England and to Vienna.

The police, meanwhile, learned that in 1974 he took a course on how to drive the Métro in Paris. Then they lost track of him. Since then, there has been no news from the one who, for a year-and-a-half, was my constant companion.

I still owe Daniel Waterlot $300. I don't know if he is still alive to claim it from me.

By 1974, the time had come for me to leave police work. The FLQ was dead: I had been present when it gasped out its last fantasies of rebirth by carrying out a kidnapping. The chief conspirator, whose name I will not reveal, put an end to the plot by committing suicide with a shotgun.

In 1974, a new period began in my life. I fell in love with a Czech musician whom I met when he came on a brief trip to Montreal. In the summer of 1974 I was doing research in Vienna on the Treaty of Munich and we went out together. It was all Europe that I loved in him and we decided to get married. On November 21, 1974, we were married in the church of Sainte Anne de la Pérade.

My husband was jealous; he did not want me to keep my former friends. I had to cut my links with the past.

In January 1975, I met my controller, Germain Tourigny, for the last time. It was a farewell dinner that we shared together; farewell to the police, farewell to the FLQ, farewell to the most intense moments of my life. My husband never knew anything about these things. He never succeeded in gaining my confidence.

Psychologically and morally, I left present-day Quebec. I withdrew from the Parti Quebecois and from active politics. I took up the study of German, the reading of Hugo and Balzac. For five years, until my divorce, I led a very private life. But I kept my memories. Some day, I didn't know when or how, I would speak out.

PART THREE

CHAPTER 29
The Return of the Past

On the night of July 26, 1974, a bomb exploded in the hands of a man who was about to plant it at the residence of the president of Steinberg. The man was wounded, and his bomb soon had political repercussions, for he was Robert Samson of the Royal Canadian Mounted Police.

The scandal spread. Samson revealed that he had taken part in a burglary that the three police forces had committed at the headquarters of a left-wing organization, the Agence de Presse Libre du Québec. Rumours flew. What else had the police permitted itself in the name of the fight against terrorism and subversion?

On June 16, 1977, the Parti Quebecois government announced the creation of a Commission of Enquiry into Illegal Police Actions in the Territory of Quebec. The Commission, headed by the Péquiste lawyer Jean-François Keable, progressively widened the scope of its investigation. The inquiry eventually considered police behaviour during the October Crisis of 1970 and during all of 1971.

Through its analysis of police reports, the Commission learned that a woman had provided the police with information about the FLQ under the code number SAT 945-171 and the code name of Poupette. The Commission showed a particular interest in her.

The dead walk again. That was the feeling I had on the rainy morning of May 24, 1979. At seven-thirty I was in the Métro on my way to Rose-Marie Parent's place. I was trembling all over. In my purse, I had a subpoena which ordered me to appear that morning before the Keable Commission. What would happen there? What secrets would at last come out in broad daylight?

I rang the doorbell. Rose-Marie answered, her face pale under her make-up. She, too, had to appear that morning before the Keable Commission.

"I am afraid of going to jail! They're going to send me to jail!" she wailed.

She had prepared toast and coffee. We tried to eat but the pieces stuck in our throats. As Rose-Marie tried to drink her coffee I could hear the cup rattling against the saucer. My legs felt rubbery. Why were we so afraid? To look at us, we were a pair of respectable middle-class women. Rose-Marie wore an elegant navy-blue suit, and I, a violet skirt with peach flowers, a beige blouse, and a black blazer.

Rose-Marie anxiously recalled her participation in the FLQ at the end of 1970 and the beginning of 1971. Would the Commission ask her about plotting to kidnap one of the Steinberg brothers? About storing dynamite in her apartment? About planting a bomb behind a post office? They were old stories, almost forgotten. Would the past come back and claim its due? Rose-Marie was afraid of prison. I had a more diffuse fear of what might await me.

We went off together in a taxi. The Keable Commission had subpoenaed us to appear at the headquarters of the provincial police on Parthenais Street. That is where the people arrested under the War Measures Act were detained in the fall of 1970. That, too, is where Paul Rose and his brother Jacques stood trial for the kidnapping and murder of Pierre Laporte.

"Carole, I am embarrassed about asking the taxi driver to take us to Parthenais. He will take us for criminals," said Rose-Marie, as though just to go to that building already implied an admission of guilt.

"But Rose-Marie, the Parthenais building also houses the morgue. The driver might think we're going to the morgue."

The taxi stopped before the glass tower of the Quebec police. In front of us, I saw a man step out of another taxi; he was slender, with French-style glasses and a little moustache. My heart leapt. Robert Comeau! The one who got me into the FLQ in the first place! I had not seen him for years. He, too, had come because of the subpoena of the Keable Commission.

We went into the main hall without exchanging a word, just as though we had never known one another. We had to form a line in front of a table. Not just anyone could walk into Quebec police headquarters. Rose-Marie, in front of me, showed a policeman seated there the subpoena of the Keable Commission and an identification card. She was asked to give name, address, telephone number, and occupation. Then it was my turn. I spoke softly because I didn't want Robert Comeau, right behind me, to hear my address. The policeman gave each of us a card hanging from a cord on which was written: *"Commission Keable."* With the card dangling from our necks, accompanied by a policeman, we rode an elevator up to the sixth floor. Comeau and I still didn't speak, but with furtive glances I noted that he had not changed much in five years. Only the glasses were different.

We left the elevator and walked into a hall where a dozen people were seated on benches along the wall. Here we were to wait until we were called. We could see the closed door that led to the court-room where the Keable Commission was preparing to question us. There was an unoccupied bench at the far end of the hall. Rose-Marie and I sat down there together.

In front of us we could see two men whom we did not recognize. Were they from the FLQ? To the left I spotted a familiar trio: François Séguin and Jean-Pierre Piquette, now joined by Robert Comeau. Three members of the Viger Cell, who delivered the letter and the photos of James Cross. I looked them over. Piquette now had longer hair, tied in a ponytail at the back of his head. I never did like him! Well, Comeau now smoked! He held his cigarette with a nervous hand, smoking it rapidly. Just as nervous as he always had been. And François Séguin? He hadn't changed at all. Still in jeans, still paunchy. He looked calm. Was he really? Like me, he bore a heavy secret. What was he thinking about at that moment?

At the far end of the hall I noticed Michel Frankland. He was reading a newspaper; with a pencil, he was filling in the crossword puzzle. I hadn't seen him for at least five years. His hair was turning grey.

I tried to read my newspaper, but the headlines danced before my eyes. I couldn't recall anything that I had read. I closed it, got up, sat back down, lit a cigarette, forgot it in the ashtray, lit an-other one. I got up and went to the washroom. I felt as though my legs would hardly carry me.

Rose-Marie never stopped smoking her long brown cigarettes. She said to me:

"Carole, who is that girl over there with the long hair, sitting not far from Frankland?"

I looked at her without recognizing her.

At last they opened the heavy wooden doors.

"If you please, everyone into the courtroom!"

I stood up. I felt as though I were suffocating. I could feel drops of sweat moving down my face.

They directed us to the wooden benches. Everyone sat down. It was as though we were before a tribunal. At the far end, on a dais, a seated man observed us. It was Commissioner Keable, younger-looking than I had imagined him. In front of him, five or six others waited in silence. One of them got up and began to read a long message that I didn't grasp at all, because all I could hear was my beating heart.

The reading finished, Mr. Keable told us that he would call upon us in turn, and that the person named was to stand and say whether he or she was represented by a lawyer.

"Jean-Guy Baril!"

A man stood. I looked at him. It was the first time I'd ever seen him. His name meant nothing to me. What could he be doing here?
"Nigel Hamer!"
I turned to look. He was standing diagonally behind me. No, I had never seen him before, even though I felt as though I knew him. It was he I had denounced in 1970 as one of those who took part in the kidnapping of Cross. The police still had not charged him. Was he also frightened, now?
"Michèle Léger!"
I looked around the room. Did she arrive without my seeing her, the woman who threw the Molotov cocktail with Michel Frankland? Then I saw, on her feet, the woman that Rose-Marie had asked me if I knew. I had not recognized her, and neither had Rose-Marie.
"Look, she has changed the colour of her hair," Rose-Marie whispered.
And the names followed each other. Piquette, Séguin, Comeau, Frankland. Each name evoked its own memories. What did the Commission hope to accomplish? Could it bring the past back to life?
"Carole de Vault!"
"No, Mr. Commissioner, I am not represented by a lawyer."
When the roll-call of the witnesses was over, they told us to go back and wait in the hall outside. Each one would be recalled alone, in turn.
Rose-Marie and I joined Michel Frankland. He greeted us warmly, but he was no longer the same Frankland. He had aged. I asked him what he was up to.
"Oh, I'm very quiet. I have four and a half children. I have nothing to do with politics any more. I've stopped smoking and I'm getting ready to run in the marathon. Apart from that, I have returned to Catholicism. I go to Mass every Sunday and I raise my little family."
I could hardly believe my ears. Where was the Michel Frankland who had talked of kidnapping, ran after his *princesses* and tapped himself on the head, crying out how wonderful we were?
Not far away, Michèle Léger talked with her lawyer. Frankland went over to greet his former friend, the one he had introduced to the terrorist adventure. She received him coldly, barely speaking to him. Frankland returned to sit with us.
I was restless, my hands were damp and my blouse was sticking to my skin. My anxiety must have been showing. Normand Marion, the lawyer for Nigel Hamer and Gilles Cossette, came up to me. He had observed that I was very nervous.
"Your situation is that serious? Would it go as far as dynamite?"
"Oh, yes."
"As far as communiqués?"

"Yes, and worse than that."

Marion asked me if I had a solicitor.

"No, I don't. I didn't know any, and I couldn't tell just anyone that I was in the FLQ."

Marion talked and talked. He spoke of Noel Vallerand, then deputy minister of cultural affairs in Quebec.

"We're going to have to involve him as much as possible, we have to incriminate him. He is in the PQ, and we have to knock him to get at the PQ. Keable is also in the PQ. It will really get them that we can implicate Vallerand, and thus the PQ, in this business."

Marion, as I knew, was part of the Trotskyist movement En Lutte, as were Comeau, Hamer, and Séguin. This movement considered the Parti Quebecois to be bourgeois and anti-revolutionary, the most harmful of all to the cause of the workers. What did Marion know of the role played by Noel Vallerand? Did Comeau tell him that it was Vallerand who had sent Comeau to me at the end of October, 1970?

He asked me whether I knew his client, Nigel Hamer.

"No, I don't know him. I have heard a lot about him, but I had never seen him before this morning."

Marion told me that Hamer had also heard of me without having met me. And Marion was aware of the quarrel between Robert Comeau and me over his accusation that I worked for the police. Indeed, his colleague from the same law office, Alain Beauvais, was representing Comeau before the Commission. I quickly made Marion aware that I wanted to have nothing to do with Robert Comeau, who had denounced me in 1971 as an agent of the RCMP in front of professors and students at the UQAM.

"Yes, I think it is just childishness on Comeau's part," Marion told me. "I will speak to him about it, as well as to Alain Beauvais. This is no time for us to be divided among ourselves."

He offered to represent me before the Commission. He was insistent that I must not go in to testify alone. I didn't know how to refuse. I certainly didn't want an adherent of En Lutte, the lawyer of Nigel Hamer and of Gilles Cossette, to represent me before the Commission.

One by one, each person disappeared into the courtroom. Now it was Rose-Marie who testified for three-quarters of an hour. What questions could they be asking her? Rose-Marie came out at last, but very nervous. She passed in front of me as though she had not seen me and pushed the button for the elevator. I went over to join her. To see her in that state made me even more nervous. What could they have said to her? Could she have learned of my identity?

I asked her what had happened. She answered that she could tell me nothing because she had been ordered not to speak of her appearance to any one.

"All right, but you forgot your umbrella."

They called Michèle Léger. She also spent about three-quarters of an hour before the Commission. Then it was the turn of Michel Frankland.

I felt as though I had the flu. Normand Marion was still beside me, insistently offering to represent me. I told him that I would think it over.

"But this isn't the time to think it over! At any moment they will call you to testify!"

I saw Frankland leave the courtroom and a bailiff cried out: "Carole de Vault!"

As though on springs, I rose and darted into the courtroom. The heavy doors closed. I was alone before the Commission.

"Place your right hand on the Bible and swear to tell the truth, the whole truth and nothing but the truth."

"I swear it."

For half an hour, they questioned me. I told them of how I began in the FLQ, how I was approached by Robert Comeau, how he proposed a hold-up, and how I went to the police. I was ready to answer all their questions; behind closed doors, I had nothing to hide. It was terribly hot and I took off my blazer. With both hands I grasped the edge of the witness stand.

When I had confessed that I had become a police informer, Commissioner Keable adjourned my questioning until the following week. Meanwhile, he forbade me to talk to anyone about what had gone on in the courtroom.

Jacques Bellemare, one of the Commission lawyers, accompanied me as I left the courtroom in case any Felquistes were still hanging around. I had been the last to testify, and the hall on the sixth floor was empty. When we emerged from the elevator on the main floor, though, we saw Niger Hamer and Normand Marion. Jacques Bellemare raised his voice to mislead them.

"Do you know, *Mademoiselle*, what perjury means under the law?"

I took a taxi and left, my secret entrusted to the Keable Commission. I put my confidence in the Commissioner. I felt confident then that he would not betray it.

CHAPTER 30
Shaking My Recollections
❦

My in-camera testimony lasted fourteen days. Looking back on it today, I feel that the Keable Commission took me in, confused me in my convictions, shook me in my loyalties. Under the pressure of its intense questioning, everything became the contrary of what it had been for me.

After the general convocation on Parthenais Street, I testified for one day the following week, at the offices of the Commission on Peel Street. The day passed pleasantly enought: the counsel asked me to draw psychological portraits of, among others, Michel Frankland, Robert Comeau, and Noel Vallerand. I talked at length and everyone laughed heartily. No wonder. What a cast of characters!

Then the Commission took holidays, postponing my further questioning until September. I learned from a policeman close to the Commission that they had hesitated before making their decision.

"They're afraid that you might pack your bag, take a plane, move to Europe, and never come back." I found that amusing.

In September, they called me again for four days, this time to a Quebec City hotel. Why in Quebec City? Because the Commission's stenographer felt that he was being followed and thought he recognized Nigel Hamer dogging him. Paranoia was rife among the members of the Commission. They already thought they were being spied on by the Montreal police, and now the leftists were involved too.

Indeed, a few days before, I had met my former controller, Julien Giguère, to discuss the Commission with him. I noticed that while driving, Julien often looked in his rear view mirror.

"I think we are being followed," he said suddenly.

He continued to make detours, glancing into his mirror. He was soon convinced that it was the Keable Commission that was having us followed.

"We'll give them a fright, we'll go to Mirabel airport. They'll think that we're taking a plane and running."

When we arrived at the airport, we parked the car and Julien led me to the counter of an Egyptian airline.

"They'll be so frightened. The fellows from the provincial police will think that we're taking a plane for Egypt. They'll phone and tell Keable."

We spent an hour in the bar, and then Julien came by my apartment. As we walked in, he put his finger to his lips and motioned me to disconnect the phone.

"Electronic surveillance doesn't work when the phone is unhooked," he told me. Then we talked freely.

His suspicions were not groundless. Some time later, the Commission's counsel Mario Bilodeau told me:

"You met Mr. Giguère recently. We know you went to Mirabel airport. We even have a picture of the two of you together."

I answered, "Yes, you put us under surveillance, and we noticed it."

Then Mr. Bilodeau began to deny it, saying that we had been seen by chance.

Nearly two years later, in 1981, a police officer from the provincial police told a police officer friend of mine that my apartment had been under electronic surveillance from May, 1979, until October, when I moved away from Montreal.

But to return to Monday, September 11, 1979: I took the seven o'clock bus for Quebec City to begin my questioning there. Rather anxious, I wondered why the Commission wanted me for four days. I closed my eyes behind my tinted glasses, trying to relive the fall of 1970 and all of 1971. Nearly ten years had gone by. Would I be able to answer all their questions?

At the Auberge des Gouverneurs in Quebec City, they gave me my key. Then I went to suite 996 to meet the Commission. There were five men seated in armchairs, sipping coffee. Mr. Keable offered me coffee and a pastry when I confessed that I hadn't yet eaten that day. Then, about ten-thirty, Mr. Keable invited us to move into the next room, which was furnished only with a rectangular table and seven chairs.

How many hours I was to spend there! How many doubts and uncertainties I would experience. Commissioner Keable sat down at the head of the table. I sat alone on his left. Across from me sat the three solicitors of the Commission — Mario Bilodeau, Jean-Pierre Lussier, Jacques Bellemare — and the criminologist Jean-Paul Brodeur, the Commission's director of research. Finally, there was Mr. Vilaire, the stenographer, with a pair of earphones over his head, who sat at the far end of the table.

The questioning began. Bilodeau asked the first questions.

"Miss de Vault, tell us about the Ouimet Cell. Who set it up? Who belonged to it?"

And I told how Michel Frankland, after his meeting with Robert Comeau, had hastened to set up his own cell, the André Ouimet Cell.

Mario Bilodeau began to ply me with questions, to form hypotheses. In each hypothesis was a sub-hypothesis, and then another, and another. He confronted me with reports, with other testimonies. He tried to catch me out. He suggested. Little by little, through the line of questioning, the hypotheses, and the insinuations, I saw what he was getting at. It was his complete version of the October Crisis that he was trying to get me to confirm. He thought that the police, if they did not concoct the kidnapping of Cross themselves, at least took part in it. Nigel Hamer, one of the kidnappers, was likely a police agent. Robert Comeau, of the Viger Cell, was likely a police agent. François Séguin, another member of the Viger Cell, was probably not simply a police informer, but a policeman working under cover. Gérard Pelletier, a Felquiste imprisoned for armed robbery, was likely a police informer.

And the Machiavellian mind who was supposed to have staged the whole thing? Julien Giguère, my controller and my friend. Now it was Julien the lost soul, the sinister conniver, the dark angel of the October Crisis. And I?

I thought they were crazy, absolutely crazy! Morning, noon, sometimes at night, during the formal sessions of the Commission, during coffee breaks, over meals or drinks shared together, Jean Keable and Mario Bilodeau returned with the same theme: "You were taken in by Giguère. Mr. Giguère is brilliant. You were duped by him, yes, by him in whom you had placed all your trust. He was taking advantage of you the whole time. It's terrible, isn't it?"

The biggest sucker of the October Crisis was Poupette. I protested. I knew Julien too well for that. It was impossible that he had taken advantage of me. We had lived through that crisis together.

"It's impossible. Julien used to call me every day to find out what was happening. And we met almost every day in November and December of 1970. If he was making a fool of me, he wouldn't have acted that way. He wouldn't have wasted his time with me."

Mario Bilodeau stated one of his hypotheses with the multiple sub-hypotheses, saying to me, in substance:

"Yes, but has it never occurred to you that Mr. Giguère needed you to protect someone else? Just imagine, for a moment, the following scenario: Mr. Giguère has an informer who is involved in the kidnapping of Cross, perhaps even in the Liberation Cell. The police, therefore, are direct accomplices of the kidnappers and know the place where the diplomat is hidden. That is serious business. The police don't act because they want to prolong the crisis to crush and destroy the left in Quebec. But that informer is terribly hot, dangerous for Mr. Giguère. If it ever got out, what a bombshell! Can you imagine it in the newspapers: police accomplices in the kidnapping of James Cross! But one day Detective-Sergeant Fernand Tanguay drops in on Mr. Giguère with a report on a woman who has just told him to expect pictures of Cross seated on a case of dynamite. Mr. Giguère can't get over it! It seems to him that heaven sent you. Mr. Giguère, of course, already knows that the pictures are to appear, thanks to his informer, so he knows at once that you probably know the same people as his informer. He is jubilant. At last he has a cover for his hot informer: *you*! Why, of course, he will hide his reports from his informer under your code number, SAT 945-171. All the reports, yours as well as his, will carry number 945-171 and will be attributed to Poupette. Mr. Giguère used you marvellously. But he didn't suspect that one day we would come along and conduct a little investigation into his affairs. So you are and you are not 945-171. But you were duped by Julien Giguère."

They were crazy! Or was I the one who was crazy?

"But if what you say is true, that person would have to know the same people I do, be very close to me?"

They had an answer for everything.

"Did you ever think of Comeau? Yes, Comeau: he knows the same people as you. You are the best cover for Robert Comeau! Isn't it possible that Comeau was a police source?"

No. It was impossible.

"Comeau is not capable of being a police informer, he doesn't have the ability, he doesn't have the temperament. I swear that it's impossible."

"If you wish, but we don't reject the possibility that Comeau was also 945-171."

Everyone in the room was experiencing intense emotions, but for different reasons. They were off on a glory trip. They were hot on the trail of the plot of the century. They believed that the police had foully betrayed the citizens of Quebec. All they had to do was prove it. And I was to help them by confirming their hypotheses and their scenarios. That was why they assailed my perception of the past, they poured scorn on my confidence in Julien Giguère. I had been proud of what we had done together, unknown to the world. Now they insisted that I had been a dupe when I thought I was living the most important moments of my life.

One day while Mr. Bilodeau was putting forward one of his hypotheses, I looked at a police report in front of me. I interrupted the solicitor's flight of rhetoric.

"But, that doesn't make sense. Look at the report in front of you! What you are proposing and what the report says can't be reconciled."

Mario Bilodeau leapt from his chair. Excited, he seized the report, glanced at it, and looked at me as though my objection were naïve in the extreme.

"Come on now, they just redid the reports. When they saw us coming, they were frightened enough to destroy their old documents. They burned them and they made up others that were not as compromising. On their new records they just applied the old stamps of the policemen, and the deed was done. It's easy to doctor records. And stamps can be kept. The stamp of Julien Giguère might have been kept and used again. They say they have burned part of their records, but that is so we won't notice that they have really burned all their records and made up new ones. They are cunning, you know!"

At the end of the second day of hearings, I was about to go to my room when Mr. Keable asked me how things were going.

"Badly, very badly."

"Come here, we'll talk about it. But first, we'll have a drink."

The Commissioner ordered two warm beers for himself, and everyone put in an order for gin or scotch. We were seated on sofas.

"You understand, Miss de Vault," said Mr. Bilodeau, "we don't have it in for Mr. Giguère. If he has done nothing, let him come and tell us, we'll listen to him."

And Mr. Bellemare added: "We don't have it in for the police. What we want is for the police to be honest."

They were taking my account of my experiences in the FLQ and were turning it upside down. I told them that Robert Comeau had sent me dynamite and official FLQ paper through the person who called himself Jean. This Jean bothered them. They spent a lot of time on Jean, and Mr. Bilodeau got lost in contradictory hypotheses.

One hypothesis: Jean didn't exist and I had made him up to explain how I received the dynamite. I was the only one to have seen Jean, because, according to Mr. Bilodeau, Michel Frankland said he never saw him. And yet Frankland and I were together in his office at Collège Bois de Boulogne when Jean came. I asked the Commission to have Frankland come so that I could confront him, but they refused.

Next hypothesis: Jean existed and I did see him. But he was a policeman. It was, therefore, a policeman who brought me explosives, plans for making bombs, and official FLQ paper. Jean might have been sent by Robert Comeau, who might have been a police informer.

"Did you ever think about the fact that the police never saw your Jean? You spotted him immediately from the window of Frankland's office. But the police, whose job it is, didn't see him, and they were a whole team! Have you thought of that? You said yourself that you told off Mr. Giguère because he hadn't seen your Jean. Don't you find that strange?"

They did everything they could to get me to admit that Julien Giguère had played a double game. For instance, they showed me a report by Julien in which he said that, according to source 945-171 — me — all the members of the Viger Cell were going to go dancing one night at a place called Casse-Noisettes. They asked me if I had really reported that. I said no.

"And yet, it does say that comes from source 945-171?"

I continued to deny that I had ever said such a thing.

"But did you ever think, Miss de Vault, that Mr. Giguère could have given your number, 945-171, to someone else? To another informer that he was hiding under your number?"

My confidence was shaken. Why was it that I couldn't recognize some of the reports attributed to me? Could Julien have hidden someone under my code number? Why had he not arrested Nigel Hamer after I had given him the address of this kidnapper of Cross? Why did he never arrest Robert Comeau, Michel Frankland, and other Felquistes whose actions he knew of?

At night, alone in my room, I cried out of anguish. I wanted terribly to speak to Julien. But I didn't dare call him, because I supposed that my telephone must be tapped.

Tired after the second day of my questioning, I had put in hair curlers for something to do, and had gone to bed early. I was dozing when, in the next room, they begin partying and ringing a bell. I looked at my watch: it had stopped. I telephoned the suite of the Commission and asked Mr. Bilodeau for the time; I told him I couldn't sleep because of the bells. It was nine o'clock. A few minutes later, my telephone rang: it was Commissioner Keable.

"Good evening, are you sleeping?"

"No."

"Then do you want to come for a drink? I am in the Commission suite."

I got up, and wrapped my head in a silk scarf to hide the curlers. I was wearing a black silk nightie, so I put on over it a black lace negligee with long sleeves. With my keys and my cigarettes in one hand, I knocked at the door of suite 996.

Jean Keable and Mario Bilodeau were waiting for me. Mr. Keable ordered beer and scotch from room service. Then we talked of every subject under the sun for two or three hours.

"I keep wondering how you dressed at that time," Jean Keable said. "You don't strike me as the kind of woman to go about in jeans."

"What gets me," said Mario Bilodeau, "is how Michel Frankland got all those names of priests for the FN. Sometimes I imagine an old *curé* from the Gaspé who is eighty and, one morning, with his eggs and bacon, his old housekeeper brings him a letter inviting him to join a terrorist movement and asking him to go and plant a bomb!"

Jean Keable was exactly my age, thirty-four years old. He, Mario and I were all born in 1945. Mr. Keable was neither tall nor handsome. But he had a lot of charm, he was very gallant, and very polite. He was always elegant in his well-pressed suits. His shoes were perfectly polished. He never had a wrinkle, a spot, or a hair out of place. He had blue eyes and brown hair which was slightly wavy. You could sense that he knew he was brilliant, and liked to be flattered. He was a specialist in labour law, and once a Parti Quebecois candidate in the provincial elections.

He showed a constant gallantry towards me. When I arrived in the morning, he ordered coffee and biscuits, and sat in front of me to serve me coffee while the others had to serve themselves. He didn't smoke, and did not allow Mario to smoke during the hearings, but he allowed me one cigarette.

Mario Bilodeau was thin and puny, fair-haired, but balding in front. His hair fell halfway down his neck and the police working with the Commission nick-named him "the hairy caterpillar." A criminal lawyer who loved his work, he gave the impression, like Keable, of being proud of himself. In fact, Mario made no secret of it.

"You know, I'm well known in Quebec City, I am quite a personality here."

Of a nervous temperament, he smoked up to three packages a day of unfiltered Celtiques. He was never still, gestured constantly, talked without a pause. He ate a lot, but also expended a lot of energy. Keable, on the other hand, watched his waistline and arrived each morning with a brown bag containing apples and yogurt. He ate about a dozen cups of yogurt a day. Mario was always late. He would come hurrying in thirty to forty-five minutes after the time set for the start of the hearings.

"Damn it, Mr. Commissioner, I went to bed late and I had trouble getting up. You'll have to excuse me, Mr. Commissioner. Tomorrow I'll try to do better." The next day, the same delay, but a new excuse.

Mario tried to act as my friend, as someone of my age and my generation who understood me perfectly. Why would I hide anything from him?

On the level of personal relations, we felt increasingly at ease with one another. But, on the strength of their great stacks of files from every police force, and carried away by their dreams of a superplot, they constantly led me into a surrealistic world. I couldn't get my bearings. They suggested, for instance, that Julien was the man in uniform the Quebec police surveillance squad saw going by in a car in front of Brink's a few moments after Michel Frankland and Michèle Léger tossed their Molotov cocktail. Why Julien, who hadn't been in a uniform for years? Because it supported their theory of a plot.

"Miss de Vault, what makes you think that Mr. Giguère gave you fake dynamite and not real dynamite?"

"Well, I don't know — Julien would not have made me sleep over a case of dynamite, he wouldn't have let me give real dynamite to Primeau for him to make a bomb. I don't know, I just have confidence that he would not do such a thing."

But they had shaken my confidence. They seemed so sure of themselves, so well informed. And they hated Julien Giguère so much. I was beginning to have doubts about him, about myself, about everything in the past.

One morning, on awakening, I couldn't bear the light. My eyes hurt terribly. I had conjunctivitis. And I had a cold. I appeared before the Commission wearing dark glasses. Mario Bilodeau, surprised, said:

"But why are you wearing those glasses? I like to see the eyes of the people I am questioning."

They drew the curtains and I was able to take off my glasses. The state of my eyes reflected faithfully the disturbance in my head. I could no longer see.

The attitude held by Commissioner Keable and Mario Bilodeau toward me had changed since the early days of my questioning in Quebec. Little by little, they no longer treated me as the co-conspirator of Julien Giguère in the plot to destroy the left and the Parti Quebecois in Quebec. They spoke to me more and more openly.

The turning point, I remember, came when Mr. Bilodeau was questioning me on the FLQ paper that I had received from Jean. My memory tricked me. To the question: "How many kinds of paper did Jean give you?" I answered "two." So it was. But, in describing the two kinds of paper, I confused one of them with the paper that Michel Frankland and I had made up ourselves for the communiqué of the André Ouimet Cell on December 16, 1970. Jean had only brought me the FLQ paper a few weeks later.

I could see that something was wrong. Mario Bilodeau wore an ironic smile. Commissioner Keable put before me the communiqué of the André Ouimet Cell, with its date of December 16.

"How do you explain that?"

Astounded, I stared at the communiqué. For twenty minutes they had been questioning me so as to lead me into a trap, and I had fallen into it. All the solicitors were laughing. I stuck my tongue out at them. Commissioner Keable brought his fist down on the table.

"Answer! This is not a circus!" He was furious.

I burst into tears. It was all so many years ago. The communiqués blurred into each other. The past was out of focus. If they would only allow me to consult reports, documents, to stimulate my memory. But no.

Keable saw the tears falling on the copy of the communiqué. He motioned for the others to leave. Then he tapped my hand paternally.

"Come, Carole. May I call you Carole? You can call me Jean."

Together, we clarified the origin of the three kinds of paper. That evening, Keable and Bilodeau took me out for dinner to a restaurant near Place Royale.

"Let's go, we'll have a good meal together. You'll see that we don't mean you any harm."

Bottles of wine, frogs' legs, liqueurs.

"You know, we're not so bad, we don't have it in for the police nor for Mr. Giguère. But we want to know the truth. We understand you, we know it must be hard to realize that you were taken in by the man in whom you had placed all your confidence. But the truth will be your revenge."

During the whole meal, Keable and Bilodeau excitedly developed their version of the plot.

Keable explained to me that the police had been much more closely involved than is generally believed in the kidnapping of Cross. Once Cross was freed, the police decided to prolong the crisis.

What suppositions! My head reeled. I returned to my hotel room not knowing what to think. Was it possible that I understood absolutely nothing about the events in which I had been involved?

And the examination continued.

"Miss de Vault, did you deliver the communiqué with Miss Parent or Miss Lavergne?"

I couldn't remember. We were studying some eighth or tenth communiqué.

"Oh, no, I couldn't have delivered it with Rose-Marie, she was in Algeria at that time."

"All right, did you deliver it with Miss Lavergne or Miss Lamarche?"

"I can't remember."

"Oh, so you can't remember? And yet you have a phenomenal memory."

I pondered. Perhaps with Miss Lamarche, but I was not certain. My nose was running, and I felt sick.

Mr. Lussier asked a question.

"Was it Miss Lavergne or Miss Léger?"

I answered at once, almost without taking time to think: "Miss Lavergne or Miss Lamarche, but not Miss Léger. She was in the hospital at the time."

Yes, now I remembered, Michèle Léger spent a week in Fleury Hospital.

On the weekend I returned to Montreal tired, upset, my trust in Julien shaken. And I had to go back to testify again in a few days. I met my friend and my second controller, Germain Tourigny. In tears, I threw myself into his arms.

"Germain, I don't ever want to return to testify before the Commission. I can't stand it any more. I am all muddled up."

Germain contacted the legal branch of the Montreal police, which hired a former employee, the lawyer Yvan Roy, to accompany me to my second week of examination. Mr. Roy was familiar with the files from having read, day by day, the reports of Poupette drawn up by Julien Giguère. But soon, he was as shaken as I. He began to believe in the theory of a great conspiracy. He started to fear that Julien Giguère had diabolically organized everything from behind the scenes.

Before leaving me at the end of the second week, Roy told me: "When I get to Montreal, I will have to call Guy!* I am sure he never could have imagined that such things were going on!"

As for me, my spirit was bruised. I had had so much confidence in Julien Giguère, I had believed in him and in our common undertaking. I had carried a secret pride for years. Now I could only see my past as a mockery.

On my return to Montreal, I was like someone coming out of a closed retreat, shaken to the depths of my soul. I returned a few times to the offices of the Commission on Peel Street. Mario Bilodeau wanted to check a few more details.

One day, returning from one of these interviews, I noticed a man standing idly near the front door. Public transportation in Montreal was on strike, so I began to walk towards Place des Arts. My man, in his twenties, slender, in jeans, followed about twenty feet behind me. I turned around from time to time during that twenty-

---

* Guy Lafrance was the head of the Montreal police's legal branch.

five minute walk, and he was always there. I went into Place des Arts and started walking though its labyrinths. He still followed me. I walked through the tunnel to Place Desjardins, and took the elevator to the Meridian Hotel. He took the next elevator. I went to a public phone and called Mario Bilodeau, to tell him that I was being followed. Mario told me to go to the entrance of the Four Seasons Hotel and that he would send someone from the Commission to meet me.

I went to the Four Seasons Hotel in a taxi and met Louise Beaudoin, one of the two secretaries of the Commission. We went into the hotel bar to await further instructions. A second secretary, Lise Gervais, arrived in turn. We chatted together over several drinks. I couldn't see my man anymore. Louise Beaudoin spoke to Keable on the telephone, and he told her to go to his room at the Ritz Carlton. We went there and waited, ordering gin and tonics from room service. Finally Keable and Mario Bilodeau arrived. I went down the Maritimes Bar with the two men, where we had drinks and Keable ordered two dozen oysters.

Mario, although less charming than Keable, liked women too much for his own good, at least so he had told me in Quebec City. "I like women too much, it will be my ruin." But, much as he liked women, he feared even more being one day compromised by the ill will of the police.

"There is nothing in the world as bad as being under surveillance. It's as dangerous as it can be."

In the bar of the Ritz, without even noticing, I put my arm negligently on the back of Mario's chair. He leapt up as though I had pinched him.

"Carole, don't do that! What if the police are here and take a picture!"

A few days later I met him in Quebec and he brought up the incident again. "You know, I spoke to my wife about what happened the other night." I didn't know what he was talking about.

"You know, at the Ritz Carlton! I told my wife that she might receive in the mail a picture showing you sitting beside me with your arm around my shoulders. She told me she would immediately throw the picture into the garbage. Damn it, Carole! Be careful of police surveillance. You should know, you have experience!"

This fear of the police often came up among the members of the Commission. Keable, who lived in Quebec, stayed at the Ritz Carlton when he was working in Montreal. One night, two women of blatant charms knocked at the door of his room and offered their services. Keable slammed the door. He suspected the police of being behind the nocturnal visit. Soon after, he met the solicitor for the police.

"Did your guys send me someone? If it's your people, tell them next time to send someone a little more attractive."

CHAPTER 31
Interlude

In mid-October, I received a phone call from Mario Bilodeau. He invited me to supper that very evening with Jean Keable and himself. I accepted. What could they want now?

I arrived at seven o'clock at the Commission office. A guard seated before the always-locked door was listening to music. I gave my name and he let me in. The Commissioner and Mario arrived and we left on foot for Café Martin, where Mario had reserved a small private dining room. We sat down at the table. Keable ordered two warm beers, Mario and I two double scotches apiece. Then I asked my question.

"Now, gentlemen, I would like to know why you invited me here for supper. I am certain it's not to look into my beautiful eyes!"

They turned to me and exclaimed, with one voice: "Why not?"

I didn't insist. It was an agreeable evening, and the conversation was stimulating. I ordered sweetbreads, Mario, kidneys with Madeira sauce, Keable, tournedos Rossini. We drank down a bottle of Bordeaux, and then a second.

Keable confided to me his suspicions that I had not only been a police informer, but actually a regular member of a police force, working under cover.

"You know, if we ever discover that you have a badge number, it will be worse for you than an earthquake!"

I was astonished that he could still think this of me after the ninety hours examination and all the hours we had spent together in easy camaraderie.

It must have been midnight by the time we got to the dessert. So far, we had only bantered about the FLQ and the police. Then it was time for coffee and liqueurs. It was now nearly two o'clock in the morning, and I still didn't know why they had invited me here.

Suddenly Jean Keable reached into an inside pocket of his jacket and took out a folded sheet of paper which he handed to me, saying: "Now, I would like you to sign this for me."

In a flash I understood. It was a form whereby I would consent to testify publicly! I, Carole de Vault, source 945-171! I looked at Keable.

"Ah! So that was it!"

I had a moment of dizziness. In spite of the alcohol, I had a terrible, crushing intuition: I was dead. I could not imagine a life when all Quebec would know that I had betrayed the FLQ. I could see the tough, ruthless men in the movement: what would they say and do, when they knew everything?

And yet I never thought of refusing. Events were following a course that I couldn't stop. I had taken part, in spite of myself, in a sinister plot. I had helped the police to fool the population. How could I make amends, except by testifying publicly, by telling the whole truth?

I answered Jean Keable that I would testify under certain conditions. I would have to leave Montreal. I would need police protection. I would require money to live on for the time of my testimony, because I would have to quit my job in Montreal. And when it was all over, I had to have a guarantee of employment.

"Who will want to hire Carole de Vault after my testimony?"

Keable took note of my conditions. He obviously couldn't give me an answer then and there. But he was all smiles, reassuring. He proposed to move me to Quebec. He would see me in a few days with the answer. He paid the bill of about $250 and we left.

Two days later Mario called me to ask me to meet him and Mr. Keable at Curly Joe's Restaurant. When I arrived, Jean Keable told me that he had good news.

"We saw the minister, we told him of your conditions, and they have been accepted. But the minister added on his own that, if he could not get you a job after your testimony, he would give you a lump sum of money in compensation. So you had better give me your curriculum vitae as soon as possible so that I can send it to the ministry."

My conditions were accepted. And I would therefore testify in public. It was not very good news for me. I did not demand in writing the guarantees I had asked for. I believed in the honour of Jean Keable and of Mario Bilodeau and their word seemed to me sufficient guarantee. I would discover my mistake a few months later.

I packed my bags and said farewell to Montreal. The next time I came back, it would be to confess publicly my role as an informer. Montreal, my city, would become a forbidden territory. I returned to Quebec City and moved once again into the Auberge des Gouverneurs. It was October 27. Mario Bilodeau soon arrived and introduced me to Sergeant Marcel Ste-Marie of the Quebec police and to Major Pierre Ricard, owner of the security agency charged with my protection. Mario told me that two bodyguards would protect me, and that I would have to inform them of my every movement. "You will not leave your room, even to buy a newspaper, without warning them and having them accompany you."

The major brought in two giants and introduced them to me. One was named Jean-Claude, the other François. Thus began our strange life *à trois*.

I went everywhere followed by the two incredible hulks. When I got up in the morning and wanted to go down for breakfast, I had to telephone their room on the same floor and warn them that I would be at the elevator door in two minutes. They met me there and we went down together, I and my two mascots. They alone almost filled the elevator. If I went to the newsstand to buy newspapers and cigarettes, they followed me and stood guard. I went into the restaurant for breakfast, and they were two tables away. With nothing to do, I wandered after my meal around the boutiques of Place Québec, in which the hotel was located. They followed along ten feet behind me. And they didn't go unnoticed. Jean-Claude must have weighed at the very least 220 pounds. He had a great belly that he covered with a tomato-red windbreaker. He and his faithful companion were very conspicuous in the bourgeois atmosphere of the Auberge des Gouverneurs.

A stranger started talking to me, flirting a bit, in the elevator. Jean-Claude — or was it François? — crossed his arms ponderously, loomed over him and stared at him threateningly.

"Could you tell me what it is you want?"

The man wanted nothing except to escape from the elevator in one piece. The same fate awaited another man who tried to be friendly in the tobacco store. Curtly addressed from behind, he took quick stock of the situation and retired from the field.

My guardian angels kept a log of my daily activities. Every time I left my hotel room, they recorded the time and the route. If I spoke to someone, they asked his name. With these two watchdogs constantly at my heels, I felt increasingly isolated, a prisoner.

After a week of this regimen I decided to treat myself to a few hours of freedom. One afternoon I left my room without warning my guards. I felt like breathing fresh air, belonging to myself, going where I wanted to, and lingering with whomever I wanted, without this constant surveillance, without those two masses intervening between me and my life.

I fled quickly from the area of the hotel. Almost running, I went up to the Plains of Abraham. Seated on a bench, I looked at the river at the foot of the escarpment, and smoked a cigarette. A handsome fair-haired man, a tourist from Norway, began to speak to me and I answered, delighted at being able to chat normally with someone.

My escape lasted two hours. I returned to the hotel biting into an apple. In the main hall I encountered the bigger of my watchdogs. His face unhappy, and his arms crossed, he stared at me. "Can we ask you where you were?"

I, proud of my feat, answered nonchalantly, taking a bite of my apple, "Of course. I went for a walk on the Plains."

He could not get over it. "You went for a walk on the Plains! Alone!" The other watchdog came over to us quickly. "She was taking a walk on the Plains!" he exclaimed, as flabbergasted as the first.

They soon informed me that they had contacted the Major. He had telephoned Sergeant Ste-Marie, who in turn had gotten in touch with Mario Bilodeau. When I arrived smiling, with an apple in my hand, they were about to broadcast my description over the provincial police radio.

I had to wait a month before my public appearance. They were weeks in which I felt more and more out of touch with normal life. I was someone who had been sentenced. I was waiting for justice to take its course, fearing the appointed hour, but unable to taste a moment's peace in the meantime.

And I was sinking increasingly into depression. My life was being taken away from me. My past mocked me. I could see myself losing all my friends, the former Felquistes like Rose-Marie Parent and Luc Gosselin, and those from the university. In intellectual circles, terrorism was considered an engaging foible, while cooperating with the police was an abominable, unforgivable crime.

With what relief I saw the day for testimony arrive at last. The intolerable wait was coming to an end. My guards drove me from Quebec to Montreal. I spent the night in a hotel, scarcely closing an eye, about as unhappy as on that night of November 5, 1970, when I had first decided to go to the police. I had so little idea, that night, where my decision would take me. And now, what would be the consequences of my public avowal?

I took three Valiums before leaving for the courthouse. I answered the questions of Mario Bilodeau. In a sense, it was easier than the examination in camera. Now I had before me a thick file with copies of the communiqués to refer to. The solicitors no longer tried to catch me out, or to lead me into contradicting myself. The ninety hours of questioning in camera had freshened my memory of the past. Now the object was not to discover the truth but to put on a performance for the gallery.

By his line of questioning, Mario Bilodeau took me through what he called "an overview of Miss de Vault's activities." But how tendentious, how utterly biased, was his overview! The thesis that he hammered home dozens of times was that the police knew every-thing in advance, the police prevented nothing, the police never bothered the terrorists, the police, through me, took part in every terrorist activity. What a sinister impression of the role of the police he conveyed! He asked me just enough to suggest police perfidy, but not enough for the onlookers to form an accurate idea of what had happened.

Here, as an example, was how he treated the subject of the "bomb" planted behind the post office by Jacques Primeau. (I related the incident in Chapter 22.)

"You have in front of you the Wolfred Nelson communiqué. This communiqué, dated February 19, 1971, mentions an explosion or a bombing attempt that had taken place the previous night in a postal station located on Delorimier Street, at the corner of Mont Royal and Papineau."

"Yes."

"Were the facts mentioned in this communiqué made known in advance to your controller?"

"Oh, yes. Entirely."

"Were the writing and the contents of this communiqué made known in advance to your controller?"

"Yes."

"Was the distribution of this communiqué made known in ad-vance to your controller?"

"Yes, yes, he was aware of the operation in advance."

"From beginning to end?"

"From beginning to end."

Everything he made me say was the pure truth! But his ques-tions gave an impression of criminal negligence on the part of the police, which was utterly false.

He spoke of an "explosion or a bombing attempt." He knew perfectly well that there had been no explosion, because Julien had substituted fake dynamite for the real. About that he said not one word. He left the impression that Julien had done nothing while Jacques Primeau prepared his bomb. On the contrary, Julien had made sure that Primeau would plant his bomb outside on the ground, and not in the chute or on the roof. He was on the scene with a specialist in bomb disposal. The police encircled and neutralized the FLQ so minimal damage to people and to property would occur. Few Felquistes went to jail after I began to inform on the FLQ, not because the police let them act at will, but on the contrary, because the police kept them from acting effectively. Of that, Mario Bilodeau breathed not a word.

It was the same with the Jalbert Cell's communiqué, in which Michel Frankland had warned that a bomb planted in a plane in flight would explode unless $200,000 were paid into the account of Jacques Lanctôt in Cuba. Here is what Mr. Bilodeau said:

"I want you to notice, Mr. Commissioner, that this communiqué, dated November 19, constitutes, in my opinion, a rather striking proof of extortion, and so I would like to ask Miss de Vault whether, to your knowledge, the persons who participated in the events described in the communiqué and in the writing of the communiqué or in its distribution, were ever, to your knowledge, bothered by the police and taken before the courts?"

"Those people were never bothered by the police."

"Did you, in advance, inform your controller of the events related in this communiqué?"

"Oh, yes."

"And you also informed your controller of the existence of the communiqué itself?"

"Yes."

I could understand why Mario Bilodeau thought that Julien Giguère should have put Michel Frankland and Dagobert in prison for this extortion attempt. What I couldn't accept was that the Commission counsel kept from the public that the police had controlled the operation to make sure it was harmless. Julien made sure that Michel Frankland did not even have fake dynamite to carry out his plan. The police knew, through me, that there was no bomb in a plane, that the electric detonator accompanying the communiqué was just bluff. Those in charge of the airport were advised that they were not to take the communiqué seriously. Mario Bilodeau omitted this because it did not fit his thesis of the sinister plot.

He came back constantly to his theme.

"Am I to understand that, even though Mr. Giguère knew it in advance, had the information in hand, he let the situation deteriorate?"

To my shame, I answered: "That's correct."

The counsel, on that November 21, 1979, took up each of the main moments of my participation in the FLQ, beginning with the visit of Robert Comeau and the copying of the communiqué announcing the escape of the Rose brothers and of Francis Simard from the apartment on Queen Mary. He always stressed the fact that Julien knew everything in advance.

I returned to Quebec City escorted by my guards, tired and drained. Not only did my secret no longer belong to me, but I felt obscurely that I had in some way denied my past, betrayed Julien Giguère, blackened the reputation of the police. Mario Bilodeau had succeeded in leaving the impression that it was the police who were in charge of terrorism in Quebec.

"Carole Devault [sic] admits she engaged in terrorism with the collaboration of the police," *La Presse* headlined the next day.

"On November 14, 1970, the Viger Information Cell put out a communiqué commenting on the arrest of Bernard Lortie and the flight of Francis Simard and of the Rose brothers. The author of the communiqué? Carole Devault! [sic] Captain Julien Giguère was privy to it all!

". . . Carole Devault [sic] is precise in her testimony bearing on her activities as a collaborator and a terrorist. She is no less precise when she evaluates the behaviour of her controller, Captain Giguère. She gave the information; Captain Giguère knew absolutely everything, but he let the situation deteriorate; none of the individuals involved in the terrorist actions announced in the communiqués and who actually committed these bombing attempts, or the extortion attempt, was ever bothered in any way at all."

The Montreal Gazette, in its headline of November 22, faithfully relayed the impression that the Commission wanted to convey: "Police dictated 'FLQ messages,' woman tells inquiry." The same theme was repeated in the first sentence of the story.

"Police officers themselves dictated — or at least approved in advance — many of the terrorist messages subsequently received in late 1970 by police forces and news organizations in Montreal, an inquiry commission was told yesterday."

The theory of the police as the chief agent of terrorism was well sown in the public mind.

Back in Quebec City, I had to wait almost two-and-a-half months before my second public appearance in front of the Commission. First, it heard other witnesses. Then, the hearings were postponed until the end of January 1980, when the solicitor for the police, Guy Lafrance, challenged in court the Commission's right to have a policeman testify about the informer he controlled.

I will always remember the evening of November 27, a few days after my return to Quebec. I was seated before the television set and watching the news on the CBC, which reported daily about the Keable Commission. Suddenly the announcer said that Commissioner Keable had publicly denounced François Séguin as a police informer! I was stunned, I felt sick to my stomach. How could he have done that!

Right there in the courtroom, brutally, without notice, Jean Keable denounced François Séguin. He had François and Robert Comeau in front of him in the witness box. They refused to testify on the grounds that the Commission was a form of inquisition. They had accepted in advance that they would be sentenced to prison for contempt of court. But no, Keable found the worst of all possible punishments for François Séguin. He denounced him as a police informer, revealed his code number, 945-226, and named Detective-Sergeant Emile Bisaillon as his controller. François was wracked with sobs; Robert Comeau nearly fainted and had to be treated.

Keable dramatically assigned two court security officers to protect Séguin until four o'clock in the afternoon.

"It is up to the service that employed you, the police force of the Montreal Urban Community, to provide your protection after that time."

To Comeau, the Commissioner said with contempt:

"As far back as one goes into the activities for which you are known, be they political or subversive, you were, consciously or not, the dupe of the police forces."

I shook with rage at the Commissioner. I ran to the telephone and called the number of the Commission in Montreal. Keable himself answered the phone.

"This is Commissioner Keable, can I help you?"

"Yes, you can help me. I want to know what made you denounce Fritz? By what right did you do that?"

The Commissioner spoke deliberately in a low tone of voice, and very slowly.

"Do you think that I did it lightly? It is a decision that took us a week to come to. In any case, you should ask Mario to explain."

"Well, I want to tell you that I am disgusted, that you had no right to do that!"

"That's fine. Good night!"

I saw Mario a week later in Quebec City. Before he had even taken off his coat I asked my question.

"Why did you do that to Fritz?"

He gave me a long and tortuous explanation, which ran along the following lines:

"Listen, Carole, Comeau and Fritz were up to something really awful. Just imagine that Fritz wrote a paper denouncing you, with the help of Emile Bisaillon. Then, Fritz went to see Comeau with the paper, telling Comeau that he had written it alone, of course, and he and Comeau made slight changes to the text that had been written by Fritz and Bisaillon. Don't you find that disgusting? You can see the scenario: Fritz and Bisaillon, both with the police, write a paper against a third person from the police, you. Fritz pretends to Comeau that he wrote the paper alone, and Comeau, a dupe once more, adds a few comments of his own.

"But, this time, an honest policeman warned us of what was coming and we saw the letter. I will never show it to you because you would tear down the curtains. It was a real beauty. If ever anyone was denounced, it was you, and by Bisaillon, Fritz, and Comeau. So we had to put an end to that association quickly by separating Comeau from Fritz. And, just between the two of us, the role of Séguin is much more important in the whole thing than of Comeau. Comeau is nothing, but Fritz is a police lackey who is trying to put obstacles in the way of the Commission. He deserved a far worse punishment than Comeau. The two could have been convicted of contempt of court, but it would have been unjust to give them the same sentence when one was much more guilty than the other."

To think that I believed him at the time! I believed in the existence of that terrible letter denouncing me in terms so terrible that Commissioner Keable had to act to stop François Séguin. But I have researched it since and I am now convinced that the letter composed by Detective-Sergeant Emile Bisaillon and François Séguin existed nowhere but in the fertile imagination of Mario Bilodeau. He had to calm down the chief witness of the Commission.

Why denounce François Séguin as a police informer? What crimes had he committed since he had become an informer? The Commission knew perfectly well that he had committed all his crimes at the time he was a terrorist. In what way did the public interest require that the Commission endanger his life, ruin his career, destroy all his friendships? François Séguin had answered in camera all the Commission's questions. He had hidden nothing. What he could not agree to was to be publicly unmasked as an informer. The Commission had in hand all the information required to draw up an enlightened report. Why this roman circus in which François Séguin was tossed to the lions?

It is significant that the report of the Commission, which was published in 1981, said nothing to justify this public execution.

"The Commission was then constrained to reveal that Mr. François Séguin was a source employed by the police force of the Montreal Urban Community." Why "constrained?" The report offered no explanation.

The truth lay elsewhere. François Séguin was to corroborate for the public the theory of the great plot. It was the police who had directed all terrorism, the Felquistes themselves were only their dupes and puppets. Commissioner Keable did not say that François Séguin had become an informer in May, 1972, after acting for years as a true terrorist at the side of Robert Comeau. No, he suggested that Séguin, always employed by the police, had led Comeau into terrorism. What other meaning could his words have, when he said publicly to Comeau: "As far back as one goes into the activities for which you are known, be they political or subversive, you were, consciously or not, the dupe of the police forces." Comeau had told me that he had been involved with the FLQ long before our meeting on October 31, 1970. How could he have been the dupe of the police forces?

The Commission wanted at all costs to prove that Fritz did not merely become an informer in May 1972, but had been so from his beginnings in the FLQ, and might even have been an undercover policeman.

One morning, a few days after this public denunciation, I got a phone call in my room at the Auberge des Gouverneurs. It was Mario Bilodeau. He wanted me to meet him over breakfast in thirty minutes. I looked at my watch: it was seven o'clock. It must be terribly important for Mario to be up so early!

Over coffee and toast with peanut butter, Mario asked me with great seriousness the following questions: "Is it possible that François Séguin is a real policeman with a badge number? I would like you to think it over, to note down the slightest indication of it. If we could discover his badge number, what a great thing that would be!"

They were not content with having ruined the life of poor Fritz, they insisted that he must also be a policeman. I could imagine the scenario that they must have developed over several hours: Fritz, a policeman, a member of the Viger Cell, had been in contact with Nigel Hamer, a member of the Liberation Cell which held Cross and probably a police informer, and he stole dynamite with Hamer and Robert Comeau, perhaps also a police informer. Séguin probably knew when Cross would be kidnapped and where he would be detained. What a lovely scandal, what a beautiful dream they nurtured for months and months! It was François Séguin first, and then a misled public, who would pay the price of their paranoia.

CHAPTER 32
Despair

I was sinking deeper and deeper into boredom, into a depression that was becoming despair. I lived through long, empty days in my Quebec City hotel, accompanied everywhere by my two bodyguards. I felt kidnapped.

Morning came and I went downstairs for a breakfast that I could not even prepare myself. What could I do with the long hours stretching in front of me? I had always loved reading, but now I couldn't concentrate on a book. A feverish restlessness possessed me. I had to go out! Dragging my two weights, I paced the streets of old Quebec, returning for the thirtieth time to the Plains of Abraham, inspecting the cannons, all the cannons, and God knows that there are many cannons in Quebec! My bodyguards complained: "Cannons again? But we've seen all the cannons!"

I went to cry in my room. I turned on the television, it bored me. I played solitaire, I tried to read. I had lost interest in everything. How I wished, even for one hour, to be rid of my guards and to be able to go and sit somewhere in a busy bar where I could speak to the person beside me, man or woman! I wanted to speak, exchange words with someone to prove to myself that I still existed, that I could interest and be interested.

The one subject that could hold my attention was the Keable Commission. I read everything written on the course of the hearings. I never missed the televised news. Gradually, when they spoke of me, I heard it as a reference to someone else. I even began speaking of myself in the third person: "Carole de Vault . . ." It hurt too much to be me, better to become this other person who existed only as an image.

I was waiting, day by day, but for what? I could not imagine my future life, now that all Quebec knew that I was an informer. It would now be out of the question to give lectures in a university or a college; the professors and the students would not accept me. No company would want a person as notorious as I in its public relations department. Work in an office? I could see myself alone, people greeting me politely but murmuring behind my back! "That's the woman who betrayed the FLQ. That's Carole de Vault, you know, the traitor."

Now I could not bear to hear my name pronounced out loud; I was afraid that people would recognize me, would point me out.

Sometimes, for a place to go, I walked in the underground corridors of Place Québec, connected with the hotel. I would stop for a coffee or a glass of milk with my guards. Jean-Claude had accompanied me since the end of October. François had been replaced by an anglophone named Ernest. I tried to learn every detail of their lives. Jean-Claude told me about his girlfriend whom he called "my big girl." She was six feet tall. And Ernest spoke of his wife who lived in Vancouver and whom he called almost every night.

Talking became an obsession with me — talking about anything at all — but talking. I talked to the waitresses at the hotel's restaurant, to the hostess, to the assistant manager, to the person in charge of banquets, to the woman in charge of the swimming pool, to the two chambermaids, to the salesclerk at the tobacco store, to a bellboy. I would have liked to have gone up to a stranger and asked him or her, with a smile, "Please, talk to me."

Cold was descending on Quebec, but I swam every day in the outdoor pool, even when snow fell on the water. One day I proposed to my bodyguards that they drive around the Ile d'Orléans. How they protested! To visit the island in such winds! We got into the two-door car, I alone in the back. I asked to walk along the beach in the great fall winds and thought about the river flowing towards the Atlantic. Ernest accompanied me while Jean-Claude grumbled in the car.

One evening I went to a theatre at Place Québec to see the film *Molière*. My bodyguard asked if it was a good western.

"What do you mean, a western?"

"Well, in the poster the man wears a big hat like a cowboy."

That day I laughed.

I had two bodyguards and they had only one car. Each weekend one of them spent two days in Montreal with the car. So, on the weekend, we could not leave the hotel because it would be too risky to walk around with only one watchdog. Two days enclosed in the Auberge des Gouverneurs and pacing in Place Québec, of which I now knew every nook and cranny.

I spent more and more time crying. I closed myself in the shower to burst into sobs. This was a technique I had learned when the police had placed a listening device in my apartment: when I sorrowed, I smothered my sobs under my pillow so that no one would hear, but when I cried too hard, I went into the shower so that I could sob to my heart's content.

A few days before Christmas, I left the hotel to move into an apartment on Sainte Ursule Street, in Old Quebec. My bodyguards remained at the hotel. I had to notify them a few minutes beforehand each time I wanted to go out.

My apartment looked like a doll's house: a bedroom, a tiny living room with a boarded-up fireplace, a tiny kitchen. The woodwork came up to shoulder level and was magnificent, perfectly preserved. From the ceiling hung fine brass light fixtures. I should have lived happily in this pet of a place, but I could not. My state of mind kept me from appreciating anything.

I lost weight. I could only get to sleep late into the night, I had terrible nightmares, nightmares from which I awoke screaming in the dark, and the terror possessed me long after I had opened my eyes.

One night I dreamed that I was among my father's family, and my grandmother reproached me for not having had children. All the others went off to attend a solemn mass and I had to stay in charge of the house. I got up, opened the drawer of a desk and a child was lying there. I took it in my arms, choked it, and tore open its chest. I ate the still warm heart of the child. I had blood all over my hands and around my mouth. I rushed to the bathtub where, nauseated, I vomited up the heart of the child. Then I heard terrible screams and woke up: I was the one who was screaming. Sick to my stomach, hating myself, I began to cry and to scream. I was afraid to go back to sleep: better insomnia and my sad thoughts than the demented terrors that tortured me when I closed my eyes.

On Christmas Eve, Mario Bilodeau phoned me to tell me that my bodyguards would no longer accompany me, except when I went up to Montreal to resume my testimony before the Commission. I became more anxious. And yet my guards could do nothing against my worst fears anyway, those that undermined me at night.

Christmas Eve, alone in a city where I knew no one except the landlady who looked after my apartment. I got up about noon on this Christmas Eve that I wanted to see as little of as possible. I went out for a stroll in the streets of Quebec, all lit up with coloured lights but almost deserted, because everyone was at home preparing for the great feast. I dragged my feet in the snow and I thought of all the people who spend Christmas alone. When I had returned home I began to cry and I wrote a letter to a friend, one of the only ones who had not rejected me. I watched television.

At about six o'clock, the landlady called. She was a woman of about sixty who wanted to be kind to me. She invited me to join a party being held at her place in the next street. I went, and there were about ten people in her tiny one-room apartment. Everyone was drunk. The landlady thought it was already December 25, she told us that midnight mass had been beautiful, but her sisters would be angry with her because she had promised to visit them for the *réveillon*. When told that it was still the 24th, she laughed crazily, refusing to believe us.

Everyone was drinking. I had a gin and tonic. When the men came up to dance, they pressed their bodies against me. I decided to leave. The landlady, who knew my secret, intervened.

"No, she mustn't go alone. Someone has to accompany her, it's very important."

One of the men offered to escort me home. As I opened the door to my place he put his foot in the door and pushed me towards my room. Going wild, he tore off the buttons of my blouse, the button of my skirt, and threw himself on top of me. By reflex I stuck my fingers in his eyes and I escaped. I left the door open and I ran to the landlady's place, my blouse open, my skirt undone, my hair wild, in my stockinged feet in the snow.

They all looked at me. I was crying.

"What happened?"

"He attacked me, he tried to rape me. I don't ever want to see him again."

I sobbed, and he came in.

"What did you do?"

"Nothing, nothing, nothing happened." He tried to act casual.

I didn't dare leave again. The others were preparing to go to midnight mass. I pretended to be going with them. When all of them had gotten into the car, I closed the door and ran as fast as I could back to my apartment, where I double-locked the door. I was trembling. I quickly got into the bath, wanting to wash off every trace of that disgusting man. I took a friction mitt and I scrubbed and scrubbed with Castille soap. Then I stretched out on my bed, listening to the radio, which was playing Christmas carols.

I was losing weight. I had no interest in anything. Since my bodyguards had left me, a terrible anxiety had come over me. I had the feeling that an assassin was tracking me down, spying on me, lying in wait. I try to reason with myself, to no avail. I could always feel him out there, not far from my lodging. My apartment was on ground level, and the door opened directly on the sidewalk. When I opened my windows I was at eye level with the passers-by. I closed my shutters. I installed a chain on my door. From time to time I got up to look through the slats of the shutters. If he was there, I wanted at least to see his face.

I never saw him, but that didn't reassure me. On the contrary. It meant he was well hidden. I looked at a tourist walking by my door, all innocence. Was he my assassin? At night, I didn't dare turn on the light in my living room or my bedroom. He would be able to see me, he could strike.

At the back of the house there was only one window, in the bathroom, and it was very small and very high. If he came in there I would surely hear him, because he would crash through. So he would come by the front. I scrutinized the rooms for rent across the street. My assassin might have taken a room there to prepare his attack.

In my apartment, I feared the assassin. And in the street, unprotected, I feared him more. He would surely recognize me. I did my best to elude him. Before going out, I put on my dark glasses and I covered my head and part of my face with a scarf.

I did not know how ill I was. Although I cried for hours on end, it seemed to me only normal for someone in my situation. I could not bring myself to talk about it to Mario Bilodeau. I felt that he must know the state I was in. It was because of the Commission that I was in this state. I confided only to my mirror, where I saw a woman with haggard eyes and sunken cheeks.

Gradually I resolved to put an end to my life. My life was over in any case. I had no future left. I felt as though I had followed my destiny. I had come into this world to take part in a few historic moments of Quebec. So I did. Now I had only to finish my testimony before the Keable Commission and then I would kill myself.

And yet, I found it difficult to resign myself to never fulfill all the plans for the future I had made. I had dreamed of some day writing a book about my experiences. Could I let the Keable Commission have the last word?

At the end of January 1980, the Commission resumed its public hearings and I was called again to testify. I once again lived with my bodyguards in a Montreal hotel. I returned to Quebec City on weekends.

Mario Bilodeau questioned me at greater length on the events he had treated briefly during my first appearance on November 21. He continued to use me to assail Julien Giguère. It was always the same refrain: Lieutenant Giguère knew everything beforehand through me, and Lieutenant Giguère did nothing.

It was a shell of a person who testified in January and in February 1980, but no one realized it. When I had to appear in the courthouse, I wiped my tears, I dressed with care, and I left behind my panic long enough to answer the questions of the Commission's counsel, of the many lawyers.

At last it was over, unless the Commission recalled me, and I returned to Quebec City. I had been without a job since I had moved from Montreal in October. Mario brought $500 each month to pay my expenses. My rent was $250.

One day, I think in April, Mario called to ask to meet me.

"I have to bring you some news that isn't very pleasant," he told me. "This is the last time that I can bring you money. You will have to rely on yourself from now on. This time I even had to fight with the deputy minister, René Dussault, to get the money."

"But Mario, you will at least get me a job, as Justice Minister Bédard promised?"

"What job?"

"Mario, the job we talked about at Curly Joe's one noon. Don't you remember? I remember it perfectly, I was wearing a scarf with exactly the same pattern as the Commissioner's tie, white polka dots on a black background. I am not crazy. Keable said word for word: 'The minister said that if he could not get you a job, you would get a lump of money in compensation.' And Keable added: 'You had better give me your curriculum vitae as soon as possible.' "

"But Carole, it's impossible. Can you imagine a minister employing you in his department? Can't you just see the Opposition getting up in the National Assembly to ask: 'Is it not true that Carole de Vault is employed in such and such a ministry?' It doesn't make sense, don't you see? What minister could take on such a responsibility?"

"Very well, then, give me the sum of money promised."

"What sum of money?"

"Mario, the money I just told you about."

"I'm sorry, but I don't remember that conversation."

My mouth dropped. How could he say that to me? How could he dare? I was seated there, on my chair, with my hand on the table. I could feel my pulse beating at my temples, in my hands. A lump in my throat kept me from crying, howling: "Liar! Traitor! Hypocrite!"

"Well, Carole, you didn't invent get up and go, but almost — you'll find a job."

"But Mario, who will want to hire Carole de Vault now?"

He told me lightly:

"You can always drive *calèches*. They pay well, you know, the *calèches*. That's how I paid my way when I was a student."

Before leaving, he told me, very seriously: "And above all, don't make a fuss about this with the press!"

He cut off my money. I now lived without a penny on the charity of my friends. My anxieties possessed me day and night. No one in the FLQ was ever punished as I punished myself during those months of winter, of spring, of summer.

CHAPTER 33
The Scales Are Tipped

❋

A new life started for me one afternoon. I bought a pair of skates and went skating on the rink of the Chateau Frontenac. Afterwards, taking off my skates, I was seated next to a man who started to talk to me. He invited me to have a beer with him. His name was William Johnson. I told him my name was Jeanne Duval (that's my mother's name). He was columnist with the Toronto newspaper, *The Globe and Mail*, but he spoke French very well. I told him that I worked for the Conseil de la langue française (Council of the French Language); when he seemed familiar with the council, I explained my ignorance by claiming I had just arrived in Quebec City to take up a new job.

He invited me to see a movie with him the next night. I accepted. After the film, we were chatting in front of a fireplace. He told me he would like to write a book, but he couldn't find a subject. Impetuously, I told him, "Perhaps you could write one about me."

He looked at me, nonplussed. He thought that I was joking, that I must have an inflated idea of my own importance. Then, after asking for a promise of secrecy, I told him my name was not Jeanne Duval, it was Carole de Vault. He was utterly astonished.

It was the beginning of a relationship that brought me back to life. He helped me to face my nightmares. He encouraged me to start writing a book about my experiences. He tried to help me out of my frightened isolation.

One day I gathered my courage to telephone Rose-Marie Parent, who had been my best friend for so many years, even if she was briefly seduced by terrorism while I was a police informer. Now that she knew everything, would she be able to forgive me? Would friendship be stronger than our opposing commitments in 1970?

She gave me a cold reception. "In the name of our former friendship, because I will always remember the girl who made me laugh so much, I will give you some advice. Leave everything, buy a plane ticket, go to Germany and never come back."

I called another friend, Julie. She had never taken part in terrorism, so I hoped she would not be hostile to me.

"I can't talk to you any more," she told me curtly. "I hope you understand, but I can't talk to you any more."

Society took in the former terrorists like lost sheep, but would not forgive the informer.

Encouraged by William, I tried to make new friends in Quebec City. I changed my name again: a reporter for *The Gazette* was on my trail, harassing my mother and my sister to find out where I was. He had printed the name of my mother, Jeanne Duval, in an article, and also published my picture. I feared being recognized. So, one evening when we were to have visitors, I put up my hair, wore glasses rather than contact lenses, and took the family name of my grandmother. I would be Jeanne Dusablon, a dentist. I chose that profession because people have so few embarrassing questions to put to a dentist they have just met for the first time. Or so I hoped.

Among the guests was Marcel Pépin, editorial page editor of the newspaper *Le Soleil*. At the table, eating my leg of lamb with a good appetite, he talked about the informer Carole de Vault who had just appeared on television.

"She is an adventuress," he confided. "She was the mistress of Pothier Ferland."

And he helped himself to more lamb while I struggled to contain my indignation.

I was getting bolder. I sometimes went to the press gallery of the National Assembly to meet William, and no one recognized me. I even went to a big party where almost all the guests were journalists.

That all ended one day in June. I went to a medical clinic in Old Quebec. A reporter for *The Gazette*, Michel Auger, was seated in the waiting room. He was one of those who regularly covered the public sessions of the Keable Commission, and he had seen me many times when I was a witness. In Quebec he did not recognize me; however, when I showed my medical insurance card to the receptionist, she said aloud: "Carole de Vault?"

Michel Auger heard her. Soon the news swept through the press gallery that Jeanne Dusablon was Carole de Vault. Some cried out that it was a scandal. They had been to a party where, incognito, there had been a police informer! Why, she might have spied on them!

The Toronto Star sent a journalist from Toronto, Val Sears, to do an article about me. I was not willing to cooperate. I had given an interview five hours long to two journalists of *La Presse* on March 1, and I had appeared on three television programs. I had answered all their questions. Now I wanted to protect my private life; I wanted to start my life over again. I no longer wanted to be a curiosity or a monster to be gawked at. I had considered suicide a few months before. Now I wanted to learn to live!

The journalist from *The Star* called me at home. I told him I was the cleaning woman and refused to talk to him. He returned to Toronto without having set eyes on me and wrote a long article in which he made believe that I had confessed my soul to him. How did he assemble such a masterpiece of dishonesty? By taking quotations from the article in *La Presse* and from an article I wrote for *Legion Magazine*, as though all those sentences were spoken to him.

"This attractive, dark-haired woman with a deep voice and cool manner may be at the heart of a series of political and criminal plots so bizarre, so convoluted, so downright monstrous that no thriller writer could have invented them. And yet they are the basis for a series of investigations that have stretched from the cheapest bars on Saint Denis Street in Montreal to the federal cabinet and the Supreme Court. . . .

"Only the mysterious Carole Devault [sic] can answer — perhaps in her book — why, if she was not a provocateur herself, she did not simply tell her controller where Cross, the kidnapped diplomat, was being hidden."

After the appearance of the article, everyone knew who I was and where I was living. I was pursued by television cameras. I felt exposed, and hunted. Once again, I retired completely from all human contact, with the exception of William.

But I had to earn my living. I wrote a few articles. Besides the article for *Legion* lifted by *The Toronto Star*, I published a critique of the book *Les trois derniers chagrins du Général de Gaulle*, in *Le Devoir*, another article in *Legion*, an article in *The Globe and Mail* in which I briefly recounted my experiences during the October Crisis, and a joint article with William Johnson on the editorial pages of *The Globe and Mail*, in which we did a critique of the Duchaîne Report on the October Crisis.

The fashionable press continued to take after me in a fury. Marc Laurendeau could not forgive me for saying that Suzanne Lanctôt was on des Récollets Street during the crisis. "The statements of Madame Carole Devault [sic] are, to our knowledge, calumnies," he wrote in *La Presse* in a first article. In the second, he described William and me as a "bizarre twosome" and a "curious tandem."

Lysiane Gagnon, who melted with pity in *La Presse* over the fate of the poor Felquistes, had little room in her heart for a police informer. "No one will doubt that informers can occasionally be useful to the police and to society. But an informer is someone whose career, so to speak, has been built on abuse of confidence and systematic betrayal."

And there were many other attacks in the press. My life had already been destroyed, but that was not punishment enough for the person who had informed on the FLQ; she must be trampled underfoot and publicly disgraced, her credibility destroyed.

I called a friend, Bernard, whom I had helped to get a good job a few years before in public relations at a large corporation. I asked to meet him for his advice. He set a time and place for our meeting. When the day arrived, his secretary called. Because of an unfortunate mix-up in his timetable, he could not make our meeting. Bernard never called back. I understood.

William pressed me to write my book. I made a start, but how hard it was! I couldn't look at the past without being overcome by anguish. I resisted looking within myself.

How could I return to look at Carole de Vault, the little girl so shy that she did not dare speak? How could I go back to the convent with the nuns? Why relive the anguish of my first love and my first desertion?

But gradually I withdrew from the outside world and went deep within myself. I learned to make friends with my childhood, with my life as a young woman, with even the life I had lived as an informer. It was all a nightmare. Fine. I would become acquainted with my nightmares. I would confront my terrors. I would consort with my demons.

I got caught up in my own game. My life was over? Alright, I would start a new life, all within, a life made of memories, images, emotions, words. The words lined up on the page. I was there in those words, I wrote and I was written. I composed myself, I listened to my own reasons, searched for my own truth, wrote a long letter to myself.

And it is for myself that I wrote this long letter, now almost finished. For I had learned not to believe in the justice of men. In my darkest moments I sent a cry for help to the Minister of Justice of Quebec. His answer enlightened me. Here is what I wrote.

Québec, August 9, 1980

Monsieur Marc-André Bédard
Minister of Justice
The National Assembly,
Québec, Québec.
Monsieur le ministre,

It is as a last recourse that I write to you today, because I do not know otherwise where to obtain justice.
You will be familiar with my story, at least until today. In 1970 I

made the serious decision to go to the police with information that might help save the life of James R. Cross. I became an informer, and remained so until 1974. Then I ended my relations with the police, I married, I started life over again. No one around me or in the public at large knew of the role I had played.

Last year the Keable Commission wanted to inquire into the actions of the police in 1970-71. They got in touch with me. I agreed to testify publicly on my role, but I set certain conditions. Commissioner Jean Keable told me (in front of the solicitor Mario Bilodeau) that he accepted my conditions. One of them was the promise to find me employment within the government at the end of my testimony, because I anticipated that it would be very difficult for me to find employment in universities, colleges, or elsewhere, after my role as a police informer was revealed.

As a result of the public hearings, I lost my anonymity, my reputation, almost all my friends, and perhaps my security. I do not dare return to Montreal where former Felquistes or others could want to see me dead.

But my appearance before the Commission and the notoriety which followed it had an effect on me that I had not anticipated and which, as of now, is much more serious. For the past seven months I have been undermined by anxiety. At night I have terrible nightmares. In the daytime I am obsessed by the almost physical presence of an assassin who lurks near my apartment and waits for me. I am crushed by terrible fearfulness, I who in the past did not fear to infiltrate the FLQ. It has become painful for me to leave my home. I live amid anxieties which prevent me from concentrating, and which express themselves in the form of physical pains in my arms and my legs that are almost beyond endurance. Sometimes, the thought of suicide becomes an obsession.

I am therefore in a state of depression that keeps me from functioning normally. I, so energetic in the past — during the October Crisis I only slept a few hours each night — am now overwhelmed by ordinary decisions that need to be made, by daily acts that I have to carry out. Everything has become terribly complicated for me.

It was in these circumstances — which I understood imperfectly myself and tried to conceal — that the Keable Commission notified me in April that it was cutting off the $500 that it had advanced me monthly on which to live. I had no employment — and the Commission also informed me that it had no intention of getting me any. Mr. Bilodeau even denied that it had been promised to me.

Already, with this $500 a month, in a city where I knew no one, I had mounting debts. I had root canal treatment and other dental costs. My rent was $250 a month. I borrowed.

Now I am without a cent. I am unable for the time being to look for a job and to carry out the responsibilities of one. I am no longer able to pay for my rent, my meals, my ordinary expenditures. I live dependent on others, I, a proud person who always earned my education and my living. My situation has become impossible.

What am I to do? Throw myself into the arms of social welfare? I applied for an indemnity under the law which offers compensation to people who are injured while trying to prevent a crime. They have begun an inquiry. It is uncertain what will come of it.

I would like to publish a book of my memoirs as a first step towards earning my living. But in my troubled state, aggravated by my intolerable situation, I only succeed in working two or three hours a day — except days of crisis, of course.

Monsieur le ministre, *it is thanks to justice in Quebec that I find myself in my present situation. Justice wanted to throw light on the events of 1970-71. I contributed part of myself, my health, my reputation, my serenity. I do not want to give my life.*

I wait, monsieur le ministre, *to learn from you whether justice does not owe me something.*

Yours sincerely,
Carole de Vault

Here is the answer I received to my letter:

GOUVERNEMENT DU QUÉBEC
MINISTÈRE DE LA JUSTICE
CABINET DU MINISTRE

ref: 33596
Sainte-Foy, September 8, 1980

Madame Carole de Vault
15 Haldiman Street, apt. 1,
QUEBEC (Québec)
G1R 4N3

Madame,

The minister of Justice, Marc-André Bédard, asks me to acknowledge receipt of your letter of August 9 last with respect to your testimony before the Keable Commission.

Yours sincerely,
The associate chief of staff,
Denis Blais.

ACKNOWLEDGMENTS

Translations on pages 89 to 91, 93, 95, 101 to 104, 139, 146 and 147 by Edrica Baheux. Reproduced with permission from *Canadian Annual Review for 1970*, John T. Saywell, ed., and *Quebec 70: A Documentary Narrative*, by John T. Saywell (both © University of Toronto Press, 1971).

ABOUT THE AUTHORS:

Carole de Vault became known to history when the Keable Commission, intrigued by references to an agent code-named Poupette, discovered her identity and convinced her to become its star witness. Her testimony forced her into hiding and made her an outcast in Quebec.

William Johnson has earned his reputation as the leading interpreter of Quebec affairs in English Canada through his articles, lectures, and broadcasts on radio and television, in both English and French. He is best known as a columnist for *The Globe and Mail*.